Praise for Investing with Volume Analysis

"*Investing with Volume Analysis* is a compelling read on the critical role that changing volume patterns play on predicting stock price movement. As buyers and sellers vie for dominance over price, volume analysis is a divining rod of profitable insight, helping to focus the serious investor on where profit can be realized and risk avoided."

—**Walter A. Row, III**, CFA, Vice President, Portfolio Manager, Eaton Vance Management

"In *Investing with Volume Analysis*, Buff builds a strong case for giving more attention to volume. This book gives a broad overview of volume diagnostic measures and includes several references to academic studies underpinning the importance of volume analysis. Maybe most importantly, it gives insight into the Volume Price Confirmation Indicator (VPCI), an indicator Buff developed to more accurately gauge investor participation when moving averages reveal price trends. The reader will find out how to calculate the VPCI and how to use it to evaluate the health of existing trends."

—**Dr. John Zietlow**, D.B.A., CTP, Professor of Finance, Malone University (Canton, OH)

"In *Investing with Volume Analysis*, the reader ... should be prepared to discover a trove of new ground-breaking innovations and ideas for revolutionizing volume analysis. Whether it is his new Capital Weighted Volume, Trend Trust Indicator, or Anti-Volume Stop Loss method, Buff offers the reader new ideas and tools unavailable anywhere else."

—From the Foreword by **Jerry E. Blythe**, Market Analyst, President of Winthrop Associates, and Founder of Blythe Investment Counsel

"Over the years, with all the advancements in computing power and analysis tools, one of the most important tools of analysis, volume, has been sadly neglected. Yes, it is true that it is included in all analysis programs, but the art and science has been almost lost. Buff's new book should take care of that neglect and restore volume to its rightful place. They say, 'In the land of the blind, the one-eyed man is king.' This book will give technicians both eyes. It is clear, well written, and step-by-steps give the reader the tools to understand this important tool putting volume analysis in its proper historical context. It is highly recommended."

—**Richard Mogey**, CMF Investment Advisors

"This book forced me to think in new investment directions and to re-evaluate my previous strategies.... I gained insights that were groundbreaking for me."
—Dr. Dennis Henlsey, Taylor University

"I found *Investing with Volume Analysis* of great interest. Any new study of volume and its great technical importance demands immediate attention. It is good to have Buff's new ideas and discoveries added to the history and importance of volume in technical analysis. My sincere thanks to Buff for his great work and contribution."
—Joseph E. Granville, *The Granville Market Letter*

"The author has gathered in one place all of the major methods and theories that deal with volume in the stock market and has recognized volume as an equal partner with price in the workings of market and stock movements. He puts it all together into usable and readable guidance, using effective analogies and occasional humor."
—Richard W. Arms, Jr., Arms Advisory

"Buff presents a thorough discussion of the utility of volume and volume-based market indicators, both traditional and of his own creation. Fellow market analysts can be glad for this resource and the fact that the VPCI on Buff himself is in a strongly rising trend."
—Robert Prechter, CMT, and Dave Allman, Elliott Wave International

"I really enjoyed and appreciated the author's ability to combine volume with many of the basic indicators used by technicians today."
—Ralph J. Acampora, CMT, Managing Director, Altaira Investment Solutions

"I trade for a living and don't have time for fluff and puff. Buff tossed facts and figures in my face like a silver cross in front of a werewolf. He is on to much here, as you will see. This book is not a morsel; it's a nine-course meal. Dig in."
—Larry Williams, Private Trader, World Cup Trading Champion

"For every stock trade that takes place, three key pieces of information are recorded: price, time, and size. It is from these three pieces of data that we derive all the key information that technical analysts use to examine a stock's behavior. If you are only looking at prices, then you are throwing out a whole lot of key information.

Buff's book teaches you how to take that information about the size of trades and turn it into the seven types of volume indicators. Better still, he teaches you how to use those tools to improve your own trading."
—Tom McClellan, Editor, *The McClellan Market Report*

Investing with
Volume Analysis

Investing with Volume Analysis

Identify, Follow, and Profit from Trends

Buff Pelz Dormeier

Vice President, Publisher: Tim Moore
Associate Publisher and Director of Marketing: Amy Neidlinger
Executive Editor: Jim Boyd
Editorial Assistant: Pamela Boland
Operations Manager: Gina Kanouse
Senior Marketing Manager: Julie Phifer
Publicity Manager: Laura Czaja
Assistant Marketing Manager: Megan Colvin
Cover Designer: Alan Clements
Managing Editor: Kristy Hart
Project Editor: Jovana San Nicolas-Shirley
Copy Editor: Deadline Driven Publishing
Proofreader: Language Logistics, LLC
Indexer: Larry Sweazy
Compositor: Nonie Ratcliff
Manufacturing Buyer: Dan Uhrig

This book is sold with the understanding that neither the author nor the publisher is engaged in rendering legal, accounting, or other professional services or advice by publishing this book. Each individual situation is unique. Thus, if legal or financial advice or other expert assistance is required in a specific situation, the services of a competent professional should be sought to ensure that the situation has been evaluated carefully and appropriately. The author and the publisher disclaim any liability, loss, or risk resulting directly or indirectly, from the use or application of any of the contents of this book.

Technical analysis is only one form of analysis. Investors should also consider the merits of Fundamental and Quantitative analysis when making investment decisions. Technical analysis is based on the study of historical price movements and past trend patterns. There is no assurance that these movements or trends can or will be duplicated in the future. The solutions discussed might not be suitable for your personal situation, even if it is similar to the example presented. Investors should make their own decisions based on their specific investment objectives and financial circumstances. The material has been prepared or is distributed solely for information purposes and is not a solicitation or an offer to buy any security or instrument or to participate in any trading strategy.

FT Press offers excellent discounts on this book when ordered in quantity for bulk purchases or special sales. For more information, please contact U.S. Corporate and Government Sales, 1-800-382-3419, corpsales@pearsontechgroup.com. For sales outside the U.S., please contact International Sales at international@pearson.com.

Company and product names mentioned herein are the trademarks or registered trademarks of their respective owners.

Printed in the United States of America

First Printing February 2011

ISBN-10: 0-13-708550-8
ISBN-13: 978-0-13-708550-7

Pearson Education LTD.
Pearson Education Australia PTY, Limited.
Pearson Education Singapore, Pte. Ltd.
Pearson Education North Asia, Ltd.
Pearson Education Canada, Ltd.
Pearson Educatión de Mexico, S.A. de C.V.
Pearson Education—Japan
Pearson Education Malaysia, Pte. Ltd.

Library of Congress Cataloging-in-Publication Data

Dormeier, Buff, 1969-
  Investing with volume analysis : identify, follow, and profit from trends / Buff Dormeier.
    p. cm.
  ISBN-13: 978-0-13-708550-7 (hardback : alk. paper)
  ISBN-10: 0-13-708550-8 (hardback : alk. paper) 1. Investment analysis. 2. Investments—Decision making. 3. Valuation. I. Title.
  HG4529.D667 2011
  332.63'2042—dc22
                        2010050894

Contents

Foreword

Volume, price, and time are fundamental concepts in market analysis.

Volume tracks quantities of things, whether shares of stocks, contracts in options, or commodities. In business, volume tracks sales, inventory, customers, and the amount of goods bought or sold.

In *Investing with Volume Analysis*, Buff Dormeier presents new ideas, digging deeper into volume by identifying secrets these often overlooked statistics hold. He has devised methods for identifying when to climb on board and stay with sustainable trends, and perhaps more importantly, when to bail out of trends when unsustainable.

The Volume Price Confirmation Indicator (VPCI) is his creation, and it helps identify these situations. It was a significant enough discovery to earn him the internationally prestigious Charles Dow Award in 2006, only given to a work deemed surprisingly new and innovative.

Buff's career has combined both fundamental and technical analysis. Earlier, as a student of fundamental analysis, he reviewed the business activities of management and made forecasts based on a company's financial history and forward guidance. He wanted further understanding about a stock's price behavior and began studying technical analysis.

He found that technical analysis, at its core, is about the flow of money into and out of securities. Yet these technical findings were not always consistent with what fundamental analysts and company management were saying. As an analytic approach, he settled on two primary tools: price and volume.

His Discovery

Buff learned that analysts had been combining price with many metrics in gauging market behavior, but many of the metrics did not include volume. He then remembered an important concept he used in fundamental analysis for assessing the overall health of the economy, the turnover of money. A healthy economy turns money over faster than a weak economy. So he set out to measure money flow in the markets.

He turned to one of the grandfathers of technical analysis and masters in volume analysis, Joseph E. Granville, and he studied his On-Balance Volume concepts. Many considered these concepts a hallmark in technical analysis. Granville taught that volume precedes prices. That resonated.

Buff wondered if there might be a way to measure a *dynamic* relationship between price and volume, one that one might influence the other, and he wondered whether he could design a method for discerning such nuances when they occurred.

He examined the differences between a volume-weighted *moving* price average and the corresponding *simple* moving price average. The differences he found would often expose information about the relationship between price and volume that was not visible any other way. He now had a way to assess the staying power or enthusiasm of investors, the force behind price moves. He had a metric for gauging the flow of money.

Although this topic of volume analysis is by nature quite technical, Buff is skilled at presenting and documenting the essentials of volume theory with exceptional clarity. He explains the depths of volume analysis with amazing simplicity, and he shows by example not only what works but why it works.

In *Investing with Volume Analysis*, the reader should find many pearls of wisdom from such technical giants as Charles Dow, Richard Wyckoff, and Joseph Granville. He should be prepared to discover a trove of new ground-breaking innovations, ideas for revolutionizing volume analysis. Whether it is his new Capital Weighted Volume, Trend Trust Indicator, or Anti Volume Stop Loss method, Buff offers the reader new ideas and tools unavailable anywhere else.

—Jerry E. Blythe, Market Analyst
   President of Winthrop Associates
   Founder of Blythe Investment Counsel
   Former Editor and Publisher of the Market Consensus Letter

Acknowledgments

I would like to personally thank Dr. Jerry Blythe for all his help with the book. Your broad insights, professional resources, and technical expertise have proven to be very valuable. Further appreciation goes to Joseph Granville. Thank you, Joe, for sharing your wisdom. Your depth of knowledge about volume surpasses all.

I would also like to thank Tom McClellan. Tom, you are a brilliant technician. Your expertise in market breadth has been invaluable to me. You have given me many excellent suggestions, pointed out some inconsistencies, and provided me with some great resources. Moreover, you have given me many terrific ideas about how to rephrase sentences and even paragraphs, plus you have provided many valuable quotes and charts. Thanks a bunch, Tom.

I would like to offer praise for others who helped me with this work, such as Steve Poser, George Schade, and Dr. John Zietlow. Steve, your knowledge of technical analysis and market structure is outstanding. Thank you for your help, expertise, and advice with modern volume issues! In my search for original resources, George Schade was hot on the trail like a bloodhound on a fresh scent! Thank you for your help and your pursuit and passion for truth, George. Professor Dr. John Zietlow, your assistance with financial formulas was very helpful to me in this assignment. Your depth of knowledge in finance is amazing. You reflect a spiritual light, encouraging me and many others.

Further praise goes to Scott Marcouiller. I am indebted to you, Scott, for conducting the book's compliance review. Thank you for sifting through each page for accuracy and advice. In you, our firm has a valuable resource. Thanks a bunch! A special thanks to Julia Ormond for your assistance in programming my Cap-Weighted Volume formula into Stockfinder. My appreciation to Dr. Dennis Hensley, Jeffrey Neuenschwander, and Jacqueline Ramey for your exceptional and exhaustive editorial assistance. A big thank you to my good buddy, Pep, for designing the book's website: www.volumeanalysis.com. Great work!

A tip of the hat to three former MTA (Market Technicians Association) presidents who conducted the book's primary peer review:

Ralph Acampora, Larry M. Berman, and Philip M. Roth. Thank you for volunteering to peer review this work. I know none you had the time to do it, but nonetheless you did it anyway. When I asked for your help in conducting the review, I really did not know what to expect as you are all among the most accomplished and respected technicians. Thank you for your insights, kind words, and encouragement. Your personal dedication to the elevation of our profession is something to be very much admired.

My sincere appreciation to my team who picked up the slack while I was hidden away writing. Laura Rowe, thank you for being my assistant, but you are so much more than that. Not only are you wonderful with everyone, especially our clients, but you also do a fantastic job keeping me organized. Dad, thank you for teaching me the business. You are the most honest, sincere man one could hope to know and be privileged to work with. Thank you for being my father.

I spent much time researching and writing this book. However, it was not really my time to spend; it was my families' time. So this book is dedicated to my family. Speaking of which, I want to thank the sweetest person I've ever met—my wife, Kathy. Marrying you was absolutely the wisest thing I've ever done. Our marriage is the greatest earthly blessing God could ever bestow upon me. You are wonderful, amazing, and incredibly beautiful. I could never reach my goals without you, nor would I want to without your support, my Love. I love you, Beautiful! To my sister Tiffany, thank you for your selfless act and commitment to our family. Your gift to us is hope, love, and life. We are forever grateful and indebted to you.

This book is much about price and value. I assert an item's value or worth is ultimately determined by the price someone else is willing to pay for it. With this in mind, there could be nothing more valuable than one's soul. And what is the value of the soul? Pondering this question, I am so utterly grateful to my Good Sheppard, who in love, ransomed His life, redeeming this unworthy soul. Blessed be the name of God for ever and ever, for wisdom and might are His. He changes the times and the seasons. He removes kings and sets up kings. He gives wisdom unto the wise and knowledge to them that know understanding. He reveals the deep and secret things. He knows what is in the darkness, and the light dwells with Him. I thank thee and give You my praise.

About the Author

Armed with proprietary indicators and investment programs, **Buff Pelz Dormeier**, CMT dynamically manages private investment portfolios for affluent individuals, institutions, trusts, and endowments. Buff builds customized strategies designed to meet or exceed a client's specific investment objectives in what is often uncertain market conditions. This is accomplished by utilizing proprietary state-of-the-art portfolio management tools designed to grow and preserve wealth in a risk-conscience manner.

In Buff's 15+ years in the securities industry, he has been employed as a financial advisor, an analyst, and a portfolio manager. An award-winning industry innovator, Buff is the developer of Volume Weighted Moving Averages (VWMA), the VW-MACD, the Volume Price Confirmation Indicator (VPCI), VPCI Stochastics, the Anti-Volume Stop Loss (AVSL), the Trend Thrust Indicator (TTI), Capital Weighted Volume Indexes, and a host of cap-weighted, volume-based breadth indicators.

As a celebrated source of investment knowledge, Buff's work with market indicators and trading system design has been published and/or referenced in *Barron's, Stock's & Commodities, SFO and Active Trader* magazines, and the *IFTA & MTA Journals*. A Chartered Market Technician, Buff received the 2006 Charles Dow Award recognizing research papers breaking new ground or which make innovative use of established techniques in the field of technical analysis. The Charles H. Dow Award is considered one of the most important recognitions in the field of technical analysis. He has also been a featured speaker at national and international conferences including Expo Trader Brazil, the TradeStation World Conference, and the Moneyshow International Trader's Expo.

Buff was a double major graduate of Indiana State University participating in varsity track and cross country as a student athlete. Still an avid runner, Buff is a former Indiana Marathon champion.

Presently, Buff is a member of the Markets Technician Association, Emmanuel Community Church, and he is an executive board member of the Inter-Faith Hospitality Network of Greater Fort Wayne.

Introduction

Do you believe navigating the markets in the coming decades will be as easy as it was in the 1980s and 1990s? If not, perhaps you should consider sharpening your investment skills with technical analysis, specifically volume analysis.

My exposure to technical analysis began early in my career as a financial advisor. Like in most major brokerage firms, my firm's squawk box reported various stock stories from the market analysts. These stock stories would make a case for why a particular company was undervalued, overlooked, or discounted relative to some future development or innovation. The best of these stories would be relayed to retail clients, who would invest in the stock of the companies featured in the stories. Occasionally, some of these stories came true, and the stock increased in value. Other times, the stock had to be relegated to the long-term holdings file while investors with losses waited until the company or industry group moved back into favor. Unfortunately, although many of these stories originally sounded promising, they ended up being nothing more than hyped-up fairy tales told by supposed Wall Street geniuses.

Fortunately, one analyst was different from all the others. His recommendations came without flashy stories. Speaking in terms of trend, support, resistance, patterns, breakouts, and risk management, his recommendations often showed profits immediately. When they did not, he would quickly admit his mistake, something unheard of among market analysts. His approach allowed investors to preserve their capital for the next investment opportunity. What was the difference between this analyst and the others? He was not a Chartered Financial Analyst (CFA), but he was a Chartered Market Technician

1

(CMT)—a technical analyst. I was so impressed by his technical approach that I pursued my own CMT designation.

So, what is technical analysis? Market analysis breaks down into two basic schools of thought: fundamental analysis and technical analysis. Assuming value is the sole determinant of price, fundamental analysis attempts to determine intrinsic value. The fundamental analyst collects, analyzes, and models information about a company, including earnings, assets, liabilities, sales, and revenue. Fundamental analysts embrace as core beliefs that the markets are inefficient, all necessary information is available to the public, and valuation is quantifiable. Fundamental analysts are concerned with how value is reflected within price. However, the fundamental approach cannot tell its practitioners when to buy or sell. For example, in 2000, Cisco Systems was Wall Street's darling. No one needed to look far to find many fundamental "buy" ratings on the stock. Yet, an investor who purchased Cisco on January 1, 2000, and held it until January 1, 2002, would have experienced a 65 percent loss. On the other hand, an investor who bought Cisco on January 1, 1998, and held it until January 1, 2000, would have experienced a 64 percent gain. Any investor with just a bit of experience investing during the past decade could list many more such examples. Timing represents a serious limitation to the fundamental approach in an investment strategy.

The technical analyst acknowledges that fundamental analysis plays a prominent role in security analysis. However, the technical analyst believes that price is ultimately the end result of the battle between the forces of supply and demand. Price represents all that is known, feared, and hoped for by the market. Technical analysis focuses on the forces behind supply and demand that produce price. Technical analysts hold as core beliefs that the markets are efficient at discounting even future developments, prices move in trends that can be forecast (up, down, and sideways), investors are both logical and emotional creatures, and history repeats itself—more so after it has been forgotten.

Hundreds of millions of dollars are poured into fundamental research by brokerage firms, mutual fund companies, hedge funds, and advisory services, all in an effort to determine their proper intrinsic value. With all this money invested in research, one would presume that an informed investor should know the worth of a given security. Yet, wide and violent price swings are still as prevalent as ever. Why? Perhaps because the fundamental information ignores the human element. And it is in the human mind, not theoretical models, that price is ultimately determined. For example, a fundamental analyst might perform a great amount of research to determine possible results of an important announcement. The data is the critical information. In contrast, the technical analyst focuses his or her forecast on how the market participants react after the data is released. The datum themselves are inconsequential relative to the importance of predetermining investor expectations.

A technical analyst studies four major areas: sentiment, cycles, price, and volume. Sentiment indicators monitor market participants. Insiders, specialists, and institutions generally are regarded as having superior or leading opinions, whereas advisory services, journalists, and small traders usually are seen as having stale news or inferior opinions. Cycle analysis is the study of time—the order, length, and recurrences of market trends. The preponderance of technical analysis involves price and chart analysis. The price chart represents the actions and behavioral patterns of investors—the market's testimony. Price testifies to what investors believe and how strongly they believe it. However, if price is the market's testimony, volume is the market's polygraph. As a stock rises, more and more investors should be attracted to participate in the stock's move. However, if fewer and fewer investors are willing to participate as the stock price continues to rise, then the volume contradicts the price movement. In this way, volume substantiates price by measuring the force and extent of investor convictions. When volume increases, it confirms price movements; when volume decreases, it contradicts price movements.

Therefore, volume analysis is a quest for truth in an otherwise scrambled investment puzzle. To solve any puzzle, it helps to look at the puzzle's box cover to form a perspective of the image. In volume analysis, volume is the box cover that enables us to view the markets through the lens of supply and demand. Like other skills, volume analysis is as of much an art than an exact science. And like most skills, a little knowledge without application experience could do more harm than good. Volume analysis is no different. It deals with probabilities; it leaves room for unfavorable outcomes because many factors can affect future price movements. Investors employing volume analysis should also apply a strict and rigorous, unemotional discipline to encourage long-term success. Fortunately, in volume analysis, it is not necessary to wait for the outcome of often already dated, stale fundamental figures or economic statistics to develop an informed opinion. A disciplined and planned approach of analyzing moving markets allows for decisive market action. Thus, as with fundamental analysts, successful technical analysis depends on one's ability to execute and one's ability to analyze and gauge the market.

Experience is the best teacher, but the market can charge some hefty tuition. However, the market need not be a closed-book test. We can also learn through sharing our knowledge and experience with one another other. This book shares with you what I have gleaned from my 15 years in the field of volume research. The endeavors of *Investing with Volume Analysis* are to

- Equip the savvy investor with a foundational understanding of the market, its history, and its present structure.

- Present an enlightened perspective on the role of volume in the markets, not only in terms of what may pragmatically work but also in terms of apprehending the underlying rationale of how and why.

- Review many of the traditional volume indicators and introduce my own ground-breaking methodologies.

- Arm the investor with volume-based strategies for assessing risk and gauging and tracking the market, similar to that of a GPS device.

Albert Einstein once said, "The essence of mathematics is not to make simple things complicated but to make complicated things simple." With this thought in mind, the essence of this book is to convey advanced technical concepts in an easily understood manner. As such, this book starts with the basics, and then rapidly builds on these essential concepts. For those seeking further information, including where to find many of indicators and new developments discussed in the forthcoming pages, go to www.VolumeAnalysis.com.

1

Two Perspectives of Market Analysis

"This is one of the most important points I've had to learn. For me, at least, 'why' is the most expensive and *least valuable* information. When you get 'why' wrong (and act accordingly), you lose lots of money. You only can know 'why' for sure after the fact (when it is useless). You gotta learn to live with the reality that there are things that are beyond the individual's ken. The search for 'why,' whether right or wrong, can just as easily lead you to irrelevancies, or, worse yet, to valid data that will not impact on the market. The best analog is arguing with your wife. Being right is often totally valueless if not counterproductive."

—Mike Epstein (1931–2009) Quoted on June 21, 2006

Building a Firm Foundation

We start our journey by getting acquainted with the basics, the fundamentals of technical analysis. These fundamentals are so self-evident that they are often overlooked. However, a rock-solid foundation is critical to understanding the volume analysis perspective. Your ability to succeed ultimately depends on your ability to discern. Every day, causal investors attempt to employ complicated indicators in their analyses of the market and individual securities; however, they generally do not fully understand what information the indicators are designed to reveal. When the markets turn and investors' indicators no longer work, they're at a loss.

Even when these investors experience short-term success, they are often building on sand because blind success reinforces poor practices. The difference between being wise and foolish is neither information nor intellect, but a depth of understanding. A thorough understanding of the basics enables investors to develop the necessary perspectives to build a cause for action. Building a cause for action is what analysis is all about.

As one of these investors yourself, a solid understanding of the basics is the bedrock that builds your perspective, shapes your beliefs, and influences your ideas. You can either seek to build a perspective on a solid foundation or be consumed with the moment—continually seeking the hottest tip, trying out the latest indicator, or reading about the newest five-step program to success. You can continue searching for the Holy Grail of market success or you can develop the understanding required to start believing in your own ability to discern, and thereby, gauge the market.

Two Legitimate Approaches

"It is the glory of God to conceal a thing, but the honor of kings is to search out a matter."

—*King Solomon*

There are many forms of security analysis on which to build an understanding. The two most common methods of analysis are the fundamental analysis and the technical analysis. Acknowledging these two approaches, the Financial Industry Regulatory Authority (FINRA) recognizes two types of research analysts: the Chartered Financial Analyst (CFA) and the Chartered Market Technician (CMT). Although the two schools of research may be used together effectively, they stem from vastly different perspectives. Your perspective of the market, what it is and how it works, plays a major role in your investment success.

Early in my career, while studying for my CMT designation, I taught technical analysis to many of the top brokers at the major brokerage firm where I was employed. A colleague who was part of the CFA program taught fundamental analysis. I once spent a day monitoring his crash course on fundamental analysis. His explanation of using financial ratios to assess the value of companies made sense. Despite my early concerns about fundamental analysis, formed from past unproductive experiences and my preconceived beliefs regarding the efficiencies of the markets' discounting mechanism, I was intrigued.

Like many fundamental analysts, the presenter had his favorite stock. He provided seemingly convincing reasons for why this stock was overlooked and undervalued in relation to earnings, the industry, and other comparative valuations. According to his analysis, the stock was intrinsically worth $6, although it traded slightly below $3. At $3, it was a cheap stock, so I inserted the symbol into my quote machine just to keep an occasional eye on it. Several days and weeks that turned into several months went by, and the stock did nothing but trade in a tight sideways channel despite the broader market being strongly bullish. One day, however, the stock broke through its long-standing resistance at a little over $3. I pulled it up. It had developed a huge base and was breaking out on strong volume. I bought it. In a short time, the stock ran up close to $6 and then began to wane. I sold part of my position and put a limit order in just below the round number of $6 to sell the rest based on some technical considerations. The $6 was the same price level the fundamentalist had estimated as fair value. I watched the stock closely and prepared to change the limit order to market if it showed further weakness. However, my order filled as the stock moved a bit over $6. It was at this time that I first realized that the fundamentals were indeed most likely wagging the dog, suggesting that the fundamentals were driving the technical aspects.

Believing I was bearing an olive branch, I sought out my new fundamental ally to point out that he was right and thank him for helping me make a buck. I even made a point to mention that he had bought the stock at a lower price than I had while I intentionally neglected that he had been sitting on dead money for over a year. Meanwhile, I had enjoyed participating in numerous stock issues throughout the bull market. However, I was floored when he told me he had not sold the stock. Based on revised data, he now saw the stock fairly valued at $9. I tried to inform him that the stock appeared to be weakening technically and perhaps he should sell part of it while he had a double in hand. No, he was far too excited. He proceeded to list many more reasons why the stock was still undervalued. As a staunch technician, those details were just not important to me. As he went on,

I listened politely while deliberately blocking out his arguments for fear that it might influence my own objectivity. The stock went back down to its former base at $3 faster than it rose. I felt really bad for the guy. He had finally gotten it right, and yet he had missed it! How could I face him again? I thought I might repurchase some shares with my profits as the stock met support at $3, just so misery might have some company. But, nah, I would just be wasting my good capital on bad assets. What kind of example would that be for my stockbroker students?

This anecdote shows that my colleague and I each had our own perspectives of the market. The fundamentalist viewed stocks as companies in which he could become part owner. He believed his favored company was worth significantly more than the market price, so he bought it. This perspective of the market springs from what is called fundamental analysis. My view of the market is that stocks are shares of companies. These shares go up because eager buyers push them up, and they go down because fervent sellers sell, forcing them down. When I saw a stock that had previously gone nowhere suddenly pop up, I concluded the force of buying pressure could propel the stock further, and I bought it. Our different investment approaches did not reflect a difference in intelligence, but they did reflect a difference in our perspectives. Fundamental analysis is primarily about the "what," whereas technical analysis is much about the "when." Rather than being pitted against each other, technical and fundamental analysis can be used to complement each other. With that clearly stated, *Investing with Volume Analysis* introduces you to a perspective of market analysis based on the principles of supply and demand. In security analysis, this perspective is technical analysis.

The Fundamental Approach

Fundamental analysis presumes security prices are based on the intrinsic value of the underlying company. Price is formed based on these values and facts surrounding the company. Seemingly, this is a highly logical approach, one that many assume is correct in most markets most of the time. The fundamentalist believes that with time, stocks will move up to minimize the disparity between their present value and their perceived intrinsic value. Thus, fundamental analysis presumes the future prospects of a security are best analyzed through a proper assessment of the intrinsic value of the underlying company.

Fundamental analysis is not concerned with the behavior of investors as measured through the stock price or trading volume. Rather, the pure fundamental analyst's focus is on finding the true worth of the underlying company. In pursuit of value, the fundamentalist collects, analyzes, and models company information, including earnings, assets, liabilities, sales, revenue, and other information required to evaluate the company. Assumptions of the fundamentalist include a belief that markets are not completely efficient and that all necessary information is available to the public, but the company may not always be efficiently priced. Overall, fundamentalists are concerned with what the price should be according to their valuation models. The determination of value from the collective action of these fundamentalist investors is the primary force moving today's markets.

The Technical Approach

While fundamental analysis focuses on the investment's intrinsic value, technical analysis is the study of the market through its creators, the investors. Therefore, the focus of technical analysis is the behavior and motivations of investors observed primarily through their own actions. It is imperfect people who determine market prices, not highly perfected valuation models. However, the technician does not deny that the pursuit of value is a primary source of market movement. Yet, the technical perspective deems that market price is formed by the collective opinions of market participants pursuing value. Thus, in the mind of a technician, price is less about company facts and more about investors' feelings and perceptions concerning those facts.

In the exchange markets, prices are determined by what one party is willing to pay and another is willing to accept. Therefore, price is ultimately the end result of a battle between the forces of supply and demand, manifested through the actions and behaviors of investors. Price represents all that is known, feared, and hoped for by the market. It is through the diagnostics of price, volume, and other technical metrics formed by the actions and sentiments of market participants that the technician gauges stock performance.

Technical analysis assumes that market participants are efficient in price formation, thus avoiding any judgments about the intrinsic value of the underlying company. Therefore, the technician is not concerned with what the ideal price should be; rather, he is concerned just with what it is. Consequently, the company or any dataset used to determine the company's value is not the pure technician's direct concern. The technician's objective is to develop an understanding of the behavioral forces producing price (such as supply and demand). The core aspects of the technician include believing that the markets are efficient at discounting even future developments, price moves through trends, investors are both logical and emotional creatures, and past behaviors tend to repeat themselves more so when enough time has elapsed that the behaviors have been forgotten.

Driving a Comparison Between Fundamental and Technical Analysis

The movie *Vantage Point* begins by playing out the same scene over and over again, each time from a different vantage point as experienced by each major character. From such a portrayal or depiction, the viewer can easily see that one's vantage point largely influences one's perspective. Likewise, the fundamentalist and the technician have similar objectives in analyzing securities. Their views are, however, developed from different vantage points. An analogy can be drawn between a fundamentalist and a technician who both examine a high-performance automobile. The fundamentalist looks under the hood, kicks the tires, and inspects the frame—the physical aspects of the car. The technician does not look under the hood. Rather, he evaluates how the car performs under a set of conditions, such as turning, accelerating, and shifting. The fundamentalist examining the engine notices a potential flaw in the engine design. Similarly, when the gauges exceed the threshold of the expected parameters, the technician is led to the same conclusion as the fundamentalist, but without a physical inspection of the engine.

A fundamentalist might identify a good valuation point of a stock based on his analysis of the company. The technician observing the actions of market participants through the stock's movements might identify the same price level as a potential support level. What is support? Support is demand (buyers). So where does this demand come from? Often, it originates from the fundamentalist's determination of value. In this way, the two perspectives often yield the same conclusion using different methodologies. One opinion is based on the search for intrinsic value, whereas the other is shaped by extrinsic behavior.

Whatever one's vantage point, price goes up for only one reason: Demand has surpassed available supply. When the available supply outweighs demand, the price must go back down. Volume is the scale weighing these forces of supply and demand that produce price. In this way, volume ultimately reflects the ebb and flow of money into and out of the market or the security. Therefore, my belief is that volume analysis provides a superior view of the market's internal structure that other forms of analysis do not offer. This book explores the market from this underemployed perspective of volume analysis, providing an investor with the tools and concepts to advance his or her own abilities in evaluating the market.

2

The History of Technical Analysis

"The market is people in action, acting like people."
—Bernard Baruch

In 1958, the candy company Just Born Candies introduced the marshmallow chicken, reigniting the classic debate over which came first—the marshmallow chicken or the chocolate egg? Which developed first—technical or fundamental analysis?

Most investors assume fundamental analysis preceded technical analysis. This conclusion appears logical. It takes two opposite opinions to come together to produce a price, and a series of prices creates the chart.

The First Recorded Investment—A Fill or Be Killed Order

One might logically expect fundamental analysis to predate technical analysis. But this logic presupposes that prices used to create the chart were exchanged based on the item's fundamental value alone. How much an item is worth is determined by how much one party is willing to pay to obtain it and how little another party is willing to accept to let it go. Although technical analysis utilizes charts, its essence is human behavior. And behavior might be as much a part of the price equation as value. The first recorded investment transaction occurs in Genesis, a "fill or be killed" order. Upon moving into a new territory, Abraham allowed people to believe that Sarah, his beautiful wife, was his sister. A king then mistakenly sends for Sarah to marry him.

In the Biblical account, God tells the king he has sinned and must return Sarah back to her husband Abraham, who is a prophet. In an effort to save his life, king Abimelech seeks Abraham's forgiveness over the mistake:

> Then Abimelech took sheep and oxen and servants—both men and women—and gave them to Abraham, and he returned his wife Sarah to him. "Look over my kingdom, and choose a place where you would like to live," Abimelech told him. Then he turned to Sarah. "Look," he said, "I am giving your 'brother' a thousand pieces of silver to compensate for any embarrassment I may have caused you. This will settle any claim against me in this matter." Then Abraham prayed to God, and God healed Abimelech, his wife, and the other women of the household, so they could have children.
>
> —*Genesis: 20*

From the Genesis account, the accepted offer appears to be based on technical observations and analysis rather than fundamental value. To summarize the text, Abimelech offered Abraham an unconditional lease of property, sheep, oxen, servants, and 1,000 pieces of silver in exchange for Abraham's prayers of forgiveness.

Abimelech's bid was accepted by Abraham. He forgave Abimelech and offered his prayers to God on the king's behalf.

Was this exchange based on fundamental value? Obviously not! One cannot put a price on the love and fidelity of a spouse. What's more, Abimelech had to reach a figure that he believed would be immediately acceptable to Abraham. Otherwise, he would put his life in jeopardy by trying to negotiate. Remember, he believed he was facing God's wrath. Abimelech probably had just one shot to strike an acceptable offer. If Abraham took offense at the first offer, Abimelech assumed he might die. Therefore, the first financial transaction recorded was based primarily on technical speculations of perceived acceptance—not fundamental considerations of intrinsic value.

Babylonian Charts

Another example of technical analysis in the ancient world is found in the seventh century B.C. city of Babylon, where seven commodity price logs were discovered. "Charts" of commodity exchange rates aided in forecasting future prices. The notion of unraveling the forces of supply and demand through price trends was at work even in the earliest of days.

Early European Markets

In more modern financial times, stocks were exchanged in Jonathan's London coffee shop in the 1690s. At the time, about 100 different companies were incorporated into tradable stock shares. International news carried from the local docks made the way into local coffee shops, such as Jonathan's Coffee House, owned by Jonathan Miles. News and rumors of news undoubtedly were strong motivators to exchange stocks at specific prices. These prices were based on one trader's ideas of what other parties might be willing to accept and what other investors would be willing to bid. At Jonathan's, stock prices were commonly displayed behind the bar for all to see. In 1698, John Castaing, a frequent patron and prominent broker of the Huguenot's, began recording stock prices and exchange rates in a publication called *The Course of the Exchange and Other Things*. These records were then taken back to the ships and spread internationally. After a fire in 1748, Jonathan's was rebuilt, becoming the London Stock Exchange.

This "bid-offer" premise can be seen, too, in one of the oldest books about the markets, *Confusion de Confusiones*, written in 1688 by Joseph de la Vega. Observing the Amsterdam exchange, de la Vega states, "when prices rise, we think they will run away from us." This might be the first Dutch rendering of the traders' notion that "the trend is your friend."

Samurai Trading

Although historic records of market technicians are few, they do exist. There was an ancient Japanese technical trader, Munehisa

Homma, of whom we have some knowledge. Homma's methods of recording and analyzing prices are still with us to this day in the form of candlestick charts. Using his unique charting methods, Homma became a literal samurai of trading, making a killing trading rice. ("Killing" is an intentional pun of our samurai trader.)

In 1755, Homma wrote the first book to be regarded as a true work of technical analysis, *The Fountain of Gold—The Three Monkey Record of Money*. In this book, Homma claims that the most important aspect of investment is gauging the psychology of the market. As such, he described the developments of bull (yang) and bear (yin) markets and their tendencies to run to extremes and then reverse. Homma was also believed to be a practitioner of volume and weather patterns. At his peak, Homma was rumored to earn, in today's dollars, more than $10 billion a year in trading profits. His personal fortune grew to more than $100 billion!

Early American Market Analysis

Today, in the United States, securities analysis is dominated by fundamental, not technical, analysis. One might reasonably conclude that the modern markets and exchanges have always operated under these lines of thought. Yet the use of technical analysis in the modern markets has a rich history—one predating traditional fundamental analysis.

For instance, what comes to mind when you hear *Barron's, The Wall Street Journal, Forbes*, the Dow Jones Industrial Average, and Standard and Poor's? Technical analysis? Perhaps it should. All of these publications and indexes, in fact, have their roots in technical analysis.

The Root—Charles H. Dow

The modern father of technical analysis is considered to be none other than Charles H. Dow, the founder of *The Wall Street Journal*. Dow began his career as a financial reporter in the 1870s, a time when equities were not the dominant investment vehicle. Financial information about common stocks was scarce, and the information available often was unreliable. Historical ledgers of prices were not readily kept.

Thus, much of the knowledge about the underlying companies was limited to people "in the know" who frequently used that knowledge to manipulate stock prices. Dow used his bird's-eye position as a member of the New York Stock Exchange to change much of this by introducing a newsletter called *Customers' Afternoon Letter*. This revolutionary letter contained stock-price ledgers and company financial information, plus the first ever stock index, comprised of 11 stocks.

The concept of an index was revolutionary. It freed investors from tracking individual stocks, enabling them to follow the market instead. If investors knew the collective movement of just a few prominent stocks, they would have a good idea of how most stocks behaved as a whole. If investors knew how stocks were performing, they might be able to predict the actions of the overall economy. These ideas gave rise to Dow Theory, commonly regarded as the bedrock of modern technical analysis.

Such early innovations led Dow to introduce *The Wall Street Journal* on July 8, 1889, a financial newspaper that he cofounded with statistician Edward Jones. In 1894, Dow created what is now called the Dow Jones Transportation Average from nine railroad companies. On May 26, 1896, he created its more popular companion, the Dow Jones Industrial Average, composed of 12 industrial stocks.

As editor of *The Wall Street Journal*, Charles Dow employed his remarkable theories to interpret market averages and forecast the economy in its pages. These writings are now considered to be among the most superb financial editorials ever composed. Nevertheless, Dow never penned a summary explanation of his theories, to the frustration of his followers. Yet a friend of his, Samual A. Nelson, was able to render an account of Dow's theories (hence the term Dow theory) in *The ABC of Stock Speculation*, published the year of Dow's sudden death in 1902.

The Shoots—William Peter Hamilton and Other Dow Theorists

In 1903, Dow's interests in the Dow Jones Corporation were sold to Clarence W. Barron. It was about this time that Dow's apprentice, William Peter Hamilton, took over as the fourth editor of *The Wall Street Journal*. Hamilton continued the practices of his predecessor, promoting Dow's theories in 252 exceptional editorials published in *The Wall Street Journal* newspaper and in the newly established *Barron's* magazine. In 1922, Hamilton published his own account of Dow Theory in a book, *The Stock Market Barometer*. Hamilton died in 1929, clearing the way for the next person in the lineage of Dow thinking, Robert Rhea.

Rhea was an avid follower of Dow and of Hamilton's Dow theories. Rhea developed the first set of public charts for the Dow Jones industrial and transport indexes. He was a leading advocate of volume and relative strength analysis. Above all, Rhea was a master investor. Some argue Rhea was the best of a loaded field of early investing stars including the famous Jesse L. Livermore and Richard D. Wyckoff.

In 1932, Rhea released his book *Dow Theory*, published by Barron's, which articulated and refined Dow's theories into the concepts we still use today. Also in 1932, Rhea launched his newsletter, *Dow Theory Comment*, in which he called the exact bottom of the market, on July 8, 1932, and then the market's cyclical top in 1937.

Budding Practitioners

Other early contributors to technical analysis include Leonard P. Ayers, Richard D. Wyckoff, and Richard W. Schabacker, each of whom put his stamp upon technical analysis by moving it in new directions from that of the late Charles Dow. It was Ayers who first developed and promoted market-breadth analysis. He published his work through his company, Standard Statistics. It later merged with H.V. Poor and H.W. Poor Company to form Standard and Poor's in 1941.

A contemporary of Charles Dow, Wyckoff developed the first American investment magazine, *The Magazine of Wall Street*, in 1907. Wyckoff deviated from Dow theorists because he was more interested in the underlying reasons markets moved.

Wyckoff saw the economic principles of supply and demand at work in the stock exchange. He believed that the behavior observed through price and volume movements held the key to forecasting future market movements. These observations led Wyckoff to believe that the market operated under a set of three principles: the law of supply and demand, the law of cause and effect, and the law of effort versus results.

Wyckoff understood much of the market's movements to be the actions of large stock operators who accumulated stocks only to redistribute them back to the public at higher prices. Wyckoff believed volume was the key to identifying these operations.

By applying these technically oriented ideas and principles, Wyckoff soon amassed a large fortune. His newsletter was also quite popular, reaching more than 200,000 subscribers. Toward the end of his life, Wyckoff gave back to technical analysis by teaching his theories to others in his own investment course and publishing several books expressing his beliefs about technical analysis.

Schabacker was another follower of Dow's theories but, like Wyckoff, Schabacker moved Dow's concepts into new directions. He strayed from Wyckoff in that he saw his study of the markets as a scientific inquiry into the depths of the market structure. Schabacker wrote extensively about his ideas regarding technical analysis as a weekend editor of *The New York Times* and the youngest editor ever of *Forbes* magazine. In the September 1929 issue of *Forbes*, Schabacker warned of an "impending major reaction." We now know this event as the Great Market Crash of '29. It started the next month in October.

Although his life was short, ending in 1935 at the tender age of 36, Schabacker made significant contributions to the field of technical analysis. Many, if not most, of today's modern-day technical concepts come from the Schabacker perspective. *Technical Analysis of Stock Trends*, by Robert Davis Edwards and John Magee, is considered the Bible of all technical analysis tomes, but actually it's a New Testament.

Astute technicians are aware that it was Robert Edward's brother-in-law, Schabacker, who wrote the original "Old Testament," titled *Technical Analysis and Stock Market Profits*.

The Rise of the Fundamentals

Published in 1932, two years before Benjamin Graham and David Dodd's classic, *Security Analysis*, Schabacker epitomized technical analysis in the same way that Graham and Dodd came to personify fundamental analysis. In this timeless work, Schabacker defines and defends the technical approach while contrasting it to fundamental analysis. The book also introduced various concepts behind price trends, characterized the concepts of support and resistance, and introduced many of the classic price and volume patterns. It was from this original reference and relationship with Schabacker that his close relative Robert Edwards and MIT engineer John Magee were equipped to compose *Technical Analysis of Stock Trends* in 1948.

Given this rich heritage, one might wonder why technical analysis is not more prominent today. It was commonly used in the early days of the exchange, when manipulation of the markets was widespread, both through the dissemination of company information and in the handling of floor operations.

Because of manipulation, determining a fundamental equity valuation was difficult. Many investors believed the best course of action, instead, was to observe the action and behaviors of those who might have inside knowledge.

Early technicians recognized these issues as well. In fact, the existence of market manipulation was a good reason to differentiate between the movements of the long, intermediate, and short-term trends. Although there was potential for manipulation in the short-term, the intermediate and long-term trends were too broad to be exploited. Because of this, many early technicians confined their investment operations and advice to the big picture conveyed through the long-term trend.

Volume was important to the technician, too. Although prices could be temporarily manipulated, volume data could not. By analyzing trading volume, a technician could more easily detect whether a price movement represented true commitment. In the 1914 issue of the *Magazine of Wall Street,* Wyckoff wrote of the importance of following volume (called sales back then) as the fundamentals alone were not enough to make competent investment decisions.

A turning point in the popularity of technical analysis occurred in the mid-1930s. The Securities Exchange Act of 1934 created the Securities and Exchange Commission (SEC), which was broadly empowered to legislate and regulate the industry. Any attempts to manipulate the market now met with swift and harsh penalties. These reforms provided much needed regulation of the markets and regulation of publicly traded companies.

In 1934, about the time of these reforms, Graham and Dodd at Columbia University released *Security Analysis,* now considered the Bible of fundamental analysis. The approach promised that adequate returns and safety could be achieved via a thorough analysis of the underlying company. Through such analysis, they argued that one could identify the "intrinsic value," or true worth, of a company.

Graham and Dodd discounted the importance of the short and intermediate movements of the markets. Instead, they advocated owning stocks as long-term investments, not in timing the market. Their book came at a good time because the recent reforms provided an excellent setting in which to evaluate companies. No doubt, this early stage in the history of market reforms created many market inefficiencies to exploit.

Also at this time, Alfred Cowles at Yale came out against market forecasters. Cowles specifically targeted William Peter Hamilton's work with Dow Theory. Gazing down from his ivory tower, Cowles thought stock market forecasting methods used at the time were crude. He believed that highly educated economists were better suited for such tasks. He desired a more scholarly approach to "the best guesses" of the market prognosticators of his day. That is to say, at the time Cowles did not respect the market. His views later changed, however, leading others to develop Efficient Market Theory, the notion that stock prices are always correct and no one can predict them.

Cowles's initial efforts, though, focused on discrediting the establishment. Although Hamilton was dead, his ideas were still very much alive and highly venerated by the public, representing a perfect target for Cowles's attacks. In 1932, he produced the paper "Can Stock Market Forecasters Forecast?" In this foundational work, Cowles reconstructed Peter William Hamilton's 255 market forecasts, providing his own assumptions about how Hamilton would have invested and the underlying investments Hamilton might have chosen.

Cowles compared Hamilton's fictional portfolio to his own, self-created index of stocks. The results showed that Hamilton's esteemed performance would have underperformed a fully invested index. Whereas Cowles' work was quite substantial, indeed foreshadowing the notion of indexing and efficient markets, his critique caused irreparable harm to technical analysis.

Then, in the aftermath of the Great Crash, many investors abandoned stocks entirely. As a result, equity investing became a business left to a small number of professionals. At the same time, the SEC changed the rules of how the stock game was played. The investment community felt the need to be perceived as more responsible. Meanwhile, academics elevated the fundamental approach while assaulting technical thought.

In a 2007 interview in *Technically Speaking*, Ralph Acampora recited a story to interviewer Molly Schilling:

> Now, listen to this. December 1977, I went to Springfield, Massachusetts on behalf of the Market Technicians Association and I gave a gentleman by the name of John Magee our annual award, I think he was the third or fourth recipient. We all know who John Magee is. He wrote the famous book. In 1948, his book was published, it's very important to remember the date. The Bible on Technical Analysis comes out in 1948. When I met Mr. Magee, he was visibly upset. And I said—what's the problem, Mr. Magee? And he said—they never understood the laws of supply and demand. And I said— Who? He said—the Securities and Exchange Commission. The SEC, in 1949, I believe it was, had him up on fraud charges in New York City, because he had put out a book recommending stock purchases and sales on stocks

that weren't fundamental. And they couldn't prosecute him because he wasn't regulated, he wasn't part of a brokerage company. The SEC came out in 1949 with a rule that all research on Wall Street, and here's the quote, "...has to be rooted in sound fundamental principles." Magee didn't have an MTA (Market Technician's Association) at the time to speak for him, didn't have one. So from that date forward the whole establishment says—research is all fundamental. And as a consequence the universities started to teach their students all these fundamental things, it was the law of the land—you had to do the fundamentals.

Market Analysis in Today's Efficient Markets

The end result was a strong shift to an almost exclusively fundamental approach toward investing—one that mostly continues to this day. Every year, billions of dollars are spent on investment research for a unique interpretation of Graham's idea of value. Cowles's ideas have gained so much respect that now many of his colleagues believe that markets cannot be beaten at all by anyone. Consequently, they advocate investing solely in market indexes.

Even the great Benjamin Graham said at a Donaldson & Lufkin seminar in 1976, the year of his death:

> I am no longer an advocate of elaborate techniques of security analysis in order to find superior value opportunities. This was a rewarding activity, say, 40 years ago, when our textbook Graham and Dodd was first published. But the situation has changed a great deal since then. In the old days, any well-trained security analyst could do a good professional job of selecting undervalued issues through detailed studies. But in the light of the enormous amount of research now being carried on, I doubt whether in most cases such extensive efforts will generate sufficient superior selections to justify their cost. To that very limited extent, I'm on the side of the efficient market school of thought.

Yet, market regulation now has caused the pendulum to swing back toward the market conditions of before 1930. In October 2000, the SEC passed fair-disclosure rules. These regulations were intended to keep valuable insider information from reaching the general investing public unfairly or irregularly.

But the regulations instead have caused companies to withhold too much information from the public, in fear of violating the rules. As a result, less information is disseminated. An article published by the Association for Investment Management and Research (AIMR; now the CFA Institute) states, "Companies can hide behind (Regulation FD) when their fundamentals are deteriorating." One CFA Institute respondent commented, "In the past, company management could send signals indicating trends likely to impact results." Another member wrote, "Now there are complete surprises, which result in more short-term volatility."

Yet another member commented, "...lack of information has resulted in more surprise announcements of revisions," a change that "increases the risk perception of the entire market, thereby driving down valuations."

In the same article, CFA Institute Senior Vice President Patricia D. Walters, CFA, said

> Clearly, many of our members feel that too many companies are taking an excessively conservative stance and misinterpreting the new regulation to mean that they should have no one-to-one or small-group communication with anyone at all. We don't believe that that is either the intent or the wording of the regulation. Regulation FD only prohibits selective disclosure or private communication of material, non-public information. Significantly, CFA Institute's survey of portfolio managers shows that, since the regulations "the volume of substantive information released by the public companies they research has decreased."

In addition, the methods by which the exchanges operate have changed as well. In an effort to increase competitive pricing, the exchanges have dropped the bid-ask spreads on securities from one-eighth to a penny. The role of the specialist on the exchange is to keep an orderly market. When spreads were large, specialists had plenty of room to operate and to profit from the spread.

However, there is little room when the gap is one cent. Consequently, the specialists attempt to profit by facilitating large block trades and by taking advantage of their prime view of the order flow. But what happens when the order flow becomes one-sided, as in the "flash crash" of May 6, 2010? The uniquely advantaged floor brokers are no longer compensated to absorb the risk of potential losses of stepping in order to stabilize the market.

As the crash unfolded, orders left the exchange and were routed to digital exchanges. These exchanges pride themselves on fast execution. Filling orders at lightning speed is great, but when the orders are all one sided, what happens next is a disorderly market, as demonstrated by the dramatic dive and no-less-dramatic rebound that occurred that day, which temporarily vaporized $1 trillion in wealth.

Contrasting the Ages

It's important to understand the difference between the market of Charles Dow and William Peter Hamilton and today's markets. In Dow's time, the companies that comprised the market were under-regulated. This resulted in information being held closely, resulting in an uninformed public. Today, the markets are over-regulated, resulting in information being closely held for fear of punishment.

Before, the exchanges were under regulated, resulting in bizarre runs and disorderly markets. Today's tight regulations and tight spreads also have resulted in the risk of disorderly markets, as evidenced by the flash crash.

Setting the Record Straight—Dow Theory Strikes Back

According to Graham, the markets were inefficient in Dow's time, resulting in many opportunities for value investing. Modern markets, according to Graham, are efficient, resulting in fewer opportunities to invest in misvalued stocks. Few dispute that today's markets are at risk of sudden disorder. If you are to accept Graham's view that few value opportunities remain, the result is that today you have an ideal climate for employing a technical risk-management approach to the markets.

But what about Cowles's claim that technical analysis did not work for Hamilton?

It took several decades, but Yale finally got it right. In 1998, Stephen J. Brown of the New York University Stern School of Business and William N. Goetzmann and Alok Kumar from the Yale School of Management conducted their own in-depth study on Cowles's evaluation of Hamilton's work. They concluded, "a review of the evidence against William Peter Hamilton's timing abilities suggests just the opposite—his application of the Dow Theory appears to have yielded positive risk-adjusted returns."

The researchers also noted other points of interest. First, the index Cowles created was a different set of stocks from the investments chosen for Hamilton's portfolio. If Cowles had given Hamilton the benefit of investing in the same instruments as he had chosen for his own portfolio, then the annual rates of return would have been essentially identical, 10.73 percent versus 10.75 percent.

The study's second issue with Cowles's work proves that when comparing a fully invested portfolio to an actively managed portfolio neglects the factor of risk. According to Cowles, Hamilton would be long only 55 percent of the time, out of the market 29 percent of the time, and short the market 16 percent of the time. Therefore, the risk incurred between the two portfolios would not be the same. On a risk-adjusted basis, "the Hamilton portfolio has a higher Sharpe Ratio (0.559 compared with 0.456) and a positive Jensen's Measure of 4.04 percent—more than 400 basis points per year. This high Jensen's Measure is due to a beta of 0.326 with respect to the S&P 500 index," according to Brown, Goetzmann, and Kumar. In translation, Hamilton's portfolio took significantly less risk in producing its returns.

In addition to these points made by the researchers, note that the study was done and ended in the midst of a strong bull market. This greatly benefited Cowles's fully invested portfolio. The researchers

point out that Hamilton decisively beat Cowles until the market
became excessively bullish in 1926 (see Figure 2.1).

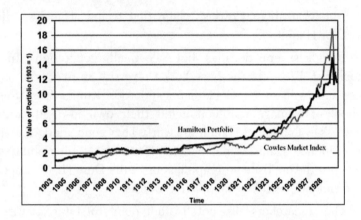

(Source: The Dow Theory: *William Peter Hamilton's Track Record Reconsidered*, William N.
Goetzmann [Yale School of Management] and Stephen J. Brown [Leonard Stern School of
Business, NYU].)

Figure 2.1   Dow theory versus Cowles' stock index.

Given these successful bear calls and the lower risk assumed in
Hamilton's portfolio, one can wonder what would happen in a secular
bear market, such as from 1929 to 1947. According to the researchers,
"Hamilton appears to have been extremely successful in his bear
calls." Armed with this knowledge, who would you want managing
your portfolio today, Hamilton or Cowles?

3

Price Analysis

"In the financial markets, a collective human bias renders a decision. This decision takes the form of price on an electronic quote machine, or at the post of a global exchange. Price influences other participants and then they make decisions according to the prevailing market trends. Price, therefore, plays a profound role in shaping the future outcome for many events (in the global stock markets)."

—*J.C. Coppola, III*

One of the most popular game shows ever to appear on daytime television was "The Price is Right." Host Bob Barker asked contestants to guess the price of various items of merchandise. There were, of course, many opinions among the contestants of what the price ought to be. But the winner was the person who guessed closest to the actual price without going over.

Many investors view the stock market as a colossal game of "The Price is Right." However, in the exchange markets, price originates from two separate parties agreeing to disagree. If I am buyer of a stock, it takes a second party willing to sell the same stock to commence the exchange. So what is this second party's opinion of the stock I want to buy? Why would he desire to sell it? Obviously, he believes it is going down. Otherwise, he would not agree sell it. Meanwhile, I believe it's going up, or I would not buy it. Thus, the seller and I disagree on the future outlook of the security, and that disagreement leads us to agree to exchange. This agreed-upon amount is called *price* in the exchange markets. Thus, price is a single point of agreement in a situation fraught with disagreement.

The Market's Price Is Right

Whether one uses the term intrinsic, fundamental, or theoretical value, value is just that: theoretical. Value represents someone's opinion. Price is truth. When intrinsic value does not equal market price, then that opinion is currently wrong. Price is the de facto belief of people. The collective knowledge anticipated by investors is manifested within price. Investors' ever-changing beliefs are priced into the stock via their actions. All new data, analysis, and events are constantly and efficiently "priced into the stock" as investors respond to these events and speculate about their consequences. As a result, all fundamental data, economic data, and any combination of financial or economic ratios lag price. No matter how well a fundamental model is constructed, the fundamentals cannot help one determine when to buy or sell. Only volume and technically manipulated data (such as derivatives of price) have been demonstrated to lead price. Unlike fundamental or economic data, price datum is not subject to constant revisions.

The Basic Building Block of the Chart

Like the DNA in living creatures, price is the basic building block of the chart. As DNA contains all genetic information of the cell, price contains the collective information known by investors about the company. A string of individual price bars drawn in sequence creates the chart's trend. As shown in Figure 3.1, a price bar contains six key pieces of information: the open, the high, the low, the close, the change, and the range.

- **The open**—The opening value is the first trade of the day. It represents the position clients want to be in at the beginning of the day. After the investors have time to review the markets overnight, the open represents the desired position of investors to begin the day. The opening trade is the change desired by investors repositioning their portfolios for a new day. The change from the previous close to the open is a reflection of these new sentiments. Also institutions looking to accumulate (or distribute) a position often place orders at the open because the open trade is often the largest, most liquid trade of the day. In this way, the open might be one of the best times to accumulate/distribute a large volume of stock while minimizing the impact on the stock's price.

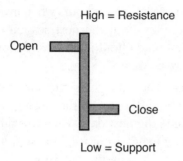

Figure 3.1   Price bar.

- **The high**—The high is the highest point the stock traded during the session. The high is the furthest point the bulls were able to advance the stock higher before sellers regained control to push the stock back down. The high represents a stronghold for sellers and a resistance area to buyers. There is one exception. When the stock closes on the high, it did not encounter any real resistance from the sellers. The buyers just ran out of time.

- **The low**—The low is the lowest point the stock traded during the session. The low is the furthest point the bears were able to force down the stock before buyers regained control to push the stock up. The low represents an area where enough supportive demand existed to prevent the price from moving lower. The exception is when the security closes on the low. When the stock closes on the low, it did not encounter buying support. Rather, the bulls were saved by the closing bell of the session.

- **The close**—The close is the last price agreed between buyers and sellers ending the trading session. It is perhaps the most important piece of information of all financial data. The close is the market's final evaluation. A lot can happen between one close to the next close. Indeed, much of the intraday activities might be considered noise. Who cares about the half-time score? Likewise, the close is the day's final score between the battle of bears and bulls. The close represents investors' sentiments and convictions of investors at the end of the day when the books are closed. It's the desired final position of investors—all in, all out, or somewhere in between. It is the position investors desire to hold after hours when investors are unable to trade with liquidity until the next session opens. The closing price is the first (and oftentimes, the only) price the majority of investors desire to know.

- **The change**—The change is the difference from close to close. This is the difference of the closing value one day versus the closing value the next day. When this difference is positive, it tells us that demand is outweighing supply. When this difference is negative, it tells us that supply is increasing beyond demand. The change is perhaps the most sought after piece of financial data on the planet.

- **The range**—The range is the spread of values within which the stock traded throughout the day. The range spans between the bar's highest point and the same bar's lowest point. It is measured from the top of the bar, where resistance set in, to the low, where support came in. The size of the range gives us important information about how easily demand can move the stock up or supply force the price down. The wider the range, typically, the easier it is for the forces of supply and demand to move the stock price.

Volume Analysis: Digging Deeper

Someone once asked me why he should believe in technical analysis. To answer this question, I first needed to establish what type of evidence he would accept. So I asked him, "Do you believe in economics?" He answered definitively in the affirmative. I then explained that technical analysis is the law of supply and demand working within the exchange markets. For example, when securities change hands on the auction markets, the volume of shares bought always matches the volume sold on executed orders. When the price rises, the upward movement reflects that demand has exceeded supply or that buyers are in control. Likewise, when the price falls, it implies supply has exceeded demand or that sellers are controlling the action. Over time, these trends of supply and demand form accumulation and distribution trends and patterns. But what if there were a way to look deep inside these price trends to determine whether current prices were supported by the volume? Well, this is the objective of volume analysis: identifying the potential implications from any imbalances within the price-volume relationship. In the next chapter, we examine the second variable of most important relationship: volume.

4

Volume Analysis

"Volume is the steam in the boiler that makes the choo-choo go down the tracks."
—*Joseph Granville*

Volume

Even the most casual investor knows what matters about a stock—price. You are taught early on to buy low and sell high. The evening news tracks the major indexes as if they were horse races, so most people naturally believe that a higher close is good news and a lower close is bad; yet you are left none the wiser about navigating your own finances by knowing this daily result.

Price surely matters. But this is a market. Waiting for the final number on a given day or week tells you what happened but not why or, more importantly, how. Picture a mall parking lot. Is it full or half-empty? Is it Saturday or a workday? How many people are walking the shops and sitting in the restaurants? Regardless of what they buy or how much they pay, what matters to the investors of that mall is that customers are showing up and participating. For a smart trader, that's understood innately as "volume."

One can track volume for just about any stock or index easily, but understanding it and using it to your advantage is a skill few investors possess. This book breaks down the fundamental ideas that constitute volume analysis and gives you the tools you need to interpret volume to help you make better, smarter trades.

Volume Terminology

Let's start by defining a few terms. *Volume* as a general term describes the amount of a given tradable entity (for example, shares of stock, commodities contracts, options contracts, and so on) exchanged between buyers and sellers. If volume is high, more units of a security have changed ownership. If it is low, then fewer units have changed hands.

There are several categories of volume to examine:

- **Market volume (also referred to as trading volume)**— The number of shares exchanged between buyers and sellers during a given period of time, typically a day.

- **Total volume (also referred to as exchange volume)**— Describes the entire volume of all issues traded on an exchange, such as the New York Stock Exchange.

- **Index volume**—The cumulative sum of the volume traded in all of the components of an index, such as the Dow or the S&P 500.

- **Total trades**—How many transactions occurred within the trading session.

- **Dollar volume**—The value of all the shares traded over the course of the trading session.

- **Float**—The number of shares owned by the public available for exchange.

- **Average volume (also referred to as typical volume)**— Computed as a moving average, which will smooth the peaks and valleys to show a more representative view of typical volume over a predefined period of time. Average volume enables the technician to discern whether volume is increasing or decreasing relative to the past. In short, is the mall fuller this Saturday compared to every Saturday in the past year—or relatively empty?

Volume Data in Market Analysis

A trade produces only two pieces of information: the price and price's neglected sibling, volume. Perhaps the least appreciated piece of the puzzle, volume represents fertile ground for technical analysis. Proficiency in volume analysis is a rare skill. Properly understood, though, volume analysis can provide its practitioner with the power to peer deeply into market mechanics.

Benjamin Graham, the father of value investing and a mentor of Warren Buffett, often called the market a "voting machine." If so, then volume is the ballot box. Volume is a literal illustration of the power behind the forces of supply and demand.

Volume is understood as the validation of price, the source of liquidity, the substantiation of information, the fulfillment of convictions, the revelation of divergent opinions, the fuel of the market, the proponent of truth, and the energy behind the velocity of money. If you believe any of this information might be important in making an investment decision, volume analysis is important to you.

Volume Validates Price

Volume plays a critical role in securities analysis. Volume answers the deceptively simple question, "How many?" As discussed previously, volume is the quantity of shares traded. But the key is that the more shares exchanged at a given price, the more that volume confirms price. More traders "vote," in the parlance of Graham, for that price at that point in time.

In the same way, low volume tells a different story. If fewer investors participate at a given price point, more doubt is cast on the validity of that price.

Let's say you are looking to buy an item on eBay and found just one seller. How much confidence would you have that the listed price is fair and reasonable? Probably not much. However, if you found an item listed by a multitude of retailers with tens of thousands of transactions occurring at a similar price, you would reasonably conclude that the price is a good representation of the item's value.

The same principle applies to trading volume. The more people participating in a price movement, the more the price movement is validated. For the technical trader, volume dictates the quality of the price.

Volume Liberates Liquidity

We can glean another valuable piece of information from the eBay example. Assume that there was only one seller and no buyers. In that case, what is the probability of being able to exchange quickly the item back into cash at about the same price? In *Mind over Markets,* Eric Jones and James & Robert Dalton address this issue, "Volume is the truest and most reliable indicator of the market's ability to facilitate a trade...A market that is not facilitating trade will not survive long."

If volume is low, the odds of selling quickly at a good price are not very good. In the high-volume scenario, though, where many transactions occur in a narrow range of prices, the opposite is true: You can sell it for cash immediately and likely at about the same price at which you bought it. High volume normally infers high liquidity, the ability to exchange an instrument or item for currency at a fair price.

Volume Substantiates Information

Volume validates price, but it also contributes to forming price. As new information is disseminated to the public, volume reveals the flow of this information. By observing the change in volume as information is released, a trader can tell how quickly new facts are absorbed by market participants.

In this way, volume substantiates the importance of the new information. As volume rises, it equates to more emphasis being placed on new information by investors. Similarly, news or information that does not greatly impact volume indicates that the information has little significance to the market.

Volume Reveals Convictions

The volume of shares traded often reveals the market's true conviction. For example, let's say you hear that a renowned investor has

bought a certain stock. Upon learning this, you buy 1,000 shares of
the same stock.

Later on, though, you learn that the famous investor bought just
100 shares. This should change your view of the security considerably.
You expect a wealthy investor to buy 1 million shares—if he or she
acted on conviction.

Volume Expresses Interest and Enthusiasm

Market volume is money searching for a place to reside. There
are only two reasons investors choose to invest. One is to seize on
an opportunity. The other is to reduce the risk of being positioned
incorrectly. Rising volume reveals that investors believe there is a
greater interest and enthusiasm, whether on the buying or selling side
of a given market or share. Falling volume shows that fewer investors
see opportunities, so they stay on the sidelines.

Volume Denotes the Disparity of Opinions

Volume can enlighten the savvy investor when there is a disparity
of opinions. Often, information and commentary in the media lead
the investing public to choose sides, regardless of the underlying facts
(or when no facts are evident). Trading activity expressed as volume is
the empirical evidence that these diverging opinions are at work, with
each side betting on its own beliefs. The greater the disparity of opinion, the greater return each side expects to realize from an investment. Thus, a wide divergence in these beliefs shows up as higher
volume as the bulls and bears take positions to attempt to profit.
Light volume, in turn, can denote equilibrium between supply and
demand, a consensus that the price is "right" for the time being.

Volume Is the Fuel of the Market

For an engine to run, it needs fuel. The fuel of the market is provided by new supply (selling) and demand (buying). Volume is a

measure of the total supply and demand produced by market participants. Volume, thus, is the fuel that enables markets to move. Trader
Billy Williams puts it this way, "Volume is literally the fuel for stock
values. Like the space shuttle when it is launched into space, the
majority of fuel is spent just to get to orbit. This explosive force of
energy to propel the space shuttle into space or new heights requires
an above average reserve of the fuel, but then the space shuttle can
then use only a small portion of the remaining fuel reserve to carry
out the rest of its mission. Volume is to stocks what rocket fuel is to
the space shuttle."

Volume Exposes the Truth

If price is truth, volume keeps price honest. It is the desire of
large institutions to buy or sell without drawing attention. The reality,
though, is that they cannot. Large institutions must carefully choose
securities to avoid those that adversely affect price from their own
trading operations. After a security is chosen for purchase (or liquida-
tion), a big institution must be cautious: If it tips its hand, others will
try to front-run the trade, that is, buy or sell early to "ride the wave"
of the coming large transaction.

One way to hide a big trade is to sell at the "offer" or buy at the
"bid," the publicly available price of the moment. But volume analysis
sees through that trick. If a trade goes through, it must be reported. A
significant increase in volume is a clear sign that a big institution is at
the table—even if price movement is subdued.

Volume Is the Cause

Early twentieth-century stock guru Richard Wyckoff once
defined his own laws of investing. One key law, for our purposes, was
that of "cause and effect." The law of cause and effect states that the
extent of a market move is directly proportional to the amount of its
cause. For volume analysts, that means that the gap between the
number of shares offered by sellers versus those bidded on by buyers
is the cause of price change.

Volume Gives Rise to Velocity

Market volume is a quantity that, when increased, tends to produce an acceleration of price direction. Charles Dow, founder of *The Wall Street Journal* and the namesake of the Dow Jones averages, believed that a high volume indicated a more accurate price and that, in turn, volume actually led price. In short, Dow felt that a substantial increase in volume often preceded significant price movements. Since that simple proclamation more than a century ago, the concept has been validated by a multitude of research studies.

5

Volume: The Force of the Market

"A Jedi's strength flows from the force."
—*Yoda*

Volume Is the Force

Although market volume is a crucial piece of investment information, the majority of the public is ignorant of volume. Financial analysts do not consider volume, whereas technical analysts underutilize it. This chapter discusses how volume provides essential information in two critical ways: by indicating a price change before it happens and by helping the technician interpret the meaning of a price change as it happens.

Volume Leads Price

Although practitioners of technical analysis and academia have often been at odds, volume information is one area where they tend to largely agree. Volume can provide essential information by indicating a price change before it happens. The message is extremely telling, particularly when the volume reaches extreme levels. During such times, volume offers far superior information than price alone could ever provide. Authors Gervails, Kaniel, and Minglegrin of "The High Volume Return Premium," a white paper from The Rodney L. White Center for Financial Research of The Wharton School, University of Pennsylvania state, "We find that individual stocks whose trading activity is unusually large (small) over periods of a day or a week, as measured by trading volume during those periods, tend to experience large (small) subsequent returns." The researchers further state, "A stock that experiences unusually large trading activity over a particular day or a week is expected to subsequently appreciate." The testing results of their 33-year study comparing stocks that experience relatively high volume surges compared to normal and low-volume stocks is illustrated in Figure 5.1. Similar conclusions were confirmed by Kaniel, Li, and Starks of the University of Texas. Their research paper, "The High Volume Return Premium and the Investor Recognition Hypothesis: International Evidence and Determinants," concludes

> We study the existence and magnitude of the high-volume return premium across equity markets in 41 different countries and find that the premium is a strikingly pervasive global phenomenon. We find evidence that the premium is a significant presence in almost all developed markets and in a number of emerging markets as well.

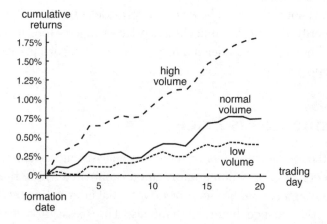

(Source: "The High Volume Return Premium," The Wharton School University, Pennsylvania.)

Figure 5.1   Average cumulative returns of stocks chosen according to the highest trading volume as experienced the day before this graph starts.

Volume Interprets Price

The second critical way in which volume provides information is by helping the technician interpret price. Volume enables the analyst to interpret the meaning of price through the lens of the corresponding volume. The authors Blume, Easley, and O'Hara (1994) reported in "Market Statistics and Technical Analysis: The Role of Volume," in the *Journal of Finance,* "volume provides information on information quality that cannot be produced by the price static. These researchers demonstrate how volume, information precision, and price movements relate, as well as how sequences of volume and prices can be informative. Moreover, they also show that traders who use information contained in market statistics do better than those trades who do not. Thus, technical analysis arises as a natural component of the agents learning process."

However, price alone represents the vast majority of the work within technical analysis. As such, this book gives volume the significance it is due as an essential element of investment analysis. Yet doing so without also discussing price is also insufficient. Volume cannot be properly understood without price any more than price can be adequately assessed without volume. Independently, both price and volume convey only vague market information. However, when examined together, they provide indications of supply and demand that neither could provide independently. Ying (1966), in his groundbreaking work on price-volume correlations, stated, "Price and volume of sales in the stock market are joint products of a single market mechanism; any model that attempts to isolate prices from volumes or vice versa will inevitably yield incomplete if not erroneous results." The mechanism to which Ying is referring is the stock market exchange.

B = S = T

Some serious misconceptions among investors exist about how the market functions. According to common perception, the market should be fairly easy to understand. Why does the market go up? The market goes up because there are more buyers than sellers, and the market goes down because there are more sellers than buyers. That's technical analysis...right? Baloney! Yet, we have heard these phrases uttered countless times by common investors and by supposed market experts. Recently, a financial commentator stated that the market was up because there were "more buyers than sellers." A few days later, another market expert said that the market was down because there were more sellers than buyers. Ils ne comprendent pas; that is, "they don't understand." You can be a far more astute technician than supposed experts by understanding this simple fact: In an auction market, price and volume are jointly determined through the agreement to trade. The easy formula B = S = T is a simple formula to help you remember this fact. B is the buyer's volume, S is the seller's volume, and T is the total trading volume. In an exchange/auction market, the number of shares *B*ought always equals the number of shares *S*old, which always equals the *T*otal number of shares traded. Trading volume, then, is the number of shares *exchanged* between buyers and sellers. Let's put this knowledge into practice by logically applying it to the following quiz.

> Quiz: Let's say that I analyzed the volume patterns in a particular stock and determined the stock to be a timely and attractive investment. As a disciplined portfolio manager, I follow such indications rigorously. To ensure that I do not miss out on any possible price appreciation, I enter a market order to buy 1,000 shares. Unbeknownst to me, a fundamentally driven fund manager somewhere has crunched some numbers and determined that the same stock has moved above its intrinsic value of $50 a share. Feeling equally strong in her convictions, the fundamentalist enters an order to sell the firm's 10,000 shares at a limit price of $50. On the exchange, our orders cross, thereby enabling me to buy 1,000 shares from the fund manager. So here is the question: Which force is in control, demand or supply? Is it me, the buyer, who has put in a market order suggesting urgency, or is it the seller, whose limit order suggests her complacency but with ten times the number of shares to distribute?

If you are not certain about the answer, do not feel alone. The theoretical and practical answers have been debated. The essential point is that price is determined by the net of demand less supply. Thus, when the trade fills on an uptick, it indicates that there is more demand than supply, whereas when the trade goes through on a downtick, supply outweighs demand. If you add up all these ticks and the price is heading down over time, they form a supply line; you have then what is called a *falling support line*. In technical analysis, this is called a *downtrend*, indicating that supply has been greater than demand over time. If after adding up all of the ticks over time they are pointing upward, you have a demand line indicating that demand has been greater than the supply over time. In technical analysis, this line is referred to as an *uptrend*.

Volume Analysis—Use the Force

What if you had a way to look deep inside the interactions of these two opposing forces, supply and demand, to determine whether the volume supported the price action. This is the objective of volume analysis. Volume analysis analyzes volume data to determine the strength of supply and demand by examining the intrinsic relationship between price and volume.

Volume analysis attempts to expose the relationship between price trends and the corresponding volume information. Bernardo and Judd (1996) described this relationship: "Volume data is informational in this setting because prices alone do not fully reveal the magnitude of the private signals and their precision." Thus, by analyzing price and volume together, you can determine whether the price-volume relationship confirms the price action or contracts it, thereby giving notice of future price movements.

Support and Resistance

In this price-volume analysis, think of volume as the force that drives the market. Force has been defined as a power exerted against support or resistance. To a technician, this definition of force is quite revealing. In technical analysis, support is a price in which buyers reside. When a stock falls to a support zone, buyers enter the market believing the stock price to be undervalued at this low level. Through their buying operations, they unknowingly "support" the stock price, effectively pushing the stock back up again. You can identify support zones by finding key low points where these buying operations have occurred in the past.

In the same fashion, resistance is an area in which sellers reside. Likewise, when a security rises to a resistance zone, sellers come in believing the stock price is overvalued at this high price level. Through their selling activities, investors "resist" the advance, forcing the stock back down again. In this way, you can view volume as the force needed to break through a support zone or breakout of a resist-ance zone (see Figure 5.2).

(Source: Tradestation. Created with TradeStation. ©TradeStation Technologies, Inc. All rights reserved.)

Figure 5.2   Support and resistance.

Trends

The concept of a price trend was mentioned previously in this chapter. But what is a price trend? An *uptrend* is simply a support line that rises during the course of time. An uptrend is representative of demand for shares that are greater than the supply of shares. An uptrend can be identified by connecting significant lows. Selling pres-sure pushes the stock price down, but this pressure is unable to push it back down beyond the previous low levels. A string of higher lows constitutes an uptrend. These rising lows that arose over time show that demand is overwhelming the supply. With each dip, buyers are eager to scoop up more shares than are shares available for sale at the given price, indicating that the security is being accumulated. In eco-nomics, you might call this trend a demand line. In this book, we use these terms interchangeably and refer to an uptrend as a rising sup-port line or demand line (see Figure 5.3).

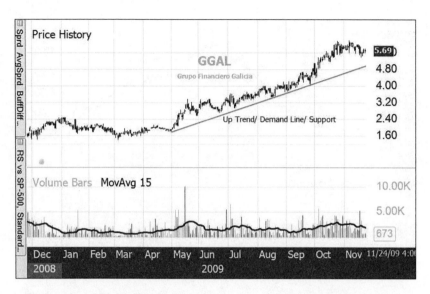

(Chart courtesy of TeleChart® by Worden Brothers, Inc. www.worden.com. Charts courtesy of TeleChart® which is a registered trademark of Worden Brothers, Inc., Five Oaks Office Park, 4905 Pine Cone Drive, Durham, NC 27707. Ph. (800) 776-4940 or (919) 408-0542. http://www.worden.com.)

Figure 5.3 Uptrend, rising support line, or demand line.

Correspondingly, a *downtrend* is simply a falling resistance line. A downtrend is a line of resistance that with time falls even lower. A downtrend indicates that demand is overrun by supply. With each advance in price, sellers are more anxious to exit a position than there are buyers at that price level, forcing the price back down because they must sell their shares at a lower price to find a willing buyer. A downtrend is identified by connecting significant highs so that each high is lower than the previous high. The downtrend reveals that, with time, sellers are willing to accept lower prices, thus indicating that the security is in a state of distribution. In economics, this falling line of resistance might be referred to as a supply line. In technical analysis, it is referred to as a downtrend. As in the case of the uptrend, we use downtrend, falling support line, and supply line interchangeably (see Figure 5.4).

(Chart courtesy of TeleChart® by Worden Brothers, Inc. www.worden.com. Charts courtesy of TeleChart® which is a registered trademark of Worden Brothers, Inc., Five Oaks Office Park, 4905 Pine Cone Drive, Durham, NC 27707. Ph. (800) 776-4940 or (919) 408-0542. http://www.worden.com.)

Figure 5.4   Downtrend, falling supply line, or falling resistance.

Every Object in a State Motion Stays in Motion Unless Acted Upon

"I can calculate the movement of the stars, but not the madness of men."

—*Sir Isaac Newton*

Now you can observe how volume interacts with price trends through Newton's laws of motion. According to Newton, a change in the motion of a body indicates a force is in operation. In security analysis, volume is the operational force behind price change.

According to Newton's First Law of Motion, every object in a state of uniform motion tends to remain in that state of motion unless an external force is applied. In other words, a body left to itself will maintain its condition unchanged. A security might have volume without change. In such cases, volume information might contain little predictive value. However, a security price without volume has no meaning and is technically impossible on an exchange market because price change cannot occur without volume.

Force = Mass × Acceleration

Newton's Second Law of Motion states that a relationship exits between an object's mass, its acceleration, and applied force. Specifically, force equals mass times acceleration. Physically, this relates to how much force it requires to move an object a given distance at a given speed. You can apply this law as a premise to understanding the markets. Understanding how much volume (force) is required to move a security (the object) a given distance (price change) at a given speed (acceleration/momentum) can be helpful in security analysis. Richard Wyckoff referred to this principal as the law of effort versus result, which asserts that the effort must be in proportion to the results.

In my first year on the colligate track team, I was designated to run in the 4-by-1 mile relay, where each of the four runners runs a 1-mile leg. I was not a miler. I primarily ran the long-distance events, such as the 5K and 10K. Interestingly, of the four relay members, none of us were milers. I led off with the first leg of the relay, and the race started out fast. I had good speed for a distance runner but was coming off of an injury and had not been training for the shorter distance events. My first lap time was 60 seconds—too fast for my taste because my heart rate was 150, but I was toward the back of the pack and did not want to let my team members down. My next lap time was 61 seconds, and again I was toward the back of the pack. Now I was dead tired, and my heart soared close to 180. I completed my next lap in a pedestrian 79 seconds and was now dead last in the race. Ashamed of myself and determined to put my team members in better position, I let loose passing a few runners on the last lap, clocking in a final lap time of 59 seconds for an unconventional 4:19 mile. I was quite embarrassed handing off the baton near the tail end of the pack. Despite my poor lead-off leg, we ended up placing second in the race and, surprisingly, I had the best split (time) on the team! This is odd because, normally, the fastest runner on a relay team runs last. However, in this relay, the fastest leg was by far the first. What happened? During this meet, the open mile was run a mere two races after the four-mile relay. Our coach pulled our miler specialists off of the 4-by-1 relay so they could run the mile race completely fresh. Meanwhile, the other teams chose to run their milers in the first leg of the 4 by 1 with the thought of maximizing their rest before their upcoming mile races. As a result, the first leg was much faster than the remaining legs.

Later, the coach told me, "Buff, if we threw out that third lap and ran it like the other three, you'd have run a 4:00 mile. We just need to get that third lap closer to par with the others. Do that, and you could be the best miler in the conference." I respectfully kept my mouth shut, but it was obvious that the only reason I could run the last lap in 59 seconds was because I completely blew off the third lap. Here, my results were the lap times (my speed) while my effort was my heart rate. The key to determining that my pace was unsustainable was the relationship between my speed and my heart rate. Between laps one and two, my speed slowed by one second, yet my heart rate jumped by nearly 20 percent. More effort yielded me an inferior result, leading to my third lap crash and burn.

Stocks operate on much of the same principles. In security analysis, the effort (force) is volume that achieves the result of price change (acceleration). In other words, it is the size of the executed bids and offers that demonstrates investors' commitment. The movement in price should not exceed the movement in volume. To discern this relationship, you must study price change (acceleration) relative to the volume change (force).

Consider this example: A stock breaks out 10 percent from its previous close on a volume 200 percent higher than normal. The next day, the stock advances another 5 percent on 300 percent higher volume. On the third day, the stock moves up 2 percent on 400 percent higher volume. The high volume on the price breakout is a bullish indication. However, with time, volume (force) expands while the price change (acceleration) wanes. In Wyckoff's terms, more effort is producing smaller results. In Newton's terms, more force (volume) produces less acceleration (price change), meaning that the mass (price) could be overly expanded (high). This situation can be an early warning signal that although the stock runs strong, it might be susceptible to its own crash and burn (see Figure 5.5).

(Chart courtesy of TeleChart® by Worden Brothers, Inc. www.worden.com. Charts courtesy of
TeleChart® which is a registered trademark of Worden Brothers, Inc., Five Oaks Office Park,
4905 Pine Cone Drive, Durham, NC 27707. Ph. (800) 776-4940 or (919) 408-0542.
http://www.worden.com.)

Figure 5.5   Law of effort versus results.

We previously described volume as a "force." The physics dictionary defines force a bit differently: "Force is a vector quantity that
tends to produce acceleration." This definition provides hints of an
important belief held by the modern founder of technical analysis,
Charles Dow. Dow believed, "Volume leads price," meaning significant volume changes tend to precede significant price movements. It
took nearly 100 years for academia to catch up with Dow's findings.
Many academics[1] (re)discovered the positive correlation between
trading volume and price change in their research. Legendary volume technician Joseph Granville said, "Volume is measured in
demand, therefore, volume must lead price." As such, volume is a
measurement of the force produced when demand and supply inter-
sect: It is the force that "pushes" price. We review more evidence of
volume leading price when discussing volume indicators.

---

[1] Ying (1966), Crouch (1970), Clark (1973), Epps and Epps (1976), Cornell
(1981), Harris (1986), Karpoff (1987), Blume, Easley, and O'Hara (1994), Harris
and Raviv (1993), Kandel and Pearson (1996), Chatrath (1996), Bernardo and
Judge (1996), Griffen (2004), and many others.

TABLE 5.1   Other Academic Studies Illustrating the Empirical Evidence on the Contemporaneous Relationship Between Trading Volume and Return

Author	Year	Data	Test Period	Time Frame
Ying	1966	Stocks	1957–1962	Daily
Epps	1976	Bonds	1971	Ticks
Morgan	1976	Stocks	1962–1965	Daily
Morgan	1976	Stocks	1926–1968	Monthly
Epps	1977	Stocks	1971	Ticks
Hanna	1978	Bonds	1971	Ticks
Rogalski	1978	Stocks and Warrents	1968–1973	Monthly
Comiskey	1984	Stocks	1976–1979	Yearly
Harris	1984	Stocks	1981–1983	Daily
Smirlock and Starks	1985	Stocks	1981	Ticks
Richardson	1987	Stocks	1973–1982	Weekly
Jain and Joh	1988	NYSE Exchange	1979–1983	Hourly
Lee and Rui	2002	S&P 500 Index	1973–1999	Daily
Lee and Rui	2002	Topix Index	1974–1999	Daily
Lee and Rui	2002	FT-SE 100	1986–1999	Daily
Tambi	2005	Stocks	2000–2005	Daily

Every Action Has an Equal and Opposite Reaction

Newton's Third Law states that for every action, an equal and opposite reaction exists. Adam Smith developed a similar theory but in the field of economics. Adam Smith believed that when demand exceeded supply, price increased, and when supply was greater than demand, price decreased.

The exchange markets operate under the same laws of supply and demand as traditional economics. Economic theory assumes that supply increases as demand rises; namely, as producers are motivated to produce more goods or services. Meanwhile, demand should rise as the available supply decreases and buyers become attracted at lower prices. However, the auction market mechanism changes the dynamics of this operation. In the exchange market, supply is mostly finite. Yes, with help of investment bankers, companies can increase the supply of shares. However, the directive of every publicly traded company is to increase shareholder wealth through dividends or stock price appreciation. The board of directors do not offer shares unless deemed necessary to *increase* (or in a crisis to stabilize) the price of the stock. Thus, both supply and demand operate on an opportunity cost model, where wealth is looking for the best opportunity for growth, or at worst the best place to preserve capital. Supply (in the form of sellers) comes from existing shareholders (or short sellers) who believe cash or another opportunity represents a greater value than the stock at its present price. Demand (or buyers) comes from investors who believe the stock represents the best opportunity for at least a portion of their wealth. (Other factors, such as trading cost, taxes, and spreads might enter into the equation, but these are not pertinent to the context of this text.)

The securities exchange markets function as an auction. The volume of shares bought always matches the volume sold on all executed orders. When the price rises, the upward movement reflects a situation in which demand exceeds supply (that is, the buyers are in control). Likewise, when the price falls, it implies that supply exceeds demand (that is, the sellers are in control). You also know that with time, these trends of supply and demand form patterns and trends of accumulation and distribution. Whether these trends are up, down, or sideways, volume is the force exerted to uphold these trends. Anna at Making Bread says, "Volume is like the water in a hose pipe, and the greater the water pressure, the more powerful the flow."

Applying the Laws of Motion in Volume Analysis

By examining Newton's first law, you learned that price change cannot occur without volume. You also learned that the imbalance between supply and demand is manifested through the trading volume as the external force causing price movements. By examining

Newton's third law, you learned that the difference between demand (buying pressure) and supply (selling pressure) determines the amount of price change reaction.

Wyckoff had a similar law called the law of cause and effect. For there to be an effect, a cause must first exist. The strength of that cause should be proportional to the effect. The asymmetry or imbalance between supply and demand, as manifested through the trading volume, is the external force causing price movements. The higher the relative volume change, the stronger this disparity force is at work. It is in these times of an unordinary high-volume surge that the market is poised for violent price swings.

6

How to Read the Market Like a Book

"In determining a value by intrinsic formulas, the investor maybe heavily influenced by subjective factors that creep into the assumptions without even being aware of them. He can thus very often mislead himself into believing that his decision is reached on the basis of 'the facts,' when in reality, his choices of assumptions has predetermined what the facts will be."

—*David Dreman*

Market news might very well be the most misused information on the planet. Market news is released and, immediately, investors read the information and judge it. Investors deem this information to be good or bad. If good, they continue to hold or buy more of the issue associated with the news. If bad, they sell. These investors don't look beyond the news story. Instead, they simply trust their ability to make sound judgments, and if the stock doesn't move in the direction they expect, they blame the market: Why is the market not responding rationally? The error, however, is not in the market, but in these investors' assumptions. They do not take into consideration that the stock's current price has been marked up in anticipation of the news announcement. Rarely are news items unanticipated; it is the job of media companies to promote news, and most market news stories are just the culmination of market expectations. If the market is up, it is because investors have previously bought. If it is down, it is because they have already sold. The most important aspect of market news is not the content, but rather the market's reaction to the news.

Reading the Tape

People have a burning need for the rational. They need explanations. I find it interesting to hear various market pundits explain why the market did what it did. Then, with the next breath, they explain what the market should have done instead. Tony Dungy, while coach of the SuperBowl champions Indianapolis Colts, had a saying: "We do what we do." Similarly, the market does what it does. We need to get to know this market by watching, observing, and listening to it. We call this practice of observing the market "reading the tape."

Understanding the Symbols of the Language

Before you can read, you must first understand the symbols of the language. Our English alphabet consists of two symbol types: consonants and vowels. Likewise, the letters in which the market communicates come in two forms: price bars and volume bars. Think of the price bars as the consonants and the volume bars as the vowels. Vlme gvs prc mng smlrl t hw vwls gv cnsnnts mng. Intrprtng th mrkt wtht vlme i lk rdng wtht vwls.

Volume gives price meaning in much the same way that vowels give consonants meaning. Interpreting the market without volume is like reading without vowels.

Combining letters forms words just as combining price and volume forms bars. A sequence of words forms a sentence, just as a sequence of price and volume bars forms' trends. A group of sentences can be combined to form a narrative, just as trends can be combined to form patterns. By relying on a basic understanding of the market's alphabet, you can uncover the messages the market sends us through its own behavior.

When I refer to reading the tape, I mean watching the price and volume change in real time to get a glimpse into the "mind" of the market. In the BC age (before computers), investors charted the markets by hand, using point and figure charts for simplicity. Many old-school technicians still practice this technique, as the sense they developed from the physical act of plotting data cannot be replicated. Modern-day traders use multiple monitors that track every tick of the market. But, if you can't follow the market in real time, tick by tick, a chart can give you the information in a historically summarized fashion. Like much of technical analysis, tape or chart reading is more art than exact science, yet the tape reflects the results of actions between buyers and sellers—actions that are based on investor beliefs.

This Is the Market, Allow Me to Introduce You

Our duty as tape readers is to know the market intimately. The market communicates to us through price and volume. In terms of developing an understanding of the market, volume is the more important statistic because volume enables the tape reader to discern the meaning of price. Although price is widely followed, the public does not typically analyze volume. As volume analysts, this is to our advantage in developing our superior perspective of the market.

To understand price, you must first understand the underlying motivation behind market movements, the basis for price change. Price change always stems from an imbalance between supply and demand. The key to understanding and analyzing the tape then is to understand the source from which supply and demand flow. This is, of course, volume. Volume measures how much demand or supply is brought to bear to move the price. If volume is expanding, then price change demonstrates that the market has the strength to continue its current course (see Figure 6.1). If volume contracts during price change, a weakening of market is expressed, which indicates that investors do not have the will to continue (see Figure 6.2).

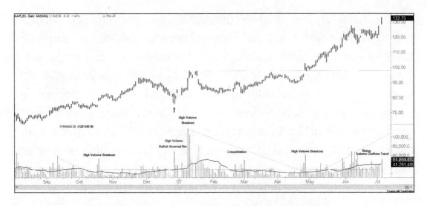

Figure 6.1   2006–2007 Apple high-volume price surge.

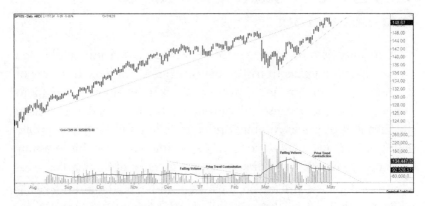

Figure 6.2   Broad market 2007 low-volume topping pattern.

Fear and Greed

As you get acquainted with the market, you learn that it appears to have a spilt personality. These personalities are represented by the two emotions that have driven humanity from the beginning.

Genesis 3:6 says, "When the woman saw that the tree was good for food, and that it was a delight to the eyes, and that the tree was desirable to make *one* wise, she took from its fruit and ate; and she gave also to her husband with her, and he ate."

The first dominating emotion of humans is lust, the desire for more and better. A wealthy friend of mind, T.P., has this motto: "I want it all." Sounds greedy, but it is unequivocally honest. We all want it all. We all want to win. It is our human nature. Buying stock gives us a crack at obtaining it.

Genesis 3:10 says, "I heard the sound of You in the garden, and I was afraid because I was naked; so I hid myself."

The most powerful of all human emotions is fear. When gripped by fear, a person is incapable of thinking rationally. Someone in a state of fear loses his or her capacity to reason; emotional instinct takes over. Intrinsic value is absolutely meaningless to a person riveted by fear. To cash is where these investors hide.

These two emotions play out every day in the stock market in the form of demand—the desire for profit—and supply—the fear of loss. As an investor, you need to determine which personality is presently the controlling market force. Is it the bears (supply) or the bulls (demand)? Price is the result of buyers and sellers telling us who is in control at any given moment. Through volume, you can gauge the price movement's legitimacy.

Thus, it is through careful study of these interactions of price and volume that the tape reader attempts to gauge the personality or attitude of the market. Similar to the development of personal relationships, you can observe others' behaviors and how they respond to conditions, such as success or adversity. Through such observation, you might develop an opinion of others' characters. If you come to know them well enough, you might be able to anticipate their behaviors under a given set of circumstances. Likewise, through close observation of the market, experience, and familiarity, you might know the market well enough to forecast how it might behave. Reading the tape has a lot to do with intuition. I cannot hope to pass on this skill anymore than one could pass on the relationship of friendship. However, if you can comprehend her language, you can understand the market well enough to form your own relationship with her.

Volume: The Technician's Decryption Device

The market just doesn't verbally tell us what kind of mood it is in today. The market speaks to us through its behavior. In a real way, though, the behavior of the market is encoded. Codes are messages containing hidden meanings. To the oblivious, a code might appear to be meaningless. For example, two lanterns can be used to form a binary encryption code: one if by land, two if by sea. To the British, the lantern is just light. To the American patriot who identifies the sign and interprets the code, the lantern contains an important meaning.

It might be helpful if you view the market as a type of Morse code. Think of the changing prices as dashes and dots coming through a telegraph. For example, dashes mean down ticks, and dots can mean up ticks. As a technician, you are now a cryptologist trying to ascertain meaning. But codes have little meaning unless they are decrypted. To interpret our dashes and dots to form meaningful letters and words, you use volume to decipher the meaning of prices. Analyzed together, this information helps us interpret price through supply and demand. It is the imbalance between supply and demand that creates price swings.

Analyzing Price and Volume Bar by Bar

Higher prices in conjunction with expanding volume reveal that more investors are willing to participate at increasing prices. This equates to stronger buying pressure, which often leads to higher future prices. Higher prices with contracting volume mean that fewer investors are willing to participate while prices increase. This signifies weakening buying pressure, an indication of falling demand.

Lower prices on expanding volume illustrate that more investors want to liquidate as the price falls. This equates to strong selling pressure, which indicates a growing supply. Lower prices with contracting volume show us that fewer holders are willing to sell while the price decreases. This reveals a reduction in selling pressure, which is falling supply.

The Four Basic Phases of Closing Price Bar Analysis

In reading the tape, the most basic form of price interpretation is comparing the closing price (close) from one bar to the next. When the change from close to close is positive, the stock is considered up on the day. When the change from one day's close to the next is negative, the stock is down for the day. This information neglects all the intraday or intra-bar action and focuses on the primary piece of information—the change from close to close.

Bar none, pardon the pun, an extraordinary high volume is the clearest technical indication that the market is poised to move. When volume is high, the market expresses firm convictions, as indicated by the high number of shares moving from bearish to bullish hands or vice versa. Such high-volume movement often signals a reversal from the present path or a fresh breath of new life in an existing trend.

Reading the tape from close to close is simple decoding. Regardless of direction in price change, increasing volume validates the movement (see Table 6.1).

TABLE 6.1   Decoding Price with Volume

Stock closing up	Volume higher	Building demand	Bullish
Stock closing up	Volume lower	Diminishing demand	Bearish
Stock closing down	Volume higher	Increasing supply	Bearish
Stock closing down	Volume lower	Drying supply	Bullish

Various Phases of Price Range Volume Analysis

A 1994 study by Blume concluded that sequences of volume and price provide information that is useful in gaining a competitive investment advantage. In 1998, Caginalp and Laurent tested short-term intraday patterns known as candlesticks and concluded that they offer significant predictive power. In price range volume analysis (also known as volume spread analysis), you combine volume and intraday price change, enhancing the effectiveness of each method.

The Price Bar Is the Market's DNA

The close gives us only information from one day to the next. In terms of studying long-term trends, in this analyst's opinion, the close is by far the most useful information. However, when analyzing shorter term movements, the intraday action reveals important information, too. The price bar represents the culmination of the interactions between demand and supply during a specific unit of time, such as a day. This price bar can be likened to another code, the DNA molecule, in that the price bar is the basic building block of the chart. The DNA molecule contains all information for an organism. In a similar manner, the price bar is formed from all the collective knowledge of the market participants who form it. As the DNA molecule has four nucleotide bases known as A, C, G, and T, the price bar has four bases of information known as O, H, L, and C.

The O, or opening, represents the price upon which market participants agree at the first trade of the day. The H is the high, representing the highest price the stock can achieve before supply overtakes demand and pushes the stock lower. In this way, the high represents resistance because sellers have resisted further price appreciation at this elevated price level. The L is the low, representing the lowest price the stock has achieved before demand elevates the stock higher. The low represents support because it is at this low point that buyers came in and supported the price. If the stock closes on the high or low, the stock does not contain a support or resistance level because demand did not overtake supply or vice versa. Rather, the time expired before a balancing point between supply and demand was achieved. The C stands for the close. The close is the most important piece of information on the chart. The close represents the conclusion where the accounts settled—the final score between the forces of bulls (demand) and bears (supply). This is especially true of the closing prices of the day, week, month, quarter, and year. The holders of these positions indicate they are willing to hold these positions overnight or over the weekend and that institutions want to report ownership on their books. Closes of intraday bars or ticks lack this finality. Neither do they presuppose any holding obligations; thus, they have much less significance.

Volume Is the Market's RNA

If price is the DNA of the chart, then volume is the RNA. Just as RNA translates DNA, volume translates price information into usable information. Thus, it is volume that ultimately gives price its meaning. Fortunately, you need not be a bioengineer to interpret the tape or the chart. Basic illustrations that might be helpful in understanding this relationship between the bar chart's price, and the corresponding volume are understood through volume and the intra day price range.

Volume Price-Spread Analysis

Moving from the simple to the complex, another factor in interpreting the price-volume relationship is measured by the relative size of the price bar and where the stock closed within the trading range. The price spread from high to low is called the range. In price range volume analysis, also known as volume-spread analysis, the analyst assesses volume based on O, H, L, and C, and on the size and range of the price bar. This is similar to candlestick analysis, except you also include volume in the evaluation.

The span of the price range is calculated from the bar's highest point to the same bar's lowest point. It is measured from the top of the bar, where resistance sets in, to the low, where support comes in driving the stock higher. The size of the range gives us important information about how easily demand can move the stock up and supply can force the price down. The wider the range, typically the easier it is for the forces of supply and demand to move the stock price. This analysis does not entirely discount the close but emphasizes the change intra-bar as opposed to closing bar to closing bar. These distinctions can be made more evident with Equal Volume Charting.

High Volume with High Stock Appreciation
(Tall Up Bar)—Bullish

When the price rises strongly on high volume, it typifies a bullish situation. In a bull market, it suggests renewed strength in the existing trend. In a bear market, it warns of an impending reversal.

The strongest bull stocks start out low, move lower, reverse, and finish higher toward the high range. Volume is very strong, confirming the reversal (see Figure 6.3 and Figure 6.4).

Another bullish formation is a stock moving much higher, closing at or near the high on high volume (see Figure 6.5 and Figure 6.8).

Figure 6.3   Most bullish (reversal); robust demand.

(Chart [or data] produced by TeleChart 2007® or StockFinder®, which is a registered trademark of Worden Brothers, Inc., Five Oaks Office Park, 4905 Pine Cone Drive, Durham, NC 27707. Ph. (800) 776-4940 or (919) 408-0542. www.Worden.com.)

Figure 6.4   Bullish volume price reversal.

Figure 6.5   Strong demand.

Moderate price movement goes up with higher volume. The stock was much higher but closes in the mid to upper end of range (see Figure 6.6). Such movements should be viewed cautiously as the stock could not maintain its momentum as supply came in negating much of the earlier advance.

Figure 6.6   Moderately bullish.

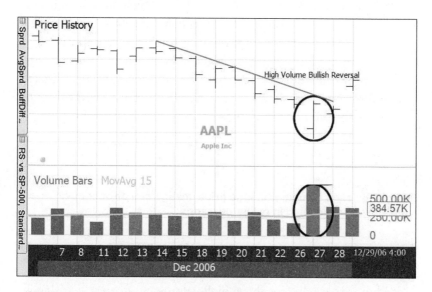

(Chart [or data] produced by TeleChart 2007® or StockFinder®, which is a registered trademark of Worden Brothers, Inc., Five Oaks Office Park, 4905 Pine Cone Drive, Durham, NC 27707. Ph. (800) 776-4940 or (919) 408-0542. www.Worden.com.)

Figure 6.7   High-volume bullish reversal.

High Volume with Low Appreciation (Short Up Bar): High Effort, Small Results; Bull Market Bearish

These moves of high volume with little appreciation are typical at the end of intermediate market trends. Such movements might indicate a turning point in an intermediate trend. In the case of an intermediate-term bull market, the market has been moving higher, pushed up by heavy demand. As the trend matures, there is still plenty of demand as indicated by the high volume. Yet, the price is unable to advance much because savvy institutions are now cashing in on the extended move. Not wanting to alert the market of their desire to liquidate, they strategically place their orders to sell at the offer. This allows the market to advance, but as bids are met with heavy supply, the price is unable to make much headway. If this occurs, the wise investor might want to sell soon, before the disparity between demand and supply is reversed.

In a bear market, if the market volume accelerates significantly and the price rises but only a little, this could be a test of the supply. Heavy buying is enough to push the price higher, but supply is still in control. This is indicative of resistance. At this point, there is adequate supply to meet demand. However, this action must be closely watched to see if the situation changes. If the price breaks through resistance, the outlook can change entirely (see Figure 6.8).

$$\mathsf{+}$$

Figure 6.8   High volume with little price change can be ominous, especially when located in extended trends.

High Volume Depreciation

When prices fall strongly on high volume, it signals a bearish condition. If occurring in a bear market, the action suggests renewed strength of the existing downtrend. In a bull market, it warns of the possibilities of an upcoming turnaround.

The strongest bear stocks start out high, move higher, reverse, and finish lower toward the high range. The volume is very strong, confirming the reversal (see Figure 6.9).

$$\mathsf{+}$$

Figure 6.9   Most bearish (reversal); robust supply.

Another very bearish formation is a stock moving much lower, closing at or near the low on high volume (see Figure 6.10 and Figure 6.13).

Figure 6.10   Strong supply.

Stock closes near low but moves down modestly, not greatly, on high volume. There is higher effort with small results (see Figure 6.11).

Figure 6.11   Modest supply; bearish.

Moderate price movement goes down with higher volume. Stock is much lower, but it closes in the mid to lower end of range (see Figure 6.12).

Figure 6.12   Moderate supply; bearish.

In a bull market, any pullback in a stock with high volume should be a warning that heavy supply is entering the market. The fact that the stock depreciates only a little indicates the stock has found some support. However, the fact that the stock is down in heavy conflict indicates the bears are gaining traction. At best, this is a sign of churn and, at worst, a sign of weakness, and the investor's position should be reevaluated.

Conversely, in a bear market, a stock down only slightly on heavy volume indicates that investors are finding value at the present price. This perception of value creates new demand, acting as support. Yet the bears are still on top, and this is frequently bearish behavior. In other times, though, these actions could indicate a stronger effort yielding smaller results. Whether the market action is a condition of

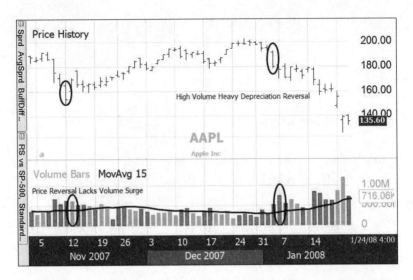

Figure 6.13 Two closing low bars: the first with modest volume and second with high volume.

high effort/low results or fresh demand, the stock should be carefully observed going forward. In either situation—bear or bull—the market is warning that the existing trend could be under scrutiny.

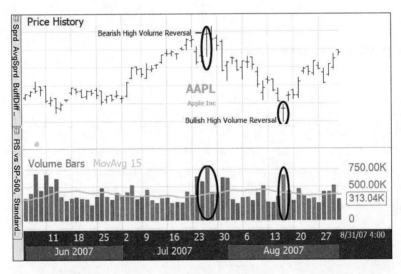

(Chart [or data] produced by TeleChart 2007® or StockFinder®, which is a registered trademark of Worden Brothers, Inc., Five Oaks Office Park, 4905 Pine Cone Drive, Durham, NC 27707. Ph. (800) 776-4940 or (919) 408-0542. www.Worden.com.)

Figure 6.14 Bearish and bullish high-volume reversals.

Low Volume Price Movements

In a bull market, when price is gaining rapidly but volume is modest or low, it suggests a greedy market. A greedy market is emblematic of small investors hearing of the success of other investors and wanting to participate and make some quick money. Often in this case, the great news is reported. Those who are last to know discover the story and want in. But savvy investors have long awaited this news. They patiently wait to see how long and far the news will propel the stock higher. However, at any sign of weakness, they begin to redistribute the stock back to the eager public.

If this action is found in a bear market, it very well could be a bearish test of resistance. Again, this explosive appreciation is usually the result of positive news. This positive news causes optimistic, generally uninformed investors to buy into the stock rise. However, the astute investors have again anticipated the news. These investors patiently await the point at which supply overtakes demand and then sell their existing holdings or add to short holdings. Regardless of whether this action is found in a bull market or a bear market, it is a bearish omen of the waning of demand.

Stocks in uptrends that moderate or stall on low volume typically occur in rounding top formations. In this situation, the market trend has matured, and the buyers have grown tired. Aging stocks often die not in an outright crash but in a dull, slow turn. Before the unwary investor knows it, the stock is firmly entrenched in the southerly direction. Another possibility is the stock encounters minor resistance and slowly moves through. However, this action should not last long. If this activity persists, then the stock is demonstrating topping behavior.

If this action of low volume and low price appreciation is found in a bear market, then the stock has temporarily caught a bid but has not displayed enough effort to affect the longer term trend. Typically, this results in just a pause of the bear trend, as not enough demand has entered to reverse it.

A string of large drops on low volume rarely occurs in the midst of a bull market trend. When it does, it usually surrounds a piece of company news or other information that was taken the wrong way by investors. Although the price movement is large, the volume is light. This suggests that uninformed investors were panicking. However,

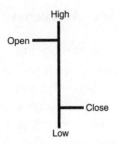

Figure 6.15   Low volume with short price depreciation (low down bar); bullish.

the smart money does not participate. The institutions anticipated the possibility of negative news and are now patiently waiting for the stock to catch support. When the sell-off moderates or begins to reverse, this indicates the stock has fallen enough, green-lighting further buying operations.

If this action is observed in a bear market, again the market is panicking. The stock price is plummeting at an ever increasing rate. Yet although the price is dropping rapidly, fewer investors will be compelled to sell at these overly rundown levels. This is often the best time to go long because the supply of stock available has faded. This action often ends in a bear market reversal, especially if low volume is accompanied by downward price gaps. When you analyze volume, you always do so in relative terms. Often in this type of bear market, the volume might appear normal or even high relative to a longer term historical norm, but it is low relative to recent volume flows, especially in light of the enormous price depreciation.

Figure 6.16   Low volume with high price depreciation (short down bar); trend continuation.

The market is down, but fewer people are willing to sell at these discounted levels. Typically, unlike bull markets, bear markets don't fizzle out. They usually are reversed suddenly. When volume and depreciation are both light, it is often just a pause or lull, indicating the bear market is just taking a nap. Should this action be found in a bull market, then, likewise, the bulls are just taking a breather and, given time, the bull trend should resume. There is a reason why they say, "Never short a dull market." Low volume with small depreciation found in a bull market is the dull market to which this rule applies. The greater concept, though, is that in a market experiencing low volume with small price depreciation, look for the market to resume its former trend.

Behind Bars

Another way of discerning information from price and volume is to note the emphasis between bars. Just as a writer denotes emphasis by capitalizing, underlining, or bolding letters, the market has ways of adding emphasis, too. Among these are through up and down side-gaps and inside and outside days.

Gaps

Strong forms of market emphasis are denoted in gaps. A gap occurs when a stock opens completely outside its previous-day range. This creates a "gap" in which no shares have been exchanged. Gaps are caused by a significant change within the balance of supply and demand that results in a significant reappraisal of the stock between trading sessions. Gaps can be used as a form of emphasis in analysis. If high volume accompanies these gaps, then the emphasis should be duly noted. If not, the gap signals a momentary gasp of excitement that might not be expected to last, especially in the case of low volume down side gaps.

Upside gaps occur when buying pressure overwhelms supply and the stock opens higher, prevailing over the previous bar's high. Unless the gap is filled, the stock will trade higher than the previous bar's high throughout the session. Ever hear of the phrase, "The stock fell out of bed?" This is a downside gap. Downside gaps occur when selling pressure overwhelms the available demand, causing the stock to open lower and surpass the previous bar's low. Overall, gaps are very powerful moves that, when accompanied by high volume, tend to move in the direction of the gap, especially when the close matches the direction of the price gap (see Figure 6.17). Gaps that lack volume might signal a reversal away from the direction of the gap.

Figure 6.17   A down side gap.

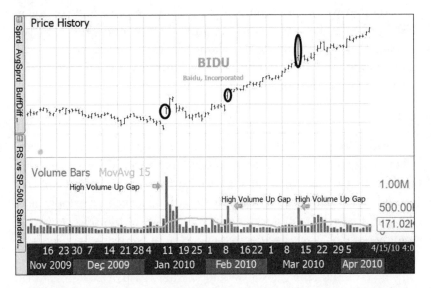

(Chart [or data] produced by TeleChart 2007® or StockFinder®, which is a registered trademark of Worden Brothers, Inc., Five Oaks Office Park, 4905 Pine Cone Drive, Durham, NC 27707. Ph. (800) 776-4940 or (919) 408-0542. www.Worden.com.)

Figure 6.18   High-volume price gaps.

Inside Days

Another form of emphasis is evaluating a bar's range compared to the previous bar's range. If the previous bar's total range completely encompasses the preceding bar, this is called an inside day (see Figure 6.19). An inside day has a low that is equal to or higher than the previous bar and be accompanied by a high equal to or lower than that of the previous bar. This indicates that the stock bar cannot violate either the previous bar's resistance (high) or the previous bar's support (low). Inside days mean that the stock is presently resting. Typically, inside days have low volume, indicating a momentary rest is needed and the prevailing trend will continue. On rare occasions, an inside bar demonstrates high volume. This might suggest the trending effort is not yielding results, indicating the prevailing trend might stall or reverse.

Figure 6.19   Inside day.

Outside Days

If the next bar's range exceeds the previous bar's range by being either higher or lower, this is called an outside bar (see Figure 6.20). This occurrence is especially significant when a stock has traded in the opposite direction for an extended period. An outside bar is pictured by a higher and/or lower bar than the previous bar. An outside bar indicates that either demand or supply has exceeded that of the previous day. Outside days that have a higher high indicate an increase in demand. Outside days with a higher low suggest that supply is gaining control. High volume confirms whether or not this break in trend might be sustainable. An outside bar exhibiting light volume suggests that any reversal may be short-lived.

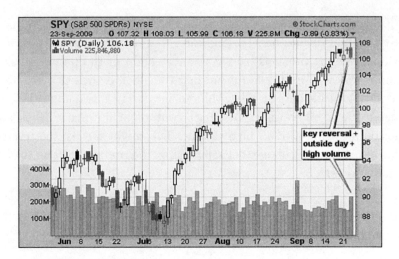

(Chart courtesy of StockCharts.com.)

Figure 6.20   Outside day.

7

Volume in Trends

"Trends are like horses; they are easier to ride in the direction they are going."
—*John Naisbitt*

Identifying Trends

Most people, when investing in a stock, believe that they are forming a relationship with a company. So they try to learn all that they can about the company and its prospects. But there is a more significant relationship that they are forming, and that is their relationship to all of the other people who own that stock. Those people can have a profound effect on the success of one's investment, irrespective of what the company itself actually does. Trend analysis is a way of studying the personality of these investors by observing their past behavior.

Previously, you viewed individual price bars as expressions of the market's emotions, convictions, and volitions. Between internal and external factors, any number of tens of thousands of fundamental and behavioral factors can affect the company, the industry, and the economy. How does anyone account for all the variables as they impact price? You track them through price and volume. Following the tracks of past behavior is trend analysis. Trends represent the dissemination and assimilation of market data by investors over time. As price imputes all the embedded knowledge and information available to the markets at a point in time, price trends are an expression of that embedded knowledge displayed over time. In this way, investing with the trend is merely participating with the consensus of market opinion. A contrarian might try to buck the trend, but it is said that the market can hold irrationality longer than the wisest of investors can hold losers.

In physics, one of the proprieties of volume is that it distributes around a mean. Likewise, a large part of volume analysis is identifying where money is flowing. The person who figures this out first is well positioned to make money. Market prices change as a result of money flowing out of one investment and into others as investors seek to optimize their returns. However, these realizations normally do not happen in the blink of an eye. They occur with the passing of time as investors assess value and gradually build positions. *Market trends* are simply prices moving directionally to solve an imbalance between supply and demand. A market trending higher represents investors accumulating shares. A market trending lower represents investors distributing shares. *Volume trend analysis* tracks the accumulation of demand and the distribution of supply.

Trends: The Words of the Market

Returning to the previous chapter's analogy, the market's sentences are trends formed through the sequential movements of individual price bars (words). Whereas the words in each sentence contain meaning, it is the overall context of the words in which the market is most appropriately understood and analyzed. Trends convey the saga of the market as it unfolds.

Individual bars move higher together form the market's uptrends. An *uptrend* is a rising support line that illustrates that demand is overwhelming available supply over time, as indicated by higher lows. At some point, the uptrend drops its rate of ascent and reverses. Downtrends are formed by individual bars moving lower together. A *downtrend* is a falling resistance line, indicating that supply is overtaking the available demand, as evidenced by lower highs.

Drawing Trend Lines

Visual aids can be helpful in recognizing trends. A *trend line* is a visual aid that identifies building forces between supply and demand.

Drawing trend lines on a chart need not be overly complicated. Your chart should be composed of several individual bars, at least 20 or more, to detect a trend properly. A *primary trend* is the trend of an investor's longest time frame. Primary trends are usually drawn with monthly charts. *Intermediate-term trends* are normally formed across the course of several weeks using weekly charts. Likewise, *short-term trends* are formed during several days by using daily charts. Intraday charts can be based on hours, minutes, or tick bars.

Trends are drawn by connecting the highs and the lows across a chart. You can identify an uptrend by connecting the significant low bars. Drawing an uptrend starts by finding the lowest bar on the chart. From the lowest bar and reading from left to right, you find the next significant low bar. The next significant low bar is where the stock has gone up then come back down (at a higher point than the lowest bar) and then gone back up again. This bar is a higher trough, where the stock meets support by being pushed back up by buying pressure. Buying pressure occurs from the purchases of buyers overwhelming the supply of sellers. This pushes the stock up to a higher point than the previous low, illustrating a new higher level of support. If there is not a higher trough, then the trend cannot be an uptrend (see Figure 7.1).

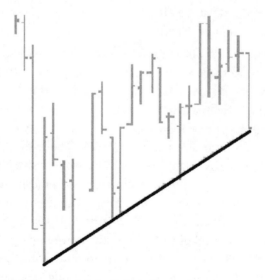

Figure 7.1   Uptrend drawn by connecting rising lows.

It takes two points to draw a line and at least three points to establish a trend. To find the next trough, look for another point where the stock has moved higher than the second trough and then comes back down to a higher point than the lowest low from which it moved back up. Again, this is where the stock finds support through buying pressure setting in, pushing the stock higher. If the point is higher than both troughs and aligns with the angle of the lowest low and previous trough, then it is a trend. This process is repeated, connecting only the troughs that align to at least three points. The more troughs that line up together, the stronger the trend is thought to be. A trend's momentum is gauged by the angle or pitch of the trend. The steepness of the uptrend reflects growing optimism in the market consensus. A downward change in the trend pitch reveals an increase in supply, suggesting weakness in an uptrend.

In the same way, a downtrend trend reflects the growth rate of pessimism as measured through the steepness of the falling peaks of former resistance. You can identify the downtrend by connecting the significant bars of falling highs. It takes at least three high bars to align to form a downtrend. The more falling highs in the trend aligning, the stronger the resistance of the downtrend. The steeper the downtrend, the more rapid the growth of pessimism. An upward change in trend indicates an increase in demand and serves as a warning to a downtrend (see Figure 7.2).

A rising tide lifts all boats. Therefore, intermediate- and short-term trends tend to be more dynamic when going with the primary trend. Whether you are a day trader or buy-and-hold investor, the most important technical assessment is the determination of the primary long-term price trend. When drawing trend lines, too often technicians overemphasize minor reactions. These short-term movements tend to counterbalance one another while distracting the technician from the big picture. A technician's foremost objective is to determine whether a primary trend exists. The next important task is to determine the direction in which the primary trend is moving. If the troughs during a period of several months move higher, then it might be concluded the stock is in a long-term uptrend. If the peaks over the course of several months move lower, then it might be concluded the stock is in a long-term downtrend. If neither or both of these occur, then you might conclude that the stock is not presently trending.

Figure 7.2 Downtrend drawn by connecting falling highs.

Evaluating the State of the Trend with Volume Analysis

"There is only one side of the market and it is not the bull side or the bear side, but the right side."

—*Jesse L. Livermore*

After a primary trend has been established and its direction confirmed, the next most important assessment is the strength and state of the trend. Ronald Reagan had a philosophy of "trust, but verify" in foreign relations. Charles Dow had a similar philosophy toward investing: "The observed trend should be assumed to continue until the weight of the evidence has shifted in favor of a reversal." Trends are constantly in a state of motion and can be changed and broken. Trend breaks or threats of trend breaks need to be closely monitored.

A price trend can be akin to an airplane in mid flight. If a plane is to maintain its flight, it must maintain minimum airspeed. If the pilot wants to increase the angle of ascent, he must change the trajectory and increase thrust. If the pilot fails to apply thrust when changing the trajectory, the plane can stall. Likewise, if a trend increases its trajectory, it needs at least an equivalent increase in volume to maintain the trajectory. If the trend does not obtain thrust through increased volume, it also risks stalling. This is the rule of trend volume, suggesting volume should expand at least relatively with the price trend, if not more. In this way, volume is the critical element vital to evaluating the stability of the trend.

Uptrends are in a state of accumulation. Downtrends should reflect a healthy phase of distribution. Low volume warns of an impending change in trend. A low-volume break of a trend discounts the validity of the counter trend. High volume legitimizes trends and trend violations. As a volume investor, you assess these conditions by verifying volume's support of the price trend. Rising volume signifies that ever more investors are eager to participate in the trend. Only after such an affirmative assessment is conducted should you look to establish positions based on the opportunities being presented over the shorter terms.

The Four Phases of Volume Analysis

"Every transaction is the result of the meeting of demand, on the one hand, with supply on the other. When demand exceeds supply, prices tend to rise. Conversely, when supply exceeds demand, prices tend to fall. Therefore: 1. Volume which occurs during advances may be designated as demand volume; 2. Volume which occurs during declines may be termed supply volume."

—*Harold M. Gartley*

Through evaluating the interactions of price and volume, the volume analyst hopes to discover pent-up supply or demand within the trend. With time, the buildup of these forces accumulates into stresses that are later exerted on the movements of the trend. These stresses come in four phases: strong demand, weak demand, strong supply, and weak supply. With this big-picture outlook, the volume analyst can evaluate the strength and state of a trend through the perspective of supply and demand.

Phase 1: Strong Demand

"When volume tends to increase during advances, it is a bullish indication."

—*Harold M. Gartley*

Generally, investors buy on hope or optimism. This optimism can be manifested through greed, the desire to obtain a profit. An uptrend can be viewed then as an accumulation of greed over time. Greed manifested in an uptrend needs fuel to build and sustain itself. Greed's growth cannot be sustained without energy. Volume is the fuel that propels the trending market.

The first phase of an uptrend is characterized by prices rising with plenty of volume to sustain the growth. This phase usually follows an exhaustion of supply. The new birth of the bull market begins with wild price swings, mostly to the upside. During the early stages of this phase, professional institutions are eager to gobble up stock on weakness, as the public views the rallies as an opportunity to exit. As the market appreciates and matures, more and more investors accept the higher prices, which in turn, restores the optimistic beliefs surrounding the underlying company. This is a market overcome by demand, as indicated by higher lows in the prevailing price trend. The higher volume provides the market with the energy it needs to continue to go higher. From these observations, an astute investor can discern that the volume confirms the uptrend and indicates the trend should continue (see Figure 7.3).

Phase 2: Weak Demand

"When volume tends to decrease during price advances, it is bearish."

—*Harold M. Gartley*

If you were to look at just the price action without examining the volume, the beginning of a second phase of an uptrend would resemble the price action of the matured half of the first phase. However, in this early distribution phase, the trend begins to destabilize. This phase can be compared to the wind down of a pyramid scheme where the last buyers on top of the pyramid are left holding the bag. In this weak demand phase, price continues to advance as evidenced by ever higher lows. However, a decrease in volume indicates fading demand or the loss of energy needed to sustain the rising trend. In simple terms, there are fewer investors willing to buy the stock as it appreciates. As the volume falls, it contradicts the price's uptrend. Such actions often denote a complacent market. Holders have enjoyed the benefits of past appreciation. Few of these investors want to sell a security treating them so well. They are motivated to do so only on higher bids. Yet increasingly fewer investors are willing to purchase the stock at these inflated levels. Mostly new, uninformed investors continue to buy the security based on its history or past performance, not necessarily the outlook. As institutions see the security becoming fully valued, they begin to work out of the stock until they push it down. After these institutions recognize the impact their operations have on price, they will change their selling tactics only to sell on rallies. However, the savvy volume analyst has already noted that the divergence between the price and volume trends signifying the trend is under a state of weak demand (see Figure 7.3).

Phase 3: Strong Supply

> "When volume tends to increase during price declines, it is a bearish indication."
> —*Harold M. Gartley*

When the primary price trend breaks down below support, the cat is out of the proverbial bag. This begins phase three of strong supply, the launching of a new downtrend. A downtrend is a supply line signifying that supply has exceeded demand over this time. Downtrends are formed by selling pressure (supply) being greater than buying pressure (demand). Many times, but not always, an investor who creates supply, a seller, is motivated by the fear of losing the value of the investment. A downtrend then can be viewed as the accumulation of fear.

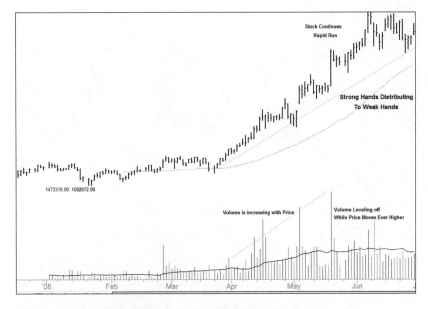

Figure 7.3   Rule of trends volume should rise with trend.

The first stage of a primary downtrend should begin on rising volume. This is indicated by more and more fearful investors willing to accept ever lower prices for their stock. As the phase begins, institutions sell into weakness. Uninformed investors buy up their shares, only at levels they view as deeply discounted. These actions create wide and erratic price movements like the beginning of the first phase, except upside down and more volatile as fear is a stronger emotion than greed. The rise in volume reveals that the supply is strong and growing. As the volume expands, it confirms the increasing strength of the supply, implying that more bearish ramifications might still loom ahead.

Weak Supply

"When volume tends to decrease during price declines, it is bullish."

—Harold M. Gartley

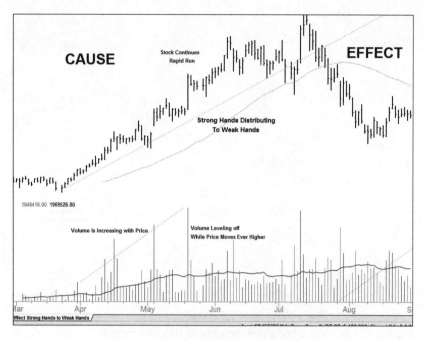

Figure 7.4   Rules have consequences.

The last stages of a downtrend are typified by diminishing volume and rapidly falling prices. Here, investors are in the final stages of a sell-off. This weak supply phase appears primarily in two forms: a panic sell-off or a dull lackluster decline. During the intermediate and short term, it is common for this phase to be the shortest, lasting only days. This is a panic sell-off, evidenced by rapid capital erosion forming a v-shaped price bottom.

However, in the primary secular trend of individual stocks, this phase is less likely to be a quick panic bottom. Rather, the weak supply phase might persist as long as any of the other phases in a dull lackluster state. In terms of market indices, if the weak supply phase persists, it might not even be recognizable using traditional volume methodologies. This is due to the secular long-term growth of index volume from stock splits, new issues, falling trading costs, and narrower price spreads that lead to volume data distortion. In such a case, volume appears to be greater than it actually is when measured in supply and demand terms. As prices rapidly fall, volume begins to become level and then subtly drop. This event might indicate that the sellers are becoming apathetic to the price decline. Many retail investors assume the stock has dropped to the point where it is no longer worthwhile to sell. They conclude they might as well ride it out with the price being so discounted. This type of fear or apathy lacks the energy needed to sustain itself. In other words, during the closing stages of weak supply, few investors remain who are willing to sell at the newly discounted prices. The lack of supply is a strong indication the security is bottoming, and the forward implications are bullish.

(Created with TradeStation. ©TradeStation Technologies, Inc. All rights reserved.)

Figure 7.5   2002 false bottom low volume trend reversal.

But what happens when you have neutral prices after a meaningful decline and volume begins rising? In terms of the volume phases, this is the end of phase 4, weak supply moving back toward strong demand. According to Ralph Acampora, portfolio manager of Altaira Investment Solutions, "This could be the sign of accumulation (buying on weakness) and the formation of a base."

March 2003 True Bottom

Volume Expansion
During Breakout

67479696.00 52506704.60

Volume Declining in Sell Off

**Figure 7.6   2003 market bottom verified with high-volume bullish
reversal and high-volume follow through.**

TABLE 7.1   Four Phases of Price / Volume Trends

Trend Up and Volume Rising (Strong Demand)	Trend Down and Volume Falling (Weak Supply)
Greed with Energy = Invigorated Greed	Fear with Entropy = Apathy
Uptrend Expansion and Volume Expansion	Downtrend Expansion and Volume Contraction
Uptrend	Downtrend
Bullish Confirmation	Bullish Contradiction

continues

TABLE 7.1   Four Phases of Price / Volume Trends (Continued)

Trend Up and Volume Falling (Weak Demand)	Trend Down and Volume Rising (Strong Supply)
Greed with Entropy = Complacency	Fear with Energy = Fear
Uptrend Expansion and Volume Contraction	Price Trend Contraction and Volume Expansion
Uptrend	*Downtrend*
Bearish Contradiction	*Bearish Confirmation*

Volume Rules and Laws: Cracking the Contradiction Code

"One of the most bullish things a stock can do is make the most of the good news and ignore the bad news. One of the most bearish things a stock can do is make the worst of bad news and ignore good news."

—*John Bollinger, CFA, CMT Bollinger Capital Management*

This brings us to another important point. You might have caught an apparent contradiction between Wyckoff's law of effort versus results and the rule of trends. To review, *the law of effort versus results* states: If more volume (force) is required to produce less price change (acceleration), then the stock is becoming overly bought or sold. Yet, the volume *rule of trends* states that more volume substantiates a stronger trend. Overall, the rule of trends applies to volume in the context of trends and the law of effort versus results to individual bar movements. However, there are times when the law of effort versus results might come into play with trends as well. For instance, which rule applies in the situation of rising volume and rising trend when the price trend change is greater than the relative volume increase? Answer: the rule of trends. Or which rule prevails when the volume expands during the consolidation points of the trend? Answer: the law of effort versus result. The key to cracking such mysteries is discovered through detecting the originating source of supply and demand.

If you are going to play the market, it might be wise to get to know the other players. These players come in two general forms: strong hands and weak hands.

Weak Hands

Weak hands consist mostly of traders and retail investors. Weak hands are frequently referred to as the public or the crowd. Weak hands are generally not well capitalized. The assets they have invested are needed to provide income either now or at some point down the road. This reality causes these investors habitually to react emotionally as opposed to rationally. They are not well informed and often find themselves caught up in the hoopla of society's latest sentiments. Unabated greed and fear drive weak-handed investors. Glimpsing at a weak holder's realized gain-loss statistics, you might perceive these investors to be geniuses. However, reading their unrealized holdings would quickly change that perception. This is due to weak holders being highly impulsive, selling profits quickly for minimal gains. However, when their position moves against them, they are reluctant to sell as pride keeps them from realizing their mistakes.

Strong Hands

Strong hands are generally considered to be large well-financed institutions that invest on the right side of the market. Knowing the landscape intimately, these investors are confident, well informed, tactical, and, above all, logical. Strong hands paddle with the tide of the major trend, leaving the smaller swales for other investors while they patiently await the big kahuna. Although many strong hands are institutions, they do not have to be. Typically, strong hands are position investors not looking to—or even be able to—take quick profits due to their massive size. Strong hands are interested in the big money. This is an important point as these institutions are often so large that their operations would significantly impact the stocks in which they participated if special precautions were not employed. When these "old turkeys" find a winner, they ride it and are not easily shaken from their positions. As buy-and-hold investors, strong hands generally hold positions until specific long-term targets are achieved or until the underlying conditions begin to erode. When repositioning their portfolios, these investors patiently work into and out of the market, executing their meticulously planned tactics with stealth and keeping the public largely unaware of their campaigns.

Figure 7.7   2000 market top expanding volume in decline followed by weak volume in subsequent advance.

Now that I have introduced the major players, we move to the important point—how each plays the game. Strong hands buy out of an expectation of capital appreciation. Weak hands buy out of greed and the fear of missing out on an opportunity. Weak hands sell from the fear of losing capital. Strong hands sell to reinvest in better opportunities (which does not have to be other equities).

The Keys to the Kingdom

The key to solving the paradox between the rule of trends and the law of efforts versus results is accomplished by detecting whether the source of supply or demand originates from strong or weak hands. Discerning this is one of the more difficult tasks in volume analysis. But if you can learn to distinguish between the two, you will have a skill few market analysts possess. Knowing your location in the battle of the trend is often the tell in making such a determination. When the market is in an early stage of an uptrend, much selling pressure still looms. This means that when the stock climbs, there are still many weak-hand investors eager to sell into the strength to pare losses or take small gains. Thus, in the early stages of an advancing trend, you should assume strong hands are driving the trend. As the price advances, you should expect heavy casualties (volume).

When the uptrend is closing into areas of resistance, strong hands take from the weak hands. Such areas include consolidation points or retracements back toward the primary trend line, moving average or linear regression line. Here in these consolidation points, the law of cause and effect prevails, implying price change should be relatively stronger than volume change. This means an uptrend does *not* need to produce a greater volume growth relative to price appreciation when the stock or market approaches a resistance area or support where many weak hands reside. Within these consolidation zones, should the volume change be greater than the price change, the market operates under the principle of conservation and effort exceeds results. In such high volume cases, the law of cause and effect suggests the stock or market is being churned. Churning occurs when strong hands distribute shares to weak-handed momentum traders who anticipate a technical breakout or breakdown to precede the consolidation basing phase. However, ongoing high volume (effort) with minimal price appreciation into these consolidation zones might actually suggest precisely the opposite scenario—a stall or reversal in trend (see Figure 7.8).

For example, in the battle between supply and demand, when the demand line (uptrend) reaches its enemy's (supply) trench line (resistance), the advance should be slowed or temporally stalled with moderate or light causalities (volume). However, should the uptrend take on heavy causalities (volume) without largely advancing the trend higher through resistance, then it might be assumed demand is losing the battle to supply. This might take the appearance of several small up or down bars clustered together. This is again affirmed by the volume expanding within the consolidation zone, a clue that the stronger hands are actually those controlling the trenches (resistance/support zones). It is important to point out this high-volume, low-price action is occurring *inside* the trenches of the consolidation zone. A price surge on extraordinary high volume should accompany any post breakout or breakdown to confirm the price break's legitimacy.

(Chart [or data] produced by TeleChart 2007® or StockFinder®, which is a registered trademark of Worden Brothers, Inc., Five Oaks Office Park, 4905 Pine Cone Drive, Durham, NC 27707. Ph. (800) 776-4940 or (919) 408-0542. www.Worden.com.)

Figure 7.8   2008 oil stock ETF top high-volume churning within consolidation.

The opposite scenario is when the trend is overly extended beyond the trend line, moving average, linear regression line, or any other trending method (not necessarily momentum) is extended. In an overextended market, it is usually best to infer that weak hands (greed/fear) are in operation. Under such weak-hand conditions, you revert back to the rule of trends, meaning the volume should *increase* at an equal or greater pace than the price change. Generally, high volume infers strong hands are in operation. If strong hands are in control in an extended market, volume should expand relatively faster than price. Thus, high and increasing high volume confirms the exaggerated price movement with the exaggerated trend (see Figure 7.9).

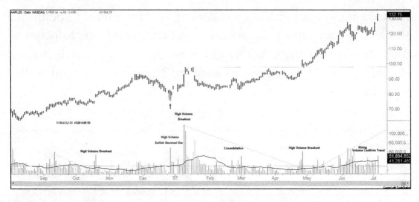

Figure 7.9 Following the rule trends 2007 APPL (Apple) high-volume breakout followed by expanding volume within the uptrend.

Often, though, these overly extended markets are controlled by the weak hands. This weak-handed extend market is evident by accelerating price change that is occurring on high volume. However, here, volume is not moving proportionally with price. Volume is high, but the price movement is relatively stronger. Here, volume lacks the force needed to sustain the exaggerated price trend. In this extended market, the absence of stronger relative volume growth to price growth indicates strong hands are distributing their shares to weaker hands (see Figure 7.10 and Figure 7.11).

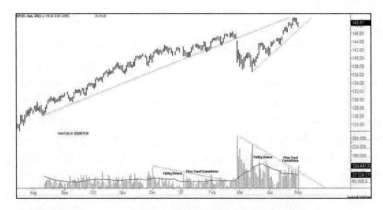

Figure 7.10 Breaking the rule trends: 2007 market surge on low and falling volume.

Figure 7.11 Consequences of breaking the rules: 2007 higher price on lower volume results.

Volume Seasonality Trends

There are some volume seasonality trends the volume investor should be aware. These volume trends in and of themselves are neither bullish nor bearish; nevertheless, the volume investor should contrast the volume in light of these trends. During holiday weeks, the volume is typically weak, especially preceding Independence Day, Thanksgiving, and Christmas. Overall, the volume in the summer is typically lighter than the other seasons, with winter typically being the heaviest season of trading. Higher volume may be associated with beginnings and endings. Volume normally expands during the end of the quarter, be it "mutual fund window dressing," quarterly portfolio rebalancing or index rebalancing. The third Friday of the month is option expiration. Generally, volume is higher on this day and the days leading up to it, especially so when the market has been strongly trending higher or volatile. The end of the calendar tax year and the beginning of a new year is normally conducted under higher market volumes conditions.

In addition, intraday volume is "U" shaped, being highest in the morning and at the close and weakest during middle lunch hours. During the lunch hour, the price action may also see a reprieve. If demand has been driving the market up, the absence of demand during the lunch hours may see the market trade temporarily lower.

Likewise, if supply has been forcing the market lower in the early session, the market may drift up higher on low volume during the lunch hours. Secular bull markets typically encounter high volume as investors are invigorated, and bear markets typically experience low volume as investors are disenfranchised. As such, bull markets may be born in low volume and die on high volume. Secular bear markets are typically birthed in high volume and die in a state of dullness.

Overall, markets are formed by people, and thus they behave like people. Decisions made today are based on what has happened to individuals in the past. Within the market exists many memories that will influence the course of the market's future behavior. These take the form of support and resistance points that in the past acted as barriers to market trends. If these memories are strong enough, they might completely reverse the market's direction. Knowing where these points reside and what actions transpired at these critical junctures in the past can be useful in determining the outcome. Next, with price patterns, we will look at what happens when trends collide.

8

Volume in Patterns

"The ticker tape is simply a record of human nature passing in review. The record gives the opinions and hopes of the people."
—*Humphrey Bancroft Neill, 1931*

Patterns: The Market's Narrative

If reading the individual price and volume bars resembles reading individual letters forming words, and if reading the trend is like reading words forming sentences, then reading market patterns is like reading the narrative.

An action movie consists of a hero, often a male, who is suddenly faced with an unforeseen problem. This causes a person or group of people closely tied to our hero to be hurt, captured, or killed. This is the low. In response, our hero stages a series of avenging acts in attempts to undo this great injustice. This is the climb. His efforts meet with weak opposition until the very end when our hero faces off with the arch villain. This is the resistance. At this point of contention, all seems to be for naught. Yet our hero miraculously defeats the villain while winning the prized affections of a distressed damsel. This is the climax, or breakout.

As you review patterns, it might help to view them as combinations of individual trends forming a broader storyline. Action movies, horror movies, chick flicks, and other movie genres have their own typical plot structures or narratives. Each movie category contains its own unique twists and turns, but generally, if you've seen one type, you've seen them all.

Likewise, markets often develop plot structures that seem to be played out over and over again. In technical analysis, these plot structures are referred to as "patterns." Patterns work because people, especially groups of people, tend to react similarly to similar events. Patterns are simply combinations of events starring either heroes as uptrends or villains as downtrends. As these seemingly independent market trends play out together, they form the "storyline." Through pattern recognition, the chartist recognizes that he's seen "this story" before. Through such a discovery, a chartist hopes to identify correctly the market's underlying "plot" and predict its inevitable outcome. Patterns exist because given similar market conditions, investors typically react with similar behavior. As in previous forms of charting, reading volume plays a major role in identifying these patterns as plots, complex plots, or subplots:

- **Plots**—Interaction of the major trends
- **Complex plots**—Multiple interaction combinations within the major trends
- **Subplots**—Minor trends within a major trend: wedges, flags, and pennants

Plots: The Interactions of Two Major Trends

Channel = Parallel Support and Resistance

The most common plot combinations are channels. Channels consist of a horizontal support line residing on the bottom of the range. Running parallel and above the support line resides a resistance line that forms the top end of the range. Channels can occur in up, down, and sideways trends (see Figure 8.1).

Here, prices fluctuate between buyers who believe the price is undervalued as it nears the lower end of the range and sellers who believe the security is overvalued as it nears the top end of the range. Unbeknownst to the typical investor, a coil forms. Think of this range as a spring being compressed. If the security is accumulated inside the range, the security eventually breaks through the supply line to higher prices. If the security is in a state of distribution in the coil, the security eventually breaks down through the demand line to lower prices. The longer the length of this coil, the more explosive the potential breakout or breakdown expected from the preceding move (see Figure 8.2).

Figure 8.1   Price channel.

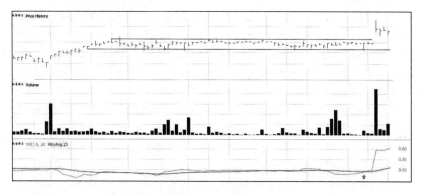

(Chart [or data] produced by TeleChart 2007® or StockFinder®, which is a registered trademark of Worden Brothers, Inc., Five Oaks Office Park, 4905 Pine Cone Drive, Durham, NC 27707. Ph. (800) 776-4940 or (919) 408-0542. www.Worden.com.)

Figure 8.2   Extended channel followed by high-volume breakout.

Observing price alone, the direction of the price break is virtually impossible to project while prices reside within the channel. However, volume indicators might give some hints about the direction of the potential breakout. When the break occurs, it should be accompanied with extraordinary volume—preferably at least 150 percent of the average daily trading volume during the trading range. The higher the volume, the more the break is validated. Sometimes, the prices slowly drift back again to the breakout point on low volume. If this happens on an upward breakout, you might expect the former resistance point to act as support as the former sellers regret their sales and wish to re-accumulate the stock at the point of their sale. Likewise, on breakdowns, the former support line acts as resistance. This retracement might offer a second chance to those who missed the initial breakout or were caught in the breakdown.

Symmetrical Triangles = Falling Resistance + Rising Support

Symmetrical triangles are born of doubt and uncertainty. A wide disparity of views causes two competing trends to emerge: one a bullish uptrend and the other a bearish downtrend. At the onset of a symmetrical triangle, neither of these trends is evident. The stock gyrates wildly up and down on very high volume. The top of the extreme forms the basis of what becomes a falling resistance line. The bottom extreme forms the rising support line, resulting in an uptrend. Unlike the channel trend lines, these trends typically begin much farther apart based on the wide disparity in beliefs between the two competing sides. Over time, the disparity grows narrower, as evidenced by the two price trends becoming closer as the volume becomes lighter. These actions symbolize the wide disparity of beliefs moving closer to parity. As prices move toward parity, less opportunity for profit is foreseen, which leads to the steadily falling volume. If left to continue, these two trends eventually meet. This would-be meeting place is the apex. The apex represents equilibrium between the two competing sides. Markets hate equilibrium. If everyone agrees, there is no money to be made.

Rarely, though, do price trends extend far enough to meet at the apex. Usually, one side or the other wins out convincingly prior to the convergence of these two competing sides. Such an event is called the *breakout* (see Figure 8.3) if up or the *breakdown* if down. When the break occurs, it is expected to create a new trend that moves in the same direction as the break. The break is identified by two simultaneous events. One is a clear and decisive break of one of the price trends. The second, just as important, is a significant rise in volume of at least 200 percent from recent low levels. The closer the break is to the apex, the higher the volume increase should be. The price break on high volume symbolizes the sound defeat of one view and the birth of a new emerging trend.

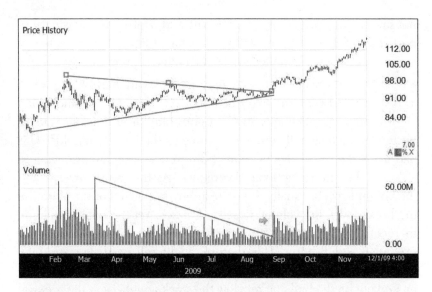

(Chart [or data] produced by TeleChart 2007® or StockFinder®, which is a registered trademark of Worden Brothers, Inc., Five Oaks Office Park, 4905 Pine Cone Drive, Durham, NC 27707. Ph. (800) 776-4940 or (919) 408-0542. www.Worden.com.)

Figure 8.3   Symmetrical triangle high-volume resolution.

According to the research of Thomas Bulkowski in *Trading Classical Patterns*, an upside breakout of a symmetrical triangle pattern results in 25 percent outperformance measured against the S&P 500, with only a 15 percent failure rate of meeting the targeted 10 percent gain. Shorting the downside breakdown of a symmetrical triangle had a 16 percent outperformance, with 24 percent of the patterns not achieving a 10 percent return.

Broadening Patterns = Rising Resistance and Falling Support

The inverse of a symmetrical triangle pattern is the broadening pattern. This pattern typically begins in a mature market that is reaching relative parity. However, over time, disparity begins to develop. The equivalent of an apex rests at the beginning of the trend. From this point of near equilibrium arise the developments of a new rising resistance line and a newly forming, falling support line. Notice I did

not say a rising uptrend or falling downtrend. Uptrends are rising support lines; downtrends are falling resistance lines. This broadening
consists of a rising resistance line and a falling support line.

At first, the swings between highs and lows are narrow. However,
as disparity between the two sides builds, the swings become wider.
With wider disparity comes more opportunity for profit. This is manifested through steadily growing volume as the pattern unfolds. This
pattern is representative of a small difference of opinion growing to
an unstable, often emotional divergence. As the trends diverge and
the volume grows, usually the pattern breaks down, not up. With the
the breakdown, the volume usually climaxes. Yet the relative volume
to recent days does not appear heavy, as the volume has already
expanded significantly. This pattern might tell us that, over time,
holders might have become overly complacent. Other investors who
missed out on the bull market view the stock's pullback as the renewal
of a once-missed opportunity. Meanwhile, new risks emerge that, at
first, are largely ignored but gradually take hold. The breakdown is
the capitulation of the bulls giving into the perceptions of a new and
dangerous reality (see Figure 8.4).

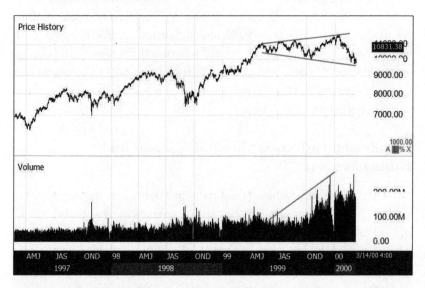

(Chart [or data] produced by TeleChart 2007® or StockFinder®, which is a registered trademark
of Worden Brothers, Inc., Five Oaks Office Park, 4905 Pine Cone Drive, Durham, NC 27707.
Ph. (800) 776-4940 or (919) 408-0542. www.Worden.com.)

Figure 8.4   Broadening pattern.

Ascending Triangles = Horizontal Resistance and Rising Support

The next pattern examined is an ascending triangle. This is the combination of a horizontal resistance line and a rising support line. In an ascending triangle, securities are accumulated, as evidenced by higher lows, forming an uptrend (rising support line). Yet these buyers run into a price extreme met with persistent supply from horizontal resistance that continually drives the prices down again. However, the buyers eventually regain control at higher levels from the previous support for another assault at the prior high. Again, the sellers push the prices down but not as low as in the previous decline. Demand regains control and the process of test the high and make a higher low begins again and again, forming the shape of an ascending triangle. The direction of the uptrend line points to the direction of the eventual breakout.

This price pattern needs to be confirmed by volume action. Each seller's throwbacks should become gradually weaker as fewer shares are desired for sale at the new resistance point. Thus, as the pattern approaches the apex of the triangle, the volume should drop lower and lower. When this pattern of a rising support line rising into a horizontal resistance line with falling volume occurs, the expectation is an upward breakout. During the breakout, the sellers become exhausted, and buyers push through the line of resistance, absorbing all the remaining holdouts. Short sellers cover, and market makers rebuild their inventory, fearing a runaway. The result is a defining upward bar closing significantly above the resistance line, accompanied by exceedingly high volume dwarfing that of recent times (see Figure 8.5). Again, the higher the volume on the breakout move, the more conviction becomes apparent in the breakout. I prefer the volume to be up more than 150 percent above normal.

Bulkowski's research shows that the ascending triangle breakout has a 21 percent outperformance over the S&P 500, with 17 percent of the patterns failing to reach a 10 percent appreciation.

(Chart [or data] produced by TeleChart 2007® or StockFinder®, which is a registered trademark
of Worden Brothers, Inc., Five Oaks Office Park, 4905 Pine Cone Drive, Durham, NC 27707.
Ph. (800) 776-4940 or (919) 408-0542. www.Worden.com.)

Figure 8.5   Ascending triangle high-volume breakout resolution.

Descending Triangles = Horizontal Support and Falling Resistance

The opposite of the ascending triangle is the descending triangle. This is a combination of a horizontal support line being persistently invaded by a falling resistance line. In this formation, sellers continue to make an assault on a firm support line. Buyers come in at the depressed level, believing it to be a good value at this "low" price, pushing the stock up again. However, each advance goes a little less high than the previous advance. This forms the falling resistance line of the descending triangle, which shows that the supply of the security is growing. The direction of the resistance line (down) points to the expected direction of the trend break. Once again, the volume needs to confirm the pattern. As the downtrend moves toward the apex of the descending triangle, volume should also wane. Thus, the pattern of the volume should almost shadow the pattern of the falling price. The breakdown occurs when the support line is violated alongside a strong volume surge. Here, the buyers who previously believed the security to be "cheap" at this level suddenly lose all confidence. They pull any remaining limit orders to buy and are motivated to sell before losses set in. I like to see the volume on the breakdown at least 140 percent of the previous trading range. According to Bulkowski, shorting a descending triangle post-breakdown has a 16 percent out-performance versus the S&P 500, with 27 percent of the patterns not achieving at least a 10 percent profit.

The Rounding Bottom: A Base-Building Trend Change

Rounding bottoms occur during a gradual shift of opinion. In a rounding bottom, pessimism slowly evaporates while being replaced by slowly building optimism. This is a downtrend dying a slow death. Prior to the formation, the stock historically has had a pessimistic outlook. The faults of the enterprise are much publicized, causing the stock to be under clear and well-known distribution. The pattern begins inconspicuously as the stock continues to fall, be it ever more slowly. The remaining holders see the security as firmly undervalued and are committed to seeing their investment through. Any residual weak-minded holders are slowly purged as the stock drops at an ever slower rate.

So far, I have only discussed price action. It is the volume, though, that tips the tape reader as to the market's hand. As the price drops at a slowing rate, the volume of shares exchanged also gradually diminishes. Over time, the rate slows to the point that the security no longer falls but moves sideways. At this point, supply and demand establish equilibrium. Volume is almost nonexistent, as those who own are unwilling to sell at depressed levels, and buyers still have little interest in purchasing shares. The pendulum swings eventually, but it is buyers who begin to push the stock up. This is weak demand as the number of shares traded remains low but slowly grows. More buyers begin to purchase the security as fundamental reasons to own the security are discovered. The stock begins a new trend, visible through an increase in price and price momentum. This new trend is confirmed by an increasing number of shares being transacted at increasing prices. If you visualize the price and volume history on bar charts, you can see that both look like a bowl. Thus, the term "rounding bottom" means the price and volume slowly fall and then slowly begin to rise, forming a bowl-shaped bottom (see Figure 8.6).

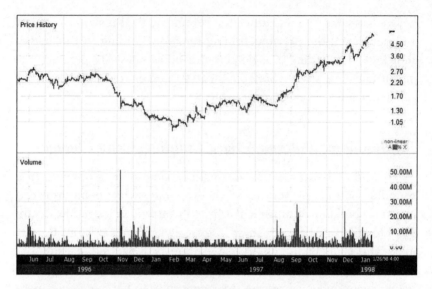

(Chart [or data] produced by TeleChart 2007® or StockFinder®, which is a registered trademark
of Worden Brothers, Inc., Five Oaks Office Park, 4905 Pine Cone Drive, Durham, NC 27707.
Ph. (800) 776-4940 or (919) 408-0542. www.Worden.com.)

Figure 8.6   Rounding saucer bottom.

Rounding Tops

In many of the prior examples, I used the analogies of war between
buyers and sellers and battles between demand and supply. I think of
rounding tops a little bit differently. Here, you have a war, but it is a war
in which the buyers have decisively won every major engagement—so
much so that over time, these owners become complacent. This market
is like an empire that outgrows itself. Who destroyed the Roman
Empire? Was it the mighty barbarians of the north? No, Rome grew
complacent in its greatness. In the process, it lost its way and was
unable to sustain its glory. Rome just fizzled out.

Stocks can have a similar demise. After a long period of time,
more and more investors develop a mentality that a certain stock
must be a core holding. Holders of the security grow increasingly
complacent. However, as the stock advances, fewer and fewer people
become interested in buying it at higher prices. This is seen on the
price chart as ever more slowly rising prices. Meanwhile, the volume
of shares traded continues to fall. Eventually, the anemic demand

equals the weak supply. At this point, stock prices peak not on a glorious high, but rather in a golden age that is not recognized as such. All appears well, but the stock is now on a slow path to disaster. This price descent starts gradually, while the volume begins to climb gently. As the downturn continues, more investors become more aware of the flaws in the company fundamentals, causing the price to drop quickly as volume increases. Thus, the stock has now moved from a defining uptrend into a new downtrend. This is seen when the price chart looks like an upside-down bowl. Meanwhile, the volume takes the shape of a bowl as it rises, falls, and regains momentum (see Figure 8.7).

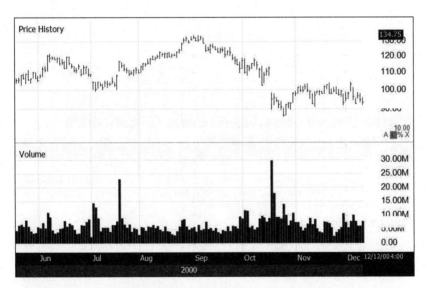

(Chart [or data] produced by TeleChart 2007® or StockFinder®, which is a registered trademark of Worden Brothers, Inc., Five Oaks Office Park, 4905 Pine Cone Drive, Durham, NC 27707. Ph. (800) 776-4940 or (919) 408-0542. www.Worden.com.)

Figure 8.7 Rounding top.

Complex Patterns Comprise Combinations of Other Patterns

Diamond Top

A *diamond top* is a bearish topping pattern. It is simply a broadening pattern that morphs into a symmetrical triangle. The formation is confirmed when the price breaks down through the downtrend line of the symmetrical triangle on heavy volume (see Figure 8.8). Diamond tops are known to be ominous. Shorting the pattern after the initial breakdown, the pattern outperforms the S&P 500 by 24 percent with a 10 percent chance of not reaching its 10 percent target, according to Bulkowski's research.

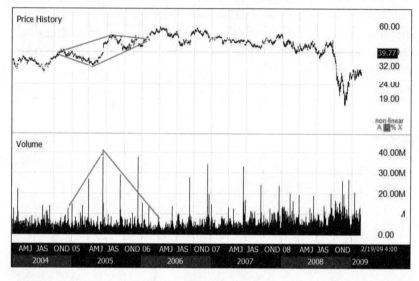

(Chart [or data] produced by TeleChart 2007® or StockFinder®, which is a registered trademark of Worden Brothers, Inc., Five Oaks Office Park, 4905 Pine Cone Drive, Durham, NC 27707. Ph. (800) 776-4940 or (919) 408-0542. www.Worden.com.)

Figure 8.8   Diamond top.

Cup and Handle

The cup-and-handle formation is a typical bullish pattern consisting of a short and shallow rounding bottom forming the "cup," followed by a horizontal or mildly tilted channel line. The cup-and-handle pattern is a shorter formation, usually forming over the course of several weeks. The cup-and-handle pattern begins in either a sideways or uptrend, but it can also form in a downtrend after a significant upward movement (greater than 30 percent). The cup is formed when the stock breaks down through minor support. As the stock continues to fall, the velocity of the drop stalls, as does the volume. After the bottom is formed on light volume, the stock begins to rise on heavier volume, forming a saucer shape for price and, to a lesser extent, the volume plotted (see Figure 8.9). This is similar to the rounding bottom, except during a condensed time period and with steeper volume on the ascent. As the stock approaches its former breakdown point, resistance sets in and halts the advance. The stock then trades sideways to slightly down on lighter volume, forming the "handle." At this point, the pattern is still subject to a high failure risk. The key to entering this trade is in waiting for the stock to break through the prior resistance, which is the high point of the initial breakdown that formed the left side of the cup. The breakout must occur on heavy volume—at least 150 percent of typical volume. If the stock breaks through without heavy volume, the pattern is null and void.

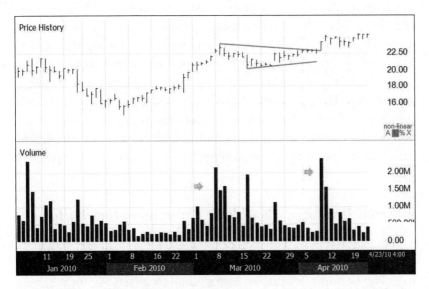

(Chart [or data] produced by TeleChart 2007® or StockFinder®, which is a registered trademark of Worden Brothers, Inc., Five Oaks Office Park, 4905 Pine Cone Drive, Durham, NC 27707. Ph. (800) 776-4940 or (919) 408-0542. www.Worden.com.)

Figure 8.9   Cup and handle.

Head and Shoulders: Three Rounding Tops

The head-and-shoulders pattern is defined by three rounding tops. The pattern arises from an established sideways or uptrend. The formation is a noted reversal pattern, meaning it reverses the direction of the prior trend and has bearish implications. The pattern begins forming a small rounding price top called and resembling a *left shoulder*. The volume of the left should be heavy as institutions sell into the rally. This is followed by a definitive rounding top called and resembling a *head*. The head is larger than the shoulder in height and width but smaller than a standard rounding top formation. The head-and-shoulders pattern is usually born of a light volume price climax. Thus, the volume is much lighter in the formation of the top of the head than at the formation of the left shoulder. However, as the price falls as it forms the head, the volume typically grows into the decline. The rounding head is halted as it runs into support from the prior trend.

A trend line is drawn connecting the bottom of this newly formed head to the former shoulder. This trend line is called the *neckline* and will become the key to the pattern. After the rounding bottom finds support, a light volume rally ensues. At the peak of the rally, the stock again falls, forming the third rounding top called the *right shoulder*. The volume should increase in the second half of the right shoulder as the stock falls. When the stock violates the neckline, the formation is complete. Heavy volume should accompany the final breakdown (see Figure 8.10). According to the historical outperformance of the S&P500 index, shorting the head-and-shoulders pattern is 19 percent with only 18 percent of the patterns failing to achieve a 10 percent gain.

Inverted Head and Shoulders: Three Rounding Bottoms

An inverted head-and-shoulders pattern is the head-and-shoulders pattern upside down. The shoulders and the head are formed by rounding bottoms as opposed to rounding tops (see Figure 8.11). As the price pattern unfolds, volume should decline in the descents and rise in the advances. According to Bulkowski, the inverted head-and-shoulders pattern produces a 25 percent outperformance to the S&P 500. The pattern fails to meet the 10 percent target only 10 percent of the time.

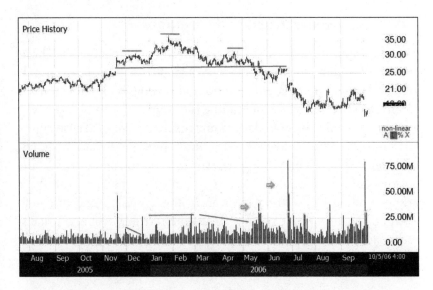

(Chart [or data] produced by TeleChart 2007® or StockFinder®, which is a registered trademark of Worden Brothers, Inc., Five Oaks Office Park, 4905 Pine Cone Drive, Durham, NC 27707. Ph. (800) 776-4940 or (919) 408-0542. www.Worden.com.)

Figure 8.10 Head and shoulders top with high-volume resolution.

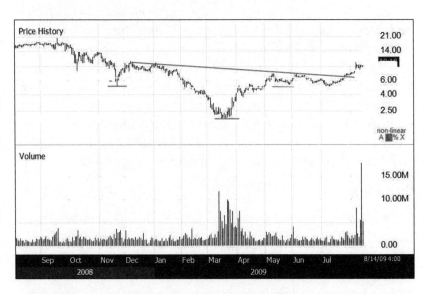

(Chart [or data] produced by TeleChart 2007® or StockFinder®, which is a registered trademark of Worden Brothers, Inc., Five Oaks Office Park, 4905 Pine Cone Drive, Durham, NC 27707. Ph. (800) 776-4940 or (919) 408-0542. www.Worden.com.)

Figure 8.11 Head and shoulders bottom with high-volume resolution.

Subplots: Counter Trending Formations

Like other narratives, stock plots often contain subplots. These consist of minor countertrends moving against the major trend. While the trend unfolds across periods of several weeks and months, countertrends usually play out during the course of several days. Typical countertrends include flags, pennants, and wedges. These countertrends represent a needed rest in the forces of demand or supply that control the primary trend. However, if these countertrends are not recognized as countertrends, they can cause trades to lose their prime position in the trend. Woven in the overall theme of countertrends is the role of volume. In a countertrend, volume usually starts high, but as the countertrend unfolds, it weakens as does the volume.

Bullish Flags and Pennant Formations

Bull market flags and pennants occur in an extended intermediate- or long-term advance. Here, a definitive uptrend is in place, which is evidenced by higher valleys (higher lows) across time. This indicates accumulation in which demand continually gobbles up supply offered by sellers. These advances can grow tired. Institutional buyers wonder how much of their own activity is pushing up the stock. Retail investors see the stock as extended and no longer want to chase it, whereas others have been waiting for the momentum to slow to take profits. These sentiments lead to a slight pause in buying activities, which, in turn, leads to an interruption in the accumulation pattern.

Bull Flag

The bull market flag formation might be identified by its appearance of a flag hanging down from the larger advance. Hence, the term bull term flag. The flag formation is a small cluster of daily bars formed by two parallel lines. The lower line is made up of lower lows (falling demand) and the upper line by higher highs (rising supply), which form the two parallel lines making the flag (see Figure 8.12).

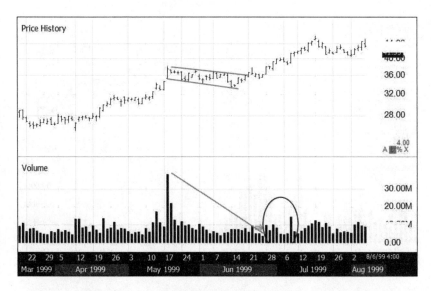

(Chart [or data] produced by TeleChart 2007® or StockFinder®, which is a registered trademark of Worden Brothers, Inc., Five Oaks Office Park, 4905 Pine Cone Drive, Durham, NC 27707. Ph. (800) 776-4940 or (919) 408-0542. www.Worden.com.)

Figure 8.12   Bull flag.

Bull Pennant

Likewise, the bullish pennant occurs amidst the course of several daily bars in the midst of the same intermediate-term uptrend conditions. The pennant formation is bounded by falling highs (reduced demand) on top, similar to the flag. However, it differs from the flag in that it is bounded by flat (stable demand) or rising (increasing demand) lows on the bottom of the countertrend, thus giving the price chart the shape of a pennant as the formation plays out.

In both of these formations, supply temporarily regains control in the midst of an impressive intermediate- to long-term advance. Volume should not expand much (less than 115 percent of 50-day average volume) during the beginning the formation. Most importantly, volume should fade the longer the countertrend plays out (see Figure 8.13). This means that the force of the countertrend gradually weakens as time passes.

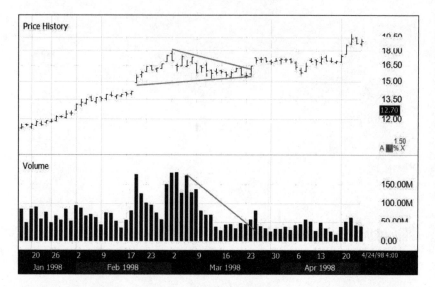

(Chart [or data] produced by TeleChart 2007® or StockFinder®, which is a registered trademark of Worden Brothers, Inc., Five Oaks Office Park, 4905 Pine Cone Drive, Durham, NC 27707. Ph. (800) 776-4940 or (919) 408-0542. www.Worden.com.)

Figure 8.13   Bull pennant.

These patterns typically break in favor of the bulls. It is healthy for a stock or a market of stock to consolidate in the midst of an advance. It is difficult for a trend to maintain a steady push. Volume is key. Volume should not be high and should gradually decrease as the countertrend weakens. Low and falling volume confirms that the countertrending force is weak and likely to fail.

Bear Flag and Pennants

Naturally, a bear flag is the opposite of a bull flag (see Figure 8.14). Bear flags occur in an extended intermediate- or long-term decline. Stock is distributed as the trend moves down, which indicates more supply than demand. If the volume expands or the price violates the primary support, then the pattern is not a flag.

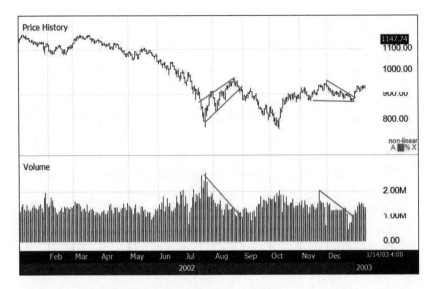

(Chart [or data] produced by TeleChart 2007® or StockFinder®, which is a registered trademark of Worden Brothers, Inc., Five Oaks Office Park, 4905 Pine Cone Drive, Durham, NC 27707. Ph. (800) 776-4940 or (919) 408-0542. www.Worden.com.)

Figure 8.14   Bear flag and pennant.

9

Measuring Volume Information

"The relationship between trading volume and securities prices is a complex one which, when understood properly, can lead to many insights in portfolio theory."

—*Walter Sun, MIT Laboratory of Information and Decision Systems, The Relationship Between Trading Volume and Securities Prices, 2003*

There are several old but elegant homes in a local community that were supposedly built by an old-time Amish master carpenter who never used a tape measure. There are also old-school master traders who can successfully trade solely on gut feel and intuition. However, I would not recommend so much as furnishing a house without a tape measure.

A book on volume analysis would be incomplete without a section on volume indicators. So far, I have discussed volume in generic terms without actually developing the concepts or indications into indicators. I have discussed mostly general principles, such as:

- High-volume movements confirm the trend.
- Low-volume movements contradict the trend.
- Volume declines in consolidation patterns.
- Volume spikes upon the onset of a new price trend.

All of these principles assume that the analyst can differentiate between normal, low, and high volume. By reading the tape and chart, indications of the tensions between supply and demand can be observed with the naked eye and a trained mind. However, a quantifiable measurement exhibiting those tensions is a more useful tool for analysis. There is a time to get out our tape measure, and likewise, there is a time to turn our general volume principles into indicators with numerical values.

Volume indicators keep score. Through mathematical computations, volume indicators provide a concrete measurement of volume and a quantitative assessment of the volume-price relationship. Unlike for the art of tape reading, you can use scientific methods to test these indicators to see if they provide useful information. Volume indicators are informative in two important ways. First, they should lead price, meaning that volume indicators often offer notification before major price breaks. When the volume indicator makes new highs or lows while the stock price does not yet change, volume indicates which direction the price might go. This enables the perceptive investor to take up or unload a position prior to a significant price move. Second, volume indicators should confirm price. Volume should rise in the direction of the trend. Should volume fall as the trend matures, the volume divergence is warning that the trend might be poised to end.

For any trade that takes place, there are three pieces of information: the price at which the trade was executed, the time when it was executed, and the size of the trade. It is from these three items that all stock market data are derived. By aggregating the sizes of multiple trades over time, we get volume. By comparing prices of each trade to prior prices, we get price trends that drive the multitude of indicators. Price indicators are devised from only five pieces of information: the open, the high, the low, the close, and time. This results in a high correlation between price and price-only-derived indicators. By taking volume into account, a trader can use volume indicators to gain insight into the inner structure of the market. In contrast to the hundreds of various price indicators that are all derived from the same data, volume indicators offer a fresh and noncorrelating alternative to price-only analysis.

Volume indicators normally appear in a box below the price chart and are set to their own scale of relative change. This enables you to make an easy comparison between the price trends and movements relative to the volume indicators' trends and movements. Interpretation of a volume indicator is generally accomplished by looking for confirmation or divergence from price. The indicator should trend in the same direction as the price. This is called *price-volume confirmation*, and it gives notice that the present price trend should continue. If the direction of the volume indicator diverges from the price trend, it is called *price-volume contradiction*, and it is an indication that the present trend might be susceptible to correction.

The Seven Types of Volume Indicators

One might suppose that volume indicators would simplify volume analysis, and they do. However, as you delve more deeply into indicators, you might open a can of worms, swimming in confusion. These "worms" are a variety of volume indicators conveying subtly different information. The objective of most of these volume indicators is to quantify the amount of money flowing into or out of the stock. A popular way to describe money flow is to say that the stock is under a state of accumulation or distribution. Each indicator represents its creator's own depiction of how accumulation and distribution should be interpreted. However, the desire to conceptualize volume indicators and market them as something the public can readily understand has led to different indicators with similar or identical names (see Figure 9.1). Because of this, many practitioners assume that all volume indicators work essentially the same way. This is an incorrect assumption that intensifies the confusion surrounding volume indicators even further.

To help clear up that confusion, I have navigated through the duplicated names and murky conceptual similarities to focus primarily on the information that is conveyed by the volume indicator, while giving proper credit to the indicator's creators and promoters.

This will enable you to overcome the perplexity and develop an understanding of the information that the various volume indicators provide, then you might be better positioned to determine leading signals, which are often not correlated to price indicators.

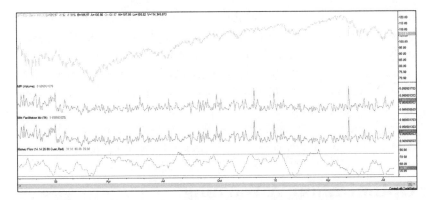

Figure 9.1 Different money flow indicators showing vastly different results.

Volume indicators provide information in seven different ways:

- **Pure volume**—A volume indicator without any price data
- **Volume accumulation based on interday price change**— Volume accumulation based on the price change from daily close to daily close
- **Volume accumulation based on intraday price change**— Volume accumulation based on intraday price movements
- **Volume-price range indicators**—Volume analysis based on the price's intraday range
- **Price accumulation based on volume**—Price accumulation based upon volume change
- **Tick volume**—Intraday accumulation of trades by each tick of the tape
- **Volume-adjusted price indicators**—Volume-weighted price based on participation

These seven classifications also represent the seven categories from which we investigate volume indicators, some of which can fit into multiple categories. This section does not present an exhaustive list of all the volume indicators ever devised, because there are far too many indicators with subtle similarities. Take, for example, the most popular of the volume indicators: on-balance volume. Seemingly, there are as many knockoff versions of on-balance volume as there are volume experts, each integrating his or her own twists into the calculation or data. The indicators reviewed are the ones I believe are most widely used or offer unique insights. This leaves out many volume indicators devised by several respected technicians who have contributed to the development of the field of volume analysis.

Optimization: A Warning

Before beginning the review of volume-based indicators, several common misunderstandings among technical indicators should be addressed. One common practice concerning technical indicators with which I disagree is the use of optimization. Most indicators provide user-defined parameters. This allows the user to choose the time periods being contrasted, such as 5 or 50 periods. Optimization is the practice of continually back testing an indicator or a combination of indicators to determine which settings should be used. I believe this practice is usually a bad idea. Habitually, optimizers tend to optimize and keep on optimizing until they have a successful combination (for example, a combination of parameters with which the indicator gives signals for profitable trades). The result is an indicator with settings that are characteristic of evolution, not mindful creation.

This is essentially just a fancy way to curve-fit to historical data. With this evolutionary design method, tens of thousands of combinations are data mined until they produce the most successful combination. However, indicators should be created under a specific set of conditions to uncover specific sets of information. Random processes simply cannot yield useful information. By applying an optimized indicator, otherwise known as curve-fitting, one simply sees that this random combination worked best in the past. But why should it work in the future? Suppose you invest money using this optimized indicator, and you enter into a long-term losing streak not experienced in the back testing. Do you keep on losing, or do you reoptimize?

I simply do not have enough faith in optimization to use it in an investment decision; it is an illogical method to be used in such a complex market structure. I suggest a simplified approach. Instead of optimizing your indicator's parameters, choose an indicator's settings based on the time frames in which you are investing. If you want to contrast what is happening over the course of a week versus a month, the proper indicator settings would be 5 days (one week) and 20 days (four weeks). Maintaining your settings to correspond to the calendar keeps it simple. My belief is that if an indicator does not "work" over the course of one time frame but supposedly does work over another, the indicator itself does not work.

Another misconception concerning indicators is that they give false signals. This might be true some of the time. Generally, however, the information calculated and displayed by the indicator is not false in itself; rather, some other force is influencing the action more than the data displayed by the indicator.

Along these lines, it is important to understand what information the indicator attempts to communicate. Too often, investors view indicators as a sort of magical phenomenon. They believe that if an indicator line crosses another line, something in the underlying price is about to happen, or they believe that if the indicator reaches a certain level, the stock's trend will suddenly reverse. Technical indicators calculate information. Therefore, indicators should be used as information, not as absolute gospel truth. As I review the volume indicators, you should view them as tools, each of which is designed to explain a distinct piece of the volume puzzle.

10

Pure Volume Indicators

"Most people look at the price of their stock and don't pay much attention to volume. But volume is a crucial component of the measure of supply and demand. When you have major volume coming into a stock, it tells you there are important players involved. So, yes, we look at volume very carefully."
—*William J. O'Neil*

Pure volume indicators are simply that; they use volume only in computations. Although volume information can be used alone, it is best used with price information.

Volume

On most charts, volume is depicted over time on a horizontal axis as a vertical line bar directly below the corresponding price bar. This allows for easy comparisons between the day's volume bar and the corresponding price bar directly above it. Also, by having a volume bar positioned right beside previous volume bars, you can easily see whether the current bar's volume is higher or lower than the previous volume bars. Trend lines might be drawn across the highs of the volume bars to help discern the trend of volume.

This method of displaying volume bars below price bars is by far the most common way to express volume. A variation on this method is to color the volume bars white or green if the price bar closes up and black or red if the price closes down (see Figure 10.1).

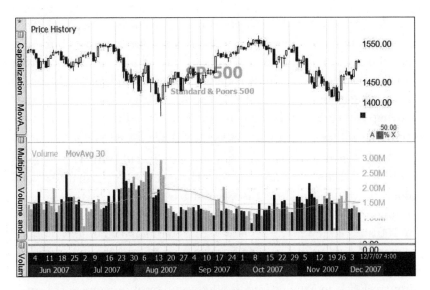

(Chart [or data] produced by TeleChart 2007® or StockFinder®, which is a registered trademark of Worden Brothers, Inc., Five Oaks Office Park, 4905 Pine Cone Drive, Durham, NC 27707. Ph. (800) 776-4940 or (919) 408-0542. www.Worden.com.)

Figure 10.1 Typical volume plot.

Other volume charts might include a zero line, which represents zero volume. From the zero line, vertical volume-bars that ascend signify that the price closed up on the day. Likewise, vertical volume-bars that descend below the zero line mean that price closed down on the day. This method allows the chartist to more easily discern how many days on the chart were "up days" versus "down days" and to compare the volume from the various days. However, I do not recommend this plotting method as a standard method because it is more difficult to compare the up volume and down volume to each other, mainly because the up and down volume bars are positioned in opposite directions from the zero line instead of appearing right next to each other.

Volume Moving Averages

Neither of these depictions of volume is of much use other than for eyeballing the various heights of the bars. Volume information is most helpful when it is illustrated in relative terms, when it can help you discern whether the volume is higher or lower than usual. The most common way to do this is to overlay a volume average horizontally moving across the volume bars. If the volume bar is below the moving average, then volume is below average. If the volume is above the moving average, then volume is above average. The length of the moving average might be customized by each individual analyst, but common volume averages are periods of 5, 20, 50, and 200.

Normalized volume (%V) is a similar concept in that it uses an average of volume to plot volume. However, with normalized volume, the volume total for the current bar is divided by the average volume (over the last n bars) to form a ratio. This ratio is multiplied by 100 and plotted in the same way that traditional volume is plotted as vertical bars on the horizontal plane, which creates a normalized volume scale of 0 to 100. This allows for easy interpretation of volume's relative movements, with 50 being typical or average volume, numbers below 50 being light volume, and numbers above 50 being heavier volume.

Volume Oscillators

A variety of other volume oscillators might be created by replicating existing price oscillators. This is accomplished by substituting volume data for the price oscillator's price data. Generally, averages of the volume data are used, as opposed to raw volume statistics because volume data are more volatile than price data. Two examples include Volume Rate of Change (V-ROC) and Volume Moving Average Convergence Divergence (V-MACD), which are also known as %Volume Oscillator (%VO). Volume oscillator indicators help identify the momentum of volume and can be contrasted to the momentum of price.

Volume Bands

Volume surges are important events that the technical analyst will almost always want to be aware of. One way to detect these unusual volume occurrences is to add a Bollinger band to a moving average of volume. This in effect displays normal two-standard deviations above and below the average volume. On those rare occasions when volume trades outside two-standard deviations from their norms, the Bollinger Bands alert you about the occurrence (see Figure 10.2).

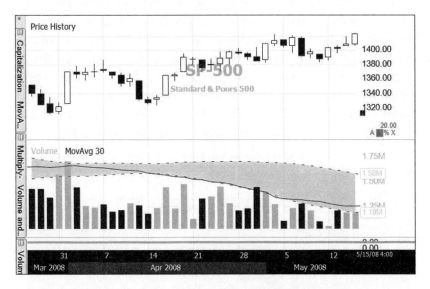

(Chart [or data] produced by TeleChart 2007® or StockFinder®, which is a registered trademark of Worden Brothers, Inc., Five Oaks Office Park, 4905 Pine Cone Drive, Durham, NC 27707. Ph. (800) 776-4940 or (919) 408-0542. www.Worden.com.)

Figure 10.2   Bollinger bands around volume average.

Volume Accumulation

Volume accumulation is a running total of the difference between the volume today versus the volume a day ago (volume today–volume yesterday). The plot looks much like a moving average. And, like a moving average, this method is another way to plot volume's trend. However, in contrast to a moving average, volume accumulation shows the accumulation of the growth or decline of volume over time. As is the case with many accumulation indicators, as time extends the data series, the less sensitive the indicator becomes to shorter term volume movements. One way to correct this limitation is to establish a strict look-back period, such as 200 volume bars. The weakness of volume accumulation is that it does a poor job of contrasting individual bar fluctuations to that of the typical bar volume. For this reason, this method of analyzing volume is rarely used except to obtain an indication of the volume trend.

Volume at Price

Another way to depict volume information is to plot volume horizontally on the vertical axis. Here, price and time are plotted horizontally, as usual. However, volume is not representative of volume during a certain time, but rather the price level at which the volume occurred. In this way, the chartist can easily discern how many shares were exchanged at various price points. This helps determine potential support and resistance levels when a vast amount of shares trade hands. Although useful, this method of displaying volume is seldom used except occasionally on intraday charts (see Figures 10.3, 10.4, and 10.5).

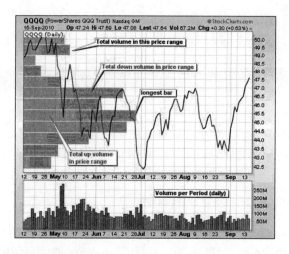

(Source: Stockcharts.com.)

Figure 10.3   Volume at price showing strong support between 44.5 and 45.

(Source: Stockcharts.com.)

Figure 10.4   Netflix finds support where volume was previously heavy.

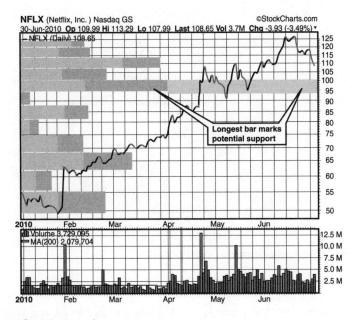

(Source: Stockcharts.com.)

Figure 10.5   Volume at price unveils heavy Netflix volume between 95-100, which might constitute strong support.

Price: Volume/Crocker Charts

Price-volume charts were created in the 1950s by Benjamin Crocker. A price-volume data point is depicted as a single point on a chart, with price determining the vertical position of the point and volume determining the horizontal position. The chart is created by connecting the data points.

It might help to conceptualize this chart by looking at the price-volume chart as a map. Price is associated with latitude, which measures north and south positions, and volume with longitude, which measures east and west positions. The coordinates of the map (chart) are the price-volume points. As price and volume change over time, the price-volume points move across the price-volume plane, forming lines that resemble a toddler's drawings on an Etch-a-Sketch (see Figure 10.6).

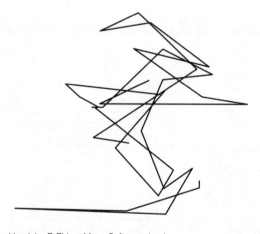

(Source: Provided by John F. Ehlers Mesa Software, Inc.)

Figure 10.6   Crocker chart.

When the price-volume line moves from the lower left to upper right, it indicates that price is moving higher on increasing volume, which is a bullish sign. When the line moves from the lower right to upper left, it demonstrates price moving higher on lower volume, which is a bearish indication. When the line travels from the upper right to the lower left, it shows the price falling on rising volume, which is also a bearish indication. When the line travels from the upper right to the lower left, it illustrates price falling on lower volume, which is a bullish indication (see Figure 10.7).

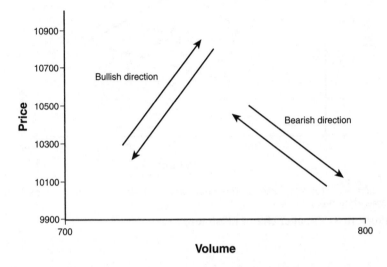

(Source: www.MarketMonograph.com Fredric Goodman, CFP Money Manager and Market Letter Writer Since 1970.)

Figure 10.7   Crocker charts straight demand supply picture.

Using the previous rules, you can observe patterns from price-volume movements. Movement of the line that goes in a clockwise direction indicates greater demand than supply (see Figure 10.8). Counterclockwise movements indicate that supply exceeds demand (see Figure 10.9). When a line crosses another line, it indicates a change in the balance of power in the direction that the line moves. These charts are quite peculiar in appearance, making the concepts in them difficult for many to grasp. However, as crazy as a Crocker chart might appear, it does hold value for those who are able to make sense of them.

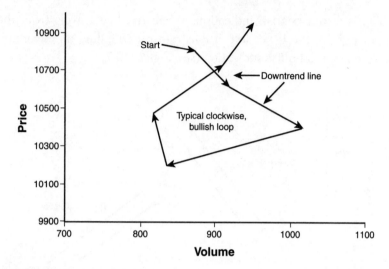

(Source: www.MarketMonograph.com Fredric Goodman, CFP Money Manager and Market Letter Writer Since 1970.)

Figure 10.8   Crocker chart bullish loop.

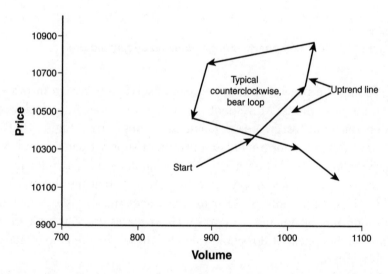

(Source: www.MarketMonograph.com Fredric Goodman, CFP Money Manager and Market Letter Writer Since 1970.)

Figure 10.9   Crocker chart patterns bearish loop.

11

Interday Volume Accumulation Indicators

"There is nothing new on Wall Street or in the school of speculation. What has happened in the past will happen again and again. This is because human nature does not change, and its human emotion that always gets in the way of human intelligence."

—*Jesse L. Livermore*

Another way to depict volume flows is by accumulating volume based on interday price change. The logic is this: If price rises on a given day, that day's volume is characterized as *up volume*. If the price falls from yesterday, then the volume is considered *down volume*. This idea was believed to have first been conceived as *cumulative volume* by Frank Vignolia, also known by his pseudonym of Woods in as early as 1946. However, the idea might have even earlier roots. Paul Clay was a highly regarded Wall Street financial statistician, economist and investment counselor. In his first ten years on Wall Street, famed analyst Edson B. Gould, Jr. worked for Clay at Moody's Investors Services. In 1932, Paul Clay gave a presentation at the American Statistical Association describing a "volume index number made by giving the sign of the price movement to the daily volumes, and accumulating the plus and minus movements." Clay described using these technical data, combined with four technical elements, to "have the very distinct merit of moving contrary to the course of the market." According to Clay, when used with economic indexes, the information has "proven more valuable than any personal judgments."

On-Balance Volume

By far the most acclaimed volume indicator is on-balance volume (OBV), a concept pioneered by Joe Granville. As a youth, Granville was a pianist, working with the likes of Orson Welles while still a teenager. He published his first book at the age of 16, called *A School Boy's Faith*, about his philosophy of life, which he claimed "has not changed one iota" since. Granville began by predicting prices of commemorative stamps, writing his first book on the subject in 1945. In 1957, he moved to predicting stock prices as E.F. Hutton's daily market commentator. In July 1961, he developed his concept of on-balance volume and began popularizing his OBV method in his 1963 book, *Granville's New Key to Stock Market Profits*. Stock market historian James E. Alphier, who was familiar with the work of Vignola was "confident Granville came upon OBV independently" and found "no reason whatever" to doubt Granville's claim of having invented it in the summer of 1961. Recognizing volume as the force behind price movements, Granville created OBV by adding positive volume on up days and subtracting negative volume on down days. Thus, if the stock's closing price is higher than the previous closing bar, then all the volume is added to the OBV totals. Similarly, if stock's closing price is lower, then all the volume is subtracted from the OBV totals.

In my present-day conversations with Granville, he still says that he "would not make a forecast without on-balance volume, the way I designed it." Granville's idea of OBV is to keep a continuous running total of volume. However, some practitioners today keep OBV history limited to a set number of rolling periods, such as 20. This adaptation allows recent historical data to have a stronger impact on the calculation. As a forecaster of the long-term market trend, Granville does not advocate this adaptation, although I believe it has merit in other settings.

The following includes OBV formulas:

- **Higher Closing Price:** OBV = Prior OBV + Current Volume
- **Lower Closing Price:** OBV = Prior OBV − Current Volume
- **Unchanged Closing Price:** OBV = Prior OBV (no change)

In essence, OBV is price-directed volume, the accumulation of +/− volume flows based on the closing price's direction. Granville's original objective with OBV was to uncover hidden building tensions in otherwise uneventful nontrending price patterns. When the OBV indicator rises, it unveils buying pressure or hidden demand. When the OBV falls, it reveals hidden selling pressure or growing supply. It is OBV's trend direction that determines whether hidden demand or supply is building inside the market. A series of new highs or lows in OBV is often a good indicator that a corresponding price breakout or down is developing (see Figure 11.1). With his OBV indicator, Granville became a renowned market strategist, and he popularized OBV and the wisdom of using volume in securities analysis. In 2002, a journalist asked him if his technical analysis still worked and whether his specific methods would work forever. Granville answered in typical Granville fashion, stating: "Of course. Truth is never out of date. There're only two things that can change the value of a stock: supply and demand, the only things I teach." Today, OBV is a standard application for charting software, and there are many OBV practitioners. However, few are able to interpret these indicators as well as Joe Granville. Granville attributes much of his market success to having a well-rounded life; the market is a lot like life, and one needs to understand the nature of people to forecast markets.

(Chart [or data] produced by TeleChart 2007® or StockFinder®, which is a registered trademark of Worden Brothers, Inc., Five Oaks Office Park, 4905 Pine Cone Drive, Durham, NC 27707. Ph. (800) 776-4940 or (919) 408-0542. www.Worden.com.)

Figure 11.1   On-balance volume.

Volume Price Trend

It did not take long for OBV to catch on. With its growth also came other ways to calculate the formula or manipulate the indicator. The first alternative version developed was volume-price trend (VPT). VPT was unveiled in 1966 in David L. Markstein's book, *How to Chart Your Way to Stock Market Profits*. Although OBV tracks change in volume based on price direction, it doesn't consider the magnitude of the price move. Thus, a stock closing up 1 point had the same impact on OBV as a stock closing up 100 points. Markstein's adaptation addressed this issue by including the relative price change in the VPT calculation. VPT is calculated in the same way as OBV, except the current volume is multiplied by the percentage in price change. In this way, VPT includes not only the change in volume, but also the corresponding change in price. For this reason, although I respect Granville's contribution, I prefer VPT to OBV. Here's the equation for VPT:

$$\text{VPT} = \text{Prior VPT} + (\text{Current Volume} - +/- \%$$
$$\text{Change in Closing Price})$$

VPT is volume accumulation based on the magnitude of the price's change. It is interpreted in the same way as OBV. Like OBV, VPT should lead or mirror the price trend. If VPT trends in the opposite direction of the price trend, then it warns that the internal pressures of supply and demand are diverging from price's present course (see Figure 11.2).

Intraday Volume Accumulation Oscillators

Although both OBV and VPT were popularized in the 1960s and 1970s, many adaptations are still being created. The most recent is the volume zone oscillator (VZO), introduced by Waleed Aly Khalil. This is a clever revision of OBV, essentially turning OBV into an oscillator. Kahalil stock oscillator is similar to Edson B. Gould, Jr.'s breadth oscillator "The Daily Trading Barometer." Like OBV, VZO considers all the volume as positive when the close is up and negative when the close is down. However, VZO replaces the cumulative running total of OBV with a smoothed 14-period exponential moving

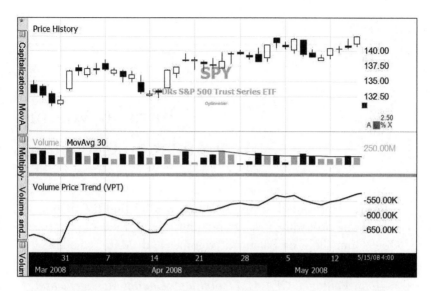

(Chart [or data] produced by TeleChart 2007® or StockFinder®, which is a registered trademark of Worden Brothers, Inc., Five Oaks Office Park, 4905 Pine Cone Drive, Durham, NC 27707. Ph. (800) 776-4940 or (919) 408-0542. www.Worden.com.)

Figure 11.2   Volume price trend.

average of +/– volume. Then VZO is made into an oscillator. This is accomplished by dividing the Exponential Moving Average (EMA) of +/– volume by a 14-period exponential average of the total and multiplying the total by 100. This will keep the VZO range bounded from as high as 100 to as low as –100. This adds the element of creating oversold and overbought ranges to the accumulated volume. As an oscillator, VZO also adds slope to the line, making the indicator's movements much more exaggerated than OBV. I believe this method might be used to add value by deducing shorter term cumulative volume trends.

E – OBV = X Exponential Periods of On-Balance Volume +/–

E – V = X Exponential Periods of Volume

VZO = 100 – (VP/TV)

12

Intraday Volume
Accumulation Oscillators

"I'm very interested in price-volume work. I find the theory
of volume preceding price to be quite useful. I'm a big fan of
Joe Granville's on-balanced volume and Marc Chaikin's
Money Flow."

—*John Bollinger, CFA, CMT Bollinger Capital Management*

Shortly after Granville began popularizing accumulative volume,
other technicians began to redefine the concept. These new concepts
accepted the role of volume but denied the use of interday closes as
the best determinants of supply and demand. Rather, these technicians believed that the best way to capture the volume flow was
through intraday activity. Similar to the beliefs involved in candlestick
charting, intraday volume analysis focuses primarily on the relationship of volume to intraday price change. These methods often focus
on the close's relationship to the low, the high, the open, and the
range (high–low). These intraday accumulation methods quantify
many of the concepts previously discussed earlier in price range volume analysis in Chaper 6, "How to Read the Market Like a Book," to
form volume indicators. Each of these indicators is intended to
unwind the market's intraday balance of power and then accumulate
these forces over time.

Intraday Intensity Index/Accumulation Distribution

Perhaps the first to depict volume accumulation in this intraday way was economist David Bostian in 1967. Bostian created the Intraday Intensity Index, which enumerates the close's position relative to that of the day's trading range. Like volume price-range analysis, this concept assumes the location of the close is the key determinant of supply and demand. The direction of the final price moves identify the position institutional investors want to hold overnight. Volume price-range analysis deems closes near the low (intraday selling) as being negative and closes near the high (intraday buying) as being positive. The Intraday Intensity Index accumulates volume as positive when closing price is near the daily highs, as zero, or neutral, for closes in middle of the range, and as negative when closes near the lower end of the range.

$$\text{Intraday Intensity Index} = (2 - \text{Close} - \text{High-Low}) / (\text{High-Low}) - \text{Volume}$$

As you will see and have previously seen from many of these volume indicators, they go by a variety of aliases. Intraday Intensity is no exception. Its most common name is Accumulation Distribution, a moniker popularized by Marc Chaikin beginning in 1975, but it also has been called "Money Flow" and the "Daily Volume Indicator." No matter what it is called, the key piece of information to recognize from this indicator is that it counts volume based on the price's closing position within the intraday price range.

Williams' Variable Accumulation Distribution

The 1960s also saw legendary trader and investor Larry Williams develop his first volume indicator, called Williams' Variable Accumulation Distribution (WVAD), although he did not reveal his indicator until the publication of his 1972 book, *The Secret of Selecting Stocks for Immediate and Substantial Gains*.

By understanding that volume is U-shaped, meaning most of the volume occurs at the open and at the close, Williams theorized that where the stock closes relative to its opening price is a key factor in determining whether the security is being accumulated or distributed throughout the trading session. If a stock rises from its opening, then the stock must be under accumulation, whereas if it falls from its opening, it is being distributed. William's theorized that this data should then be examined in the context of the stock's overall intraday range. This analysis is accomplished using Williams' WVAD formula, which accumulates the summed relationships between the open and the close and the intraday range over time.

$$\text{WVAD} = (\text{Close} - \text{Open}) / (\text{High} - \text{Low}) \times \text{Volume}$$

The most important piece of information to gather from Williams' WVAD is that it quantifies how much volume is required to drive the stock a given amount based on the intraday change from the open to the close.

Williams' Accumulation Distribution

It is a good thing Larry Williams is one of the world's greatest stock pickers because his timing was not very good in introducing WVAD. In 1975, the inclusion of the opening was dropped from most financial publications, making it difficult to calculate the WVAD. As a result, Williams amended the WVAD formula by substituting the securities opening with its "true range." True range was developed by famous market technician J. Welles Wilder. I classify indicators using true range as "tweeners" because true range uses data in between inter- and intraday. By including the previous day's close in the calculation, true range deals with the issue of trading gaps. A true range high is the higher of the previous bar's close or the current bar's high. Similarly, the true range low is the lower of the previous bar's close or the current bar's low. Williams' Accumulation Distribution (WAD) formula accumulates the summed relationships between the true range and the close over time.

The following is Williams' Accumulation Distribution (WAD) formula:

TRH = The greater of the previous bar's close or the current high.

TRL = The lesser of the previous bar's close or the current low.

If the current close is greater than the previous bar, then the WAD = (Close – TRL).

If the current close is less than the previous bar, then WAD = (Close – TRH).

If the current close is equal to the previous bar, then WAD=0.

Like OBV, WAD is accumulated over time.

WAD then measures how much volume is needed to force the stock to move up or down based on the true range change, which in the case of gaps might include the movement from the previous days' close (see Figure 12.1).

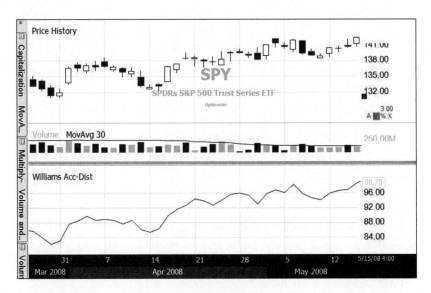

(Chart [or data] produced by TeleChart 2007® or StockFinder®, which is a registered trademark of Worden Brothers, Inc., Five Oaks Office Park, 4905 Pine Cone Drive, Durham, NC 27707. Ph. (800) 776-4940 or (919) 408-0542. www.Worden.com.)

Figure 12.1   Williams' WAD.

Intraday Volume Accumulation Oscillators

Many of these intraday volume accumulation indicators can be amended by converting them into oscillators. By viewing these indicators as oscillators, the technical analyst can gauge the momentum of the intraday volume accumulation. Ultra high readings signify large accumulation, whereas ultra low readings indicate severe distribution. Price breakouts or breakdowns without corresponding readings in the oscillator warn of an unsustainable trend. Large price increases with small readings in the intraday volume oscillators signify an overbought condition. Likewise, significant price drops without corresponding down moves in the indicator imply an oversold condition. Breakouts to new highs or lows in the indicator forecast a similar possibility in the share price.

Chaikin's Money Flow

The most popular of these intraday volume accumulation indicators is Chaikin's Money Flow. This indicator is based on the Intraday Intensity Index (Accumulation/Distribution), which accumulates positive and negative volume as defined by where the price closed within the intraday range. The oscillator is created by accumulating the Intraday Intensity Index for 21 periods (this input is customizable) and dividing the sum by the total volume for the same time period.

Sum X Periods of Intraday Intensity Index /
Sum X Periods of Total Volume

If the Chaikin Money Flow indicator is above .10, the indication is generally considered bullish. Readings below .10 are generally considered bearish. Readings between 0 and .10 are considered representative of weak buying and are interpreted as bearish, whereas readings between 0 and –.10 are considered representative of weak selling and have bullish implications (see Figure 12.2).

In addition to the typical interpretations of volume oscillators, Chaikin added an insightful twist to evaluating Money Flow. Persistency of Money Flow considers the amount of time the indicator is above or below zero over a given time. If the indicator is above zero for 9 of 10 periods, the Persistency of Money Flow would be 90 percent. It has been postulated that the Investor Business Daily (IBD) uses a similar methodology when compiling the supply and demand portion of IBD's *CANSLIM* (**C**urrent earnings, **A**nnual earnings, **N**ew products, **S**upply and demand, **L**eadership, Institutional sponsorship, **M**arket Index direction) ratings.

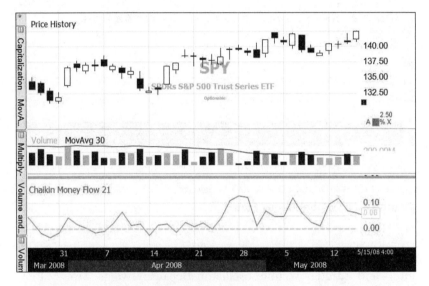

(Chart [or data] produced by TeleChart 2007® or StockFinder®, which is a registered trademark of Worden Brothers, Inc., Five Oaks Office Park, 4905 Pine Cone Drive, Durham, NC 27707. Ph. (800) 776-4940 or (919) 408-0542. www.Worden.com.)

Figure 12.2   Chaikin Money Flow.

Twiggs' Money Flow

What Marc Chaikin did to the Intraday Intensity Index (Accumulation/Distribution) to create Money Flow, Colin Twiggs closely replicated with Williams' Accumulation Distribution (WAD), creating Twiggs' Money Flow (see Figure 12.3). Using true range in the calculation solves the issues surrounding gaps between the closing and the opening prices. Twiggs added an exponential moving average to the true range calculation, smoothing the calculation while also emphasizing more recent data.

Twiggs' Money Flow = X EMA Volume – (2 – Close – True Low) / True High – True Low) –1) / X EMA Total Volume

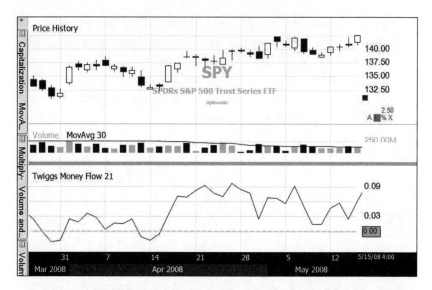

(Chart [or data] produced by TeleChart 2007® or StockFinder®, which is a registered trademark of Worden Brothers, Inc., Five Oaks Office Park, 4905 Pine Cone Drive, Durham, NC 27707. Ph. (800) 776-4940 or (919) 408-0542. www.Worden.com.)

Figure 12.3   Twiggs' Money Flow.

Like WAD, Twiggs' Money Flow is a tweener, in between an inter- and intraday volume oscillator. Because Twiggs' Money Flow includes gap information, I prefer it to Chaikin's Money Flow.

Both Twiggs' and Chaikin's Money Flow provide more momentum to the volume accumulation methods, which provide quicker signals and may be more appropriate for shorter term investment strategies.

Thus, intraday accumulation indicators look at the relationship between the stock's close and the intraday range and accumulate the volume, whereas interday and tweeners' accumulation indicators look at the relationship from close to close and accumulate the volume. Of the two types of indicators, I am strongly in the camp that interday data should be used in formulating the indicators.

It is my position that Wyckoff's "effort versus results" concept is not necessarily carried over the course of the prevailing trend. However, the primary aspiration of intraday accumulation distribution indicators is to discover how much volume is needed to push the price a certain amount intraday. This is revealed by the location of the closing price relative to the day's price range. This effort versus results concept has merit only with regard to the shorter term implications over the next few price bars. However, the intraday accumulation indicators sum these interactions over long periods. For this reason, I believe the effort versus results principles should be reserved for bar-to-bar chart reading, as opposed to accumulated over time. When I asked Joe Granville his opinion of accumulating intraday changes as opposed to the closing changes data, he emphatically stated, "They're dead wrong." My opinions on this issue are not as strong, but I do agree with Granville conceptually. The principles of the indicators are useful, but the results should not be summed up over time. I do, however, feel that intraday data are useful in bar-to-bar analysis, which brings us to the next topic, price range volume indicators.

13

Price Range Volume Indicators

"At any given time, some indicators are bullish and others bearish. They are all looking at the same indicators, but they weight them differently, so coming up with different answers. I sometimes wonder if the bullish technicians tend to give weight to indicators that agree with their own bullish inclination; and whether bearish technicians believe the bearish indicators, since they agree with their bearishness."

—*Arthur A. Merrill*

Price range volume indicators are very much like intraday volume indicators. Operating on the same effort versus results principles, price range volume indicators attempt to quantify the relationship between the price bar's close and the trading range. Like intraday volume indicators, the primary goal of a price range volume indicator is to discover whether the stock is accumulated or distributed throughout the trading session. The price range volume indicators also go about the discovery process in much the same manner as intraday price indicators. They differ in that they do not accumulate a running total over time. Rather, the information is used to visualize a perspective of the shorter term price-volume relationship. The technician then generally uses this information to help forecast the next bar or series of bars.

Market Facilitation Index

Bill Williams recognized that volume is the power behind the trend and developed an analysis system based on the close and the price range, called the Market Facilitation Index (MFI). His findings were discussed in his book, *Trading Chaos*, released in 1995. I describe MFI as a system, as opposed to an indicator, because it is more an approach to gain insights into the effort represented by volume and the results represented by price change. In essence, MFI is a mathematical depiction of price range volume analysis packaged into an easily interpreted format. MFI is calculated by dividing the trading range by the volume.

$$MFI = (High\text{-}Low) / Volume$$

A rising MFI and rising volume are considered positive. A falling MFI and falling volume are considered negative. From these two combinations, the MFI and the volume are used to produce four MFI conditions, which Williams describes as "profitunity windows." *Profitunity* windows are comparisons between the current MFI and the previous MFI. They are usually displayed via price bars color coded according to one of the four corresponding MFI conditions.

The first MFI condition is a green bar, or ++, meaning the stock has a "green light" for market movement. A green bar is formed by increasing volume and a rising MFI. This condition means that both the price range and the volume are rising. It indicates that the price trend should continue in its current direction.

The second condition is known as a fade bar, or – –, signaling that interest in the stock is fading. This condition represents a fall in volume accompanied by a drop in MFI. This type of activity is often observed toward the end of a mature trend. The drop in MFI denotes a tighter trading range. When combined with falling volume, this condition suggests the trend might be near an end.

The third condition is the fake bar or –+, representing a decrease in volume and an increase in MFI. A fake bar shows that although the price range is widening, the market lacks interest in the move as evidenced by the lower volume. This action indicates a trend reversal. Here, the smart money market operators allow the market to rise while subtly selling into its strength, thus faking out the market.

The last condition is the squat bar, or +–, an increase in volume combined with a falling MFI. This indicates rising volume but a falling price range. In price range volume analysis, this means the increase in activity is not able to produce much price change. According to

Williams, of the four conditions, the squat bar offers the most potential because it represents a buildup in pressure that eventually develops into a new trend reversal.

The MFI is often used by traders in day or intraday trading. Although Williams believes the squat bar offers the most potential, professional futures trader Charley F. Wright believes that the most powerful signal is the green bar (++). In *Stock and Commodities Magazine*, Wright published his results using MFI green ++ bars, trading the S&P 500 Futures intraday using 30-minute bars. Wright created two nonoptimized systems, both using MFI green ++ with different methods of placing buy and sell stops and different overnight holding rules. The first system, which held positions overnight, generated a return of 407 percent and posted a profit factor of 1.49 from 1986 to 1988. The second model generated a return of 312 percent and a profit factor of 2.12. The profit factor indicates how much money is made for every dollar put at risk and is calculated by dividing gross profits by gross losses. According to Wright, "MFI has shown great profits for aiding market analysis."

Equivolume Charting

According to Richard Arms, "If the market wore a wristwatch, it would be divided into shares not hours." Arms epitomizes those thoughts with equivolume charts. He sought a way to incorporate important volume information into the price chart. The result was equivolume charts, which graphically depict volume's impact on the price bar chart. This is accomplished by plotting price's height as normal via the vertical y-axis. However, the horizontal x-axis plot is based on volume. Essentially, this charting method replaces time with volume.

Equivolume charts expand the width of the price bar according to the relative volume in a given trading day. The price bar's width is created by comparing the volume of the bar to the normalized volume of the range. This process produces price bars with various widths according to their volume. Wide bars show strong volume, whereas thin bars show weak volume.

(Chart courtesy of StockCharts.com.)

Figure 13.1   Normal bar chart.

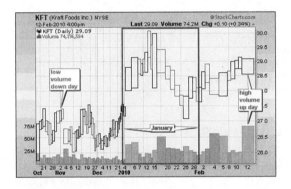

(Chart courtesy of StockCharts.com.)

Figure 13.2   Normal bar chart as displayed in Equivolume.

Arms called the tall and wide a "power box," indicating it has price movement and strong volume similar to the green bar in Williams' MFI. Power boxes are of particular importance as a stock breaks through areas of resistance and support. The existence of such power boxes during a breakout/down indicates a high probability of success. A moving average of the equivolume box can offer rich insights into the price-volume relationship, similar to volume-weighted moving averages.

This concept of amending the price chart to depict the strength or weakness of the corresponding volume is not new a new idea. It originates from Edwin S. Quinn, who created similar charts called Trendographs in the 1930s. These early precursors to Equivolume charts were applauded by Harold M. Gartley in his 1935 classic *Profits in the Stock Market*. Overall, equivolume is a unique and useful charting application that emphasizes the price-volume relationship.

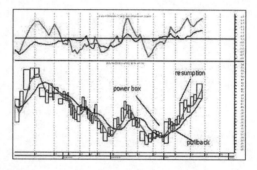

(Charts courtesy of MetaStock a Product of Thomson Reuters and Richard W. Arms, Jr.)

Figure 13.3   Arm's power box.

Ease of Movement

According to Arms, "Fundamentals do not directly determine price; they're only as important as the emphasis placed on them by the millions of minds studying them" (Trading with Equivolume at RealMoney.com). Arms certainly practiced what he preached, creating several valuable volume indicators to detect the emphasis implied by the volume. One of these is "ease of movement." Arms created ease of movement to determine how much volume is needed to facilitate a stock's movement. To calculate the ease of movement, half of today's range is subtracted from half of yesterday's range to form the midpoint move, and then a box ratio is calculated by taking today's volume divided by today's range. The ease of movement is created by dividing the midpoint (the difference between today's and yesterday's range) by the box ratio.

Ease of Movement Formula

Midpoint = Today's (High-Low) / 2 – Yesterday's (High-Low) / 2

Box Point = Today's Volume / Today's (High-Low)

Ease of Movement = Midpoint / Box Ratio

A high ease of movement reading signifies that the stock is moving higher on low volume. Low ease of movement indicates the stock is moving lower on light volume. An ease of movement near zero means the stock is not easily being moved by the volume. Often, traders apply a 14-day moving average to the ease of movement calculation. In essence, ease of movement is a day-to-day (or bar-to-bar) measurement of the volume-weighted price range. This information is then used to determine how much force (volume) was expended to produce the price change (see Figure 13.4).

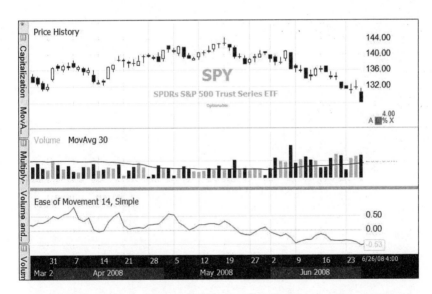

(Chart [or data] produced by TeleChart 2007® or StockFinder®, which is a registered trademark of Worden Brothers, Inc., Five Oaks Office Park, 4905 Pine Cone Drive, Durham, NC 27707. Ph. (800) 776-4940 or (919) 408-0542. www.Worden.com.)

Figure 13.4   Ease of movement.

Overall, volume-price range indicators are the tape measures of price-volume range analysis (also known as volume spread analysis). Through mathematical computations, they quantify how much effort (volume) produces the result (price). These indicators are the most useful to the tape reader when forecasting shorter term time movements.

14

Price Accumulation Based on Volume Indicators

"As we study volume, we will find that quite frequently the negative implications are the ones from which we gain the most useful conclusions."

—*Harold M. Gartley*

We have already discussed two methods of accumulating volume based on price. With the price accumulation volume indicators, you invert that process and accumulate price based on the actions of volume. Because price accumulation indicators are based on the magnitude of price change, small price moves have little effect. However, large price moves have a significant effect on price accumulation indicators.

Positive and Negative Volume Indexes

Two of these indicators are known as the Positive Volume Index (PVI) and the Negative Volume Index (NVI). Paul L. Dysart developed both in the 1930s, but they were not well popularized until econometrician Norman G. Fosback published Stock Market Logic in 1976. Dysart utilized market breadth statistics to produce these indicators but Fosback modified the indexes by employing PVI and NVI to individual security data.

Price accumulation indicators quantify the relationship between price and volume by accumulating price when volume changes. When the volume increases, the price change is counted in the PVI. PVI counts price only on the days in which the volume is higher. If the PVI is up, then price is appreciating on rising volume. If the PVI is down, then prices are depreciating on rising volume. Accumulating price change on the down-volume days is known as NVI. If the NVI is up, then price is appreciating amid declining volume. If the NVI is down, then price is depreciating on declining volume. Here are the equations:

> When today's volume is greater than yesterday's volume, then PVI = Previous PVI + Sum of (Close Today – Close Yesterday) / (Close Yesterday)

> When today's volume is less than yesterday's volume, then NVI = Previous NVI + Sum of (Close Today – Close Yesterday) / (Close Yesterday)

The logic is as follows: As institutions take long positions on individual issues, they cannot avoid influencing the price by forcing it up as they buy. However, these institutions can attempt to sell the stock in the midst of an uptrend without negatively affecting the price. This is accomplished by offering shares for sale only at the offered price, with no discounts (for example, hitting the bid). Even so, they have no way of hiding such operations in terms of volume. Such large operations are identified by a rise in volume. This makes the PVI an effective indicator for individual stock issues.

Although volume keeps large institutions from hiding their operations in the case of individual issues, such institutions do not have difficulty when it comes to the broad market. The broad market is big enough for any single institution to conduct its operations without forcing the whole market's volume higher or lower. Thus, an informed institution can buy into the market without significantly affecting the broad market's volume. In this way, NVI is a very effective indicator for use in the broad market and in market breadth analysis (see Figure 14.1).

(Chart [or data] produced by TeleChart 2007® or StockFinder®, which is a registered trademark of Worden Brothers, Inc., Five Oaks Office Park, 4905 Pine Cone Drive, Durham, NC 27707. Ph. (800) 776-4940 or (919) 408-0542. www.Worden.com.)

Figure 14.1   NVI and PVI.

In a typical birthing of a new bull market, prices should rise on increasing volume. In this state, sellers demand higher prices, as evidenced by rising volume accompanied by sharp price increases. On such high-volume days, various news and events are priced into the market. Many investors, both the informed and uninformed, want to participate. This is evidenced by a rising PVI, which is typical in the first phase of a secular bull market. However, because volume is heavy, NVI is not quick to recognize this developing trend.

As the bull market matures, stock prices can continue to rise even in the case of falling volume. Here, the PVI is not much help. However, according to price accumulation theory, this is when informed institutional investors continue to accumulate positions in anticipation of a continued economic turnaround. During these short-trend reversals, institutions steadily accumulate shares. These actions are exposed by a rising NVI in the midst of a temporary pullback in a secular bull market pullback.

A fading bull market is characterized by increases in prices with light volume. You can also use these indicators to identify a coming bear market. If the PVI drops while the market climbs, the stock or stock market is being distributed on the heavy-volume days. In this way, the PVI's divergence might help identify the maturing trend. Meanwhile, because NVI counts only the down-volume days, it might continue to track the market. However, when the market falls on heavy volume, then the NVI turns as quickly as the market drop is sharp. As you might conclude from this example, NVI is a better tool for detecting the market's major trend, while PVI might be better suited as a leading indicator.

According to Fosback's research, conducted from 1941 through 1975, when the PVI is trending above its one-year average, there is a 79 percent probability that the market is bullish. When the NVI trends above its one-year moving average, 96 percent of the market being bullish. Similarly, if the NVI trends below its one-year average, it is bullish 47 percent of the time. However, if the PVI trends below its one-year average, the market is bullish only 33 percent of the time. From this we can infer that PVI is good at identifying bear markets and that NVI is excellent at identifying a bull market trend. We revisit NVI again when market breadth indicators are reviewed.

15

Tick-Based Volume Indicators

"According to the dictionary, distribution is 'the position, arrangement or frequency of occurrence over an area or throughout a space or unit of time.' The volume of everything distributes around a mean over time. Why should trading volume be different?"

—*Market Profile, Chicago Board of Trade*

So far in the quest to better understand the relationship between supply and demand, we have investigated several methods to pinpoint whether money flows into or out of the market. These include close to close, open versus close, and various determinations of price range. All these methods represent differing opinions about how to measure the relationship.

Earlier, I discussed how stocks trade on an exchange market. You learned that an exchange market works much like an auction, where price is formed by two investors, each with a different opinion about the security's future price direction, agreeing to exchange a financial instrument. If the agreement occurs on an uptick, the buyer applied more demand than the seller exerted supply. Likewise, if the agreement occurred on a downtick, the seller's actions wielded greater force than those of the buyer. Through tick volume, you decisively quantify this relationship between price and volume.

Volume-Weighted Average Price

The Volume-Weighted Average Price (VWAP) is the average price at which investors participated over a given time period, which is typically one trading day. This is calculated by multiplying each price tick by the corresponding volume and then summing the results of all these trades and dividing the total by the number of shares traded:

$$\text{VWAP} = \text{Sum of Trade's Price} \times \text{Trade's Volume} / \text{Sum of Trading Volume}$$

The VWAP is used more as a statistic than an indicator. It is the industry standard to determine at what price a stock could have been bought or sold throughout the trading session. It might help to think of VWAP from the perspective of an institution. For example, say you are an institution and you need to buy 200,000 shares of XYZ stock today. This quantity represents 2 percent of a typical trading day's volume. If you put your order in at market, it will most likely significantly move the market, thereby raising the price you pay and making your investors unhappy. If you do this often enough, you won't have any customers left to worry about. An alternative strategy is to dollar cost average the trades incrementally throughout the day based on the common volume flow. For a nominal fee, a trader can be hired to execute such a trade. But how can you then evaluate the trader's execution? A benchmark is needed to compare the price you pay to that which the average investor pays for the stock. This benchmark is generally VWAP. VWAP is widely used by institutions to reduce the impact of their large operations (see Figure 15.1).

Money Flow/Tick Volume

When investors use the term "tick," they are referring to a trade. An uptick, or +tick, is a trade that occurs at a price higher than the previous trade. A downtick, or –tick, is a trade that occurs at a lower price than the previous trade. Tick volume refers to the volume of shares traded per tick. Tick volume analysis evaluates the change of price and volume on a tick-by-tick basis. Uptick volume is the volume that occurs on upticks. Likewise, downtick volume is the volume occurring on downticks. Where it gets murky is in the common instance of trades that occur at the previous price—an unchanged tick. Given this scenario, the commonly accepted view is to treat the unchanged tick volume as if it were a part of the previous tick. Thus, if the previous tick was up, the unchanged tick's volume would also be considered as uptick volume and vice versa. The next indicator discussed, Money Flow, views price and its corresponding volume from the perspective of ticks.

(Chart [or data] produced by TeleChart 2007® or StockFinder®, which is a registered trademark of Worden Brothers, Inc., Five Oaks Office Park, 4905 Pine Cone Drive, Durham, NC 27707. Ph. (800) 776-4940 or (919) 408-0542. www.Worden.com.)

Figure 15.1   VWAP.

Price-weighted tick volume uses tick data to weight each trade's volume by its corresponding price. The upticks are subtracted from the downticks and accumulated over time. This process used to be called Tick Volume, but now it is mostly referred to as Money Flow. In essence, Money Flow is volume weighted by the corresponding price accumulated on a tick-by-tick basis:

Tick Volume / Money Flow = Cumulative Sum (Tick Price × Uptick's Volume) – Cumulative Sum (Tick Price × Downtick's Volume)

This calculation precisely measures the supply relative to the demand on a per-trade basis and accumulates the difference over time. It reveals whether money is flowing into or out of the stock based on upticks being buys and downticks being sales. As an example, we will use two ticks to calculate Money Flow. The first tick goes through on an uptick of 100 shares at $100. Immediately, the next tick goes through on a downtick at $99.99 on 10,000 shares. The Money Flow is –$989,000 (($100 × 100 shares) – ($99.99 × 10,000)), meaning that $989,000 more in stock was sold than purchased. From this illustration, you can see how Money Flow can widely veer from the price direction by giving stronger weight to larger volume transactions. This information is used much in the same way as our other volume indicators. When Money Flow rises, it suggests demand is building, indicating the price might rise. When Money Flow falls, it suggests supply is building, an indication that price might fall.

Don Worden, president and founder of Worden Brothers, developed the concept of Money Flow in the late 1950s under the name "Tick Volume." Today, Money Flow is primarily publicized by Laszlo Birinyi. Like Worden, Birinyi parsed price-weighted tick volume into block, nonblock, and total Money Flow. Total Money Flow is the accumulation of all the price-weighted volume flows over a designated period of time. Nonblocks typically represent those trades of less than 10,000 shares. These are thought to be the increments traded by retail investors. Block trades are generally considered to be transactions of 10,000 shares or more, amounts that suggest institutional investors.

Contrasting the block from the nonblock and the total Money Flow may reveal insights as to the sentiments of the market. Institutions are regarded as being "in the know" or as the "smart money," and in theory, they are strategically well positioned. Retail investors are perceived as uninformed and weak, meaning they are seen as reactionary versus strategic. If the block trades move up while the total or nonblock Money Flow moves down, this suggests that institutions are position building, or accumulating. If the opposite is true, then Money Flow suggests the institutions are distributing.

Observing whether these trades occur in periods of strength or weakness might be helpful in establishing context for institutional behavior. If block trades are positive in periods of strength, it indicates that institutions believe more good things are to come. In a similar way, if positive block Money Flow occurs in weakness, institutional traders might well believe that eventually the fundamentals will be recognized as positive. However, if block Money Flow is negative during an uptrend, it suggests that institutions believe the stock is fully valued, and they are distributing shares to the public on strength. Likewise, if block Money Flow is negative in a falling market, institutional activity implies the sell-off might have legitimate underpinnings.

Birinyi describes Money Flow analysis as similar to tape reading, as in the days of Jesse Livermore, except with Money Flow, this process is computerized. While speaking of Money Flow, Birinyi stated in an August 1993 Bloomberg article, "It's the most useful indicator that exists, because it tells you what people are doing while they are doing it."

Worden, on the other hand, has a different take on it. According to Worden, replying to a question on Tick Volume/Money Flow in his Worden user group forum, "Originally, it (Tick Volume/Money Flow) had a phenomenal ability to contradict immediate price trends, effectively forecasting future moves in the opposite direction. However, as the market gradually went from 90 percent publicly dominated to 90 percent institutionally dominated, the large transaction developed an overwhelming negative bias." As a result, Worden dropped Tick Volume, although it carried on for a short time in the brokerage firm of Muller and Company. However, Tick Volume concepts birthed the later developments of Worden's proprietary indicators: Balance of Power (BOP), Money Stream, and Time-Segmented Volume.

Early in my career, my sentiments regarding Money Flow were closer to those of Laszlo Birinyi. However, the exchange markets have become increasingly more automated, while the decimalization of security prices has strongly reduced the reliability of this form of intraday analysis. Trades filled by scalpers and market makers are most often filled from existing inventories, making the concepts of accumulating up and downticks much more obscure. Additionally, institutions normally "work" their block trades throughout the course of the trading session to avoid making their activities transparent to the public. Often, this practice includes selling into upticks at the offer and buying into downticks at the bid. Speaking from personal experience, blocks traded on behalf of my managed portfolios are typically handled in this manner. In terms of the Money Flow calculation, such activities appear to be the inverse of what they truly are. In his book, *Value in Time, Better Trading Through Effective Volume* Pascal Willain takes on many of these post-decimalization age issues and provides a set of his own volume-based indicators designed to see through these modern institutional trading practices.

In the end, though, whether it is a daily, weekly, or monthly close, investors' behaviors are eventually reflected on the tape. Therefore, it is my belief that volume data, as opposed to tick data, is best employed via smoothing techniques that accumulate volume relative to price movements across the larger context of the overall trend. Accumulating volume relative to price trends allows the volume indicator to capture the buildup of price-volume movements in context. This type of analysis leads us to our seventh and final type of volume indicator, volume-weighted price indicators.

16

Volume-Weighted Price Indicators

"As a primary principal of economics, it is assumed that if a large number of shares are offered, the price will be depressed; or conversely, if there is a substantial demand for shares, the price will rise. However, a study of the subject indicates that this theory does not always hold true during short periods of time, although in the large and long term trends, there is no doubt of its validity."

—Harold M. Gartley

In terms of technical analysis, I believe volume-weighted price indicators represent perhaps the brightest area of exploration. It is this area where I focus the majority of my work toward the discovery of new applications. By applying the corresponding volume to price, volume-weighted price indicators expound on price to reflect volume's influence. Currently, these indicators mainly amend preexisting indicators by infusing them with volume information. Because volume leads price, it makes sense to introduce volume into momentum indicators to make them even faster. Because volume confirms a trend, you can enhance trend indicators with volume information, allowing the indicators to be more reliable. Likewise, you can combine momentum and trend principles with volume to create indicators that give you quicker and more reliable signals. In this chapter and the other chapters in this part of the book, I discuss some of these most recent revolutionary ideas and concepts.

The Money Flow Index

Not to be confused with Chaikin's Money Flow or Birinyi's Money Flow, the Money Flow Index (I warned you that it would get messy) modifies the Relative Strength Index (RSI) with volume information. The RSI is a commonly used momentum indicator developed by Welles Wilder. It is used to gauge the strength of a security with respect to its own past performance. As a stock ebbs and flows, its internal momentum can be gauged by comparing its downward momentum to its upward momentum. This is calculated by comparing the security's up days to its down days. These data are combined in such a way as to form an oscillator, creating readings that oscillate between 0 and 100. High readings indicate that the stock has bullish momentum, whereas low readings indicate it has bearish momentum. Depending on the analyst, extremely high conditions might be perceived as either situations of strength or situations of excessive strength, meaning the security is "overbought." Likewise, extremely low readings might be considered weakness or excessive weakness, meaning the security is "oversold".

The Money Flow Index is a volume-weighted form of the RSI with a slight twist. It was jointly developed by Gene Quong and Avrum Soudack, who introduced this popular indicator in the March 1989 issue of *Technical Analysis of Stocks and Commodities*. Quong and Soudack sought to improve upon the RSI by using volume to weight the index. This was a breakthrough in technical analysis, as all of the momentum indicators at the time used either price or volume, but not both merged together. Quong and Soudack weighted price with volume to form a volume-weighted momentum oscillator. By weighting price change with volume, price moves with high volume are emphasized, whereas those with low volume are minimized. Weighting price with volume accomplishes the goal of volume theory—increasing the emphasis of high-volume movements while deemphasizing movements on low volume.

Unlike the RSI, the MFI is calculated using typical price as opposed to closing price (the twist). Typical price is calculated by adding the bar high to the bar low plus the bar close, then dividing this sum by three. If the calculation is up, the total is accumulated as Positive Money Flow. If the calculation is down, it is accumulated as Negative Money Flow. Positive and Negative Money Flows are accumulated over the course of time, usually 14 periods. The accumulation of Positive Money Flow is then divided by the accumulation of Negative Money Flow over the same time period to form the Money Ratio. The Money Ratio is then converted into an oscillator.

> The Money Flow Index =
>
> Typical Price (High + Low + Close) /3
>
> Positive Money Flow = 14-Period Sum of Typical Price Current Period – Typical Price Previous Period (only when calculation is positive)
>
> Negative Money Flow = Same 14-Period Sum of Typical Price Current Period – Typical Price Previous Period (only when calculation is negative)
>
> Money Ratio = (Positive Money Flow / Negative Money Flow)
>
> The Money Flow Index = 100 – (100 / 1 – (1 + Money Ratio))

The MFI is interpreted in much the same way as the RSI (see Figure 16.1). When the MFI rises, it shows that the stock is gaining upward price and volume momentum. When the MFI falls, it suggests the stock price is falling and the downward volume momentum is growing. However, unlike typical interpretations of the RSI at extremes, the MFI's extreme high and low readings should be given less importance when showing overbought and oversold levels. Because volume is fueling price at extreme MFI levels, the extreme levels should be viewed as an increase in the fuel needed to maintain a continuation of the present trend.

Volume-Weighted Moving Averages

> "If investors have private information, they may know that the price of a security, which reflects all public information available, is incorrect. As a result, these investors will trade heavily on the issue until the price reflects the valuation of the security if the private information became public."
>
> —*Walter Sun, MIT Laboratory of Information and Decision Systems "The Relationship Between Trading Volume and Securities Prices," 2003*

(Chart [or data] produced by TeleChart 2007® or StockFinder®, which is a registered trademark of Worden Brothers, Inc., Five Oaks Office Park, 4905 Pine Cone Drive, Durham, NC 27707. Ph. (800) 776-4940 or (919) 408-0542. www.Worden.com.)

Figure 16.1   Money flow index source Worden's StockFinder.

When people hear a claim, they might respond in several different ways. One, they can accept the claim as truth. Two, they can investigate the claim and come to their own conclusions. (Most people intend to exercise the second option, but few actually get around to doing so.) Three, they can ignore or respect the claim without making any judgment as to its validity. Finally, they can outright reject the claim.

According to technical theory, volume should lead price and confirm trends. Yet technicians still predominantly consider only price and time in forming price averages. If volume theory is true, why not include volume? Volume represents the number of participants willing to wager at various points of price and time. With this in mind, I created volume-weighted price averages in the late 1990s to measure the commitment expressed through price, weighted by that day's volume compared to the total volume during the period of the average. Weighting the price average with volume gives proportional emphasis to price based on investor participation. The importance of days with greater volume would be magnified, and days with lighter volume would be proportionally reduced.

I called these new moving averages "Buff Averages" and published my results in the February 2001 issue of *Technical Analysis of Stocks & Commodities*. Buff Averages, now referred to as Volume-Weighted Moving Averages (VWMA), weighs each period's closing price with that day's volume, divided by the total volume during the period of the average (see Figure 16.2).

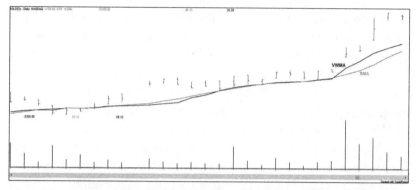

Figure 16.2   Simple Moving Averages (SMAs) – VS – Volume Weighted Moving Averages (VWMAs). Notice how much more responsive the VWMAs (the darker line) become when volume increases.

For example, to calculate a two-day moving average, using both the simple moving average (SMA) and the VWMA methods, assume a security trades at $10.00 with 100,000 shares on the first day and at $12.00 with 300,000 shares on the second day. The SMA calculation is day one's price plus day two's price divided by the number of days, or (10+12) / 2, which equals 11. The VWMA calculation is day one's price (10) multiplied by day one's volume of the total range expressed as a fraction (100,000 / 400,000 = 1/4), plus day two's price (12) multiplied by day two's volume of the total range expressed as a fraction (300,000 / 400,000 = 3/4), which equals 11.5. According to these calculations, the actual price at which investors participated was not 11, but the VWMA of 11.5.

The VWMA is calculated by weighting each time frame's closing price with the time frame's volume compared to the total volume during the range:

Volume-Weighted Average = Sum {Closing Price (I) × [Volume (I) / (Total Range)]}, where I = given day's action.

Of the possible responses to the claims mentioned previously, I chose the second option to investigate the claim for myself. If the claims I have been discussing about the importance of volume are indeed true, then the volume-weighted moving averages should be more responsive and more reliable than traditional moving averages that fail to account for volume. I chose to test the VWMA by evaluating it using four criteria: responsiveness, reliability, risk, and return (the four Rs). Responsiveness evaluates whether the volume-infused averages lead the traditional price-only averages. Reliability evaluates whether the volume-weighted averages are as reliable as price-only averages. If these two Rs are true, then I can expect improvement in at least one of the two next Rs, risk and return, which measure whether the inclusion of volume information reduces the risk taken in a trading strategy and/or increases the return.

To verify whether volume information improves performance, I tested and compared two trading systems. One system used a 5- and 20-day simple (unweighted) moving average cross, and the other system used a 5- and 20-day volume-weighted average. Both systems used the crossing of the 5-day and 20-day moving averages to generate buy and sell signals. The 5-day moving average represents the cost basis of traders with a week's time frame. The 20-day moving average represents the cost basis of traders with one month's time frame. The shorter moving average is more responsive to current price action and trend changes because it emphasizes the more recent price changes. The longer term moving average includes more information and is more indicative of the longer term trend. Because its scope is broader, the longer term moving average normally lags the action of the shorter term moving average. When a moving average curls upward (changes direction to up), the investors within this time frame experience positive momentum. The opposite is true when the moving average curls downward. When the short-term moving average's momentum is significant enough to cross over the longer term moving average, this is an indication of a rising trend, otherwise considered as a "buy signal." Likewise, when the shorter term moving average's momentum crosses under the longer term moving average, a "sell signal" is generated.

Of the securities used in the test, 1,000 shares were purchased or sold short with each cross. Commissions were not included. The testing period used was September 25, 1991, through May 14, 1999, for a total of 2,000 trading days. I selected securities from the small cap (Standard & Poor's Small Cap Index), medium cap (S&P 400 Index), and large cap (S&P 100 Index) lists. I then broke the groups down by their style characteristics of volume and volatility, forming 12 categories: small cap high volume, small cap low volume, small cap high volatility, small cap low volatility, mid cap high volume, mid cap low volume, and so on.

Five securities were studied in each of the 12 groups, for a total of 60 securities. As selection criteria, I used the five highest- and lowest-volume securities and the five highest- and lowest-beta (a measure of volatility) securities, of each of the three capitalization groups, as identified by a Bloomberg screen on June 30, 1999. Any securities that were duplicated (as high-volume and high-beta stocks were occasionally) were used only once. Securities that lacked sufficient history were removed. Again, the purpose here was not to create a profitable system, but rather to determine if the volume-infused price averages demonstrate responsiveness and reliability, and thus, the added volume information could reduce risk or increase returns.

Responsiveness

If volume leads price, I would expect volume increases to precede significant price movements, giving faster downside and upside signals, so the moving average with volume would identify the trend quicker and help us enter or exit the trade sooner.

Of the 60 securities tested, volume-weighted averages generated more signals in 56 cases, and there was one issue where the number of signals was the same (see Figure 16.3). Simple moving averages responded more quickly and more frequently only in a few large cap stocks. Overall, simple moving averages produced 6,858 trades compared to volume-enhanced averages with 7,905, for an overall 13 percent improvement.

Responsiveness of the 60 Stocks

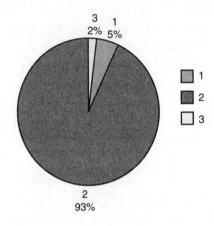

Figure 16.3   Responsiveness.

Reliability

Generating quicker signals is great but not overly difficult to achieve. All one has to do to obtain a faster moving average is shorten its length. However, the paradox one faces when generating quicker signals has always been a trade-off of the reliability of those signals, and reliability is equally if not more important than responsiveness.

However, according to our running premise, volume enhancement should improve both responsiveness and reliability. Heavy volume should affirm price movements. In addition, when volume diverges from price, volume-based indicators should give slower signals, if any at all. I tested and measured reliability by the percentage of trades profitable, again comparing the simple average method to the volume-enhanced method.

Weighting averages with volume enhancement demonstrated a higher reliability in 10 of the 12 categories. One tie occurred in the large cap low-volume category for a 10-1-1 advantage using VWMA. The simple moving averages had higher reliability in only the low-volume mid cap issues. Of the 60 securities, simple moving averages performed better in 17 occurrences (28 percent), volume-weighted averages performed better in 36 occurrences (60 percent), and there were seven virtual ties (12 percent). Thus, 60 percent of the time, weighting averages with volume enhancement helped. Only 28 percent of the time did the simple method prove more beneficial, and 12 percent of the time, it did not matter (see Figure 16.4).

60 Stocks Reliability

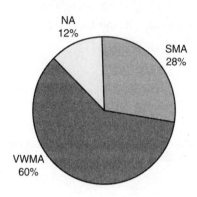

Figure 16.4   Reliability.

Therefore, by infusing price averages with volume, I simultaneously sped up the moving averages signals while obtaining more reliable signals, thereby breaking the age-old paradox of haste makes waste.

Risk

With any trading system, it is important to manage the downside of the trade. Could applying volume-weighted averages reduce downside risk? To evaluate this question, I measured risk through average drawdown, which is the average loss of all the losing trades. This statistic is used to calculate the system's typical loss potential.

In our trading system simulation, large cap stocks employing volume-weighted averages produced better results as measured by lower draw downs than the simple moving average system in 12 of the 20 stocks tested. Mid cap stocks favored the simple moving average system in 11 of the 20 occurrences. In the small cap section, volume enhancement produced superior results in 14 of the 20 stocks tested.

There were no significant differences among low-beta or low-volume stocks. High-volume stocks performed better with volume-weighted averages by a 9-to-6 margin. Likewise, high-beta stocks were more successful with volume enhancement; these highly volatile stocks proved more profitable in 11 of the 15 securities tested.

Overall, volume moving averages proved more reliable in 73 percent of the securities tested (see Figure 16.5). Volume-weighted averages had the most reliability improvement in the small cap securities and the high-volume and high-beta securities. Based on these results, I am confident that adding volume to the mix helped reduce the risk in our hypothetical trading system.

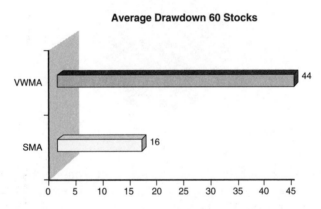

Figure 16.5   Number of issues experiencing lower draw downs.

Return

So far, volume has lived up to its reputation, leaving us only with the most pertinent of all the statistics—return. So which approach—simple averages or volume-weighted averages—makes the most money as measured by total return? For the most part, regardless of how it was divided up, by size or by style, volume was again able to add to the bottom line—return. However, some areas showed more improvement than others.

Whether the stocks were small, medium, or large, all three size groups showed improvement. Judging by the reliability statistics, I suspected that mid caps had the least chance of beating the simple moving average. However, mid caps had the largest profit improvement of the three size groups (see Figure 16.6).

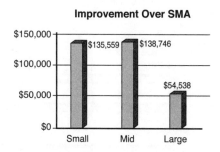

Figure 16.6   VWMA improvement over SMA by capitalization.

Similarly, whether the style was high or low volume or high or low volatility, all four style groups showed improvement. The biggest difference was between low and high volume. Definitively, the high-volume issues performed much better than the low-volume issues with the volume-weighting method. Volume Weighted Moving Averages also performed better in high volatility versus low volatility. This data confirms other academic studies showing a high correlation between volume and volatility (see Figure 16.7).

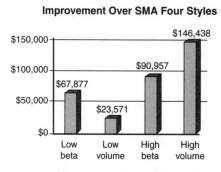

Figure 16.7   VWMA improvement over SMA by style.

Of the 12 groups, 11 (91.6 percent) favored volume-weighted averages, but of the 60 stocks, only 35 (58.3 percent) produced a higher return when using volume-weighted averages. This suggests that additional analysis techniques are needed to complement the volume-weighting methodology in individual security analysis. In total, volume-weighted averages produced $328,843 more than simple moving averages (see Figure 16.8).

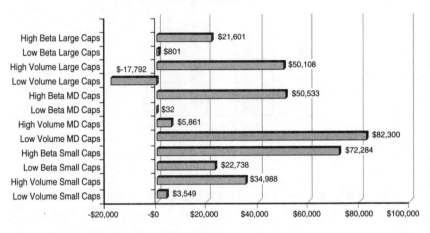

Figure 16.8   VWMA versus SMA within 12 subgroups.

Summary

This study demonstrates that an investor using volume-weighted averages generally entered a trade sooner while simultaneously increasing the probability of making a correct investment decision. When the investor is wrong, however, adding volume information keeps the losses smaller. This advantage is enhanced when trading in highly volatile and highly liquid securities and small and mid cap securities.

VW-MACD

"The average man doesn't wish to be told that it is a bull or a bear market. What he desires is to be told specifically which particular stock to buy or sell. He wants to get something for nothing. He does not wish to work. He doesn't even wish to have to think."

—*Jesse L. Livermore*

The simplicity of VWMA makes it easily amendable. The close might be substituted for the high to make a VWMA of the highs or the low might be substituted to make a VWMA of the lows. Other price-averaging methods could also be employed, such as an exponential smoothing method. An intraday trader might want to change the data setting from time to ticks, thus transform the VWMA into a modified yet customizable VWAP. In the same fashion, various filters can be applied to sort intraday ticks through sorting block sizes similar to Tick Volume/Money Flow. Analysts looking for new ideas can combine various combinations of these VWMA methodologies to formulate some enlightening analysis.

Additionally, volume-weighted averages might be used with existing indicators to form new volume-weighted indicators. One such indicator is the Volume-Weighted Moving Average Convergence Divergence (VW-MACD). I developed the VW-MACD in the early part of 2000 while working as a portfolio manager and market technician at T.P. Donovan Investments. The indicator was popularized by the esteemed market analyst John Bollinger in his 2002 book, *Bollinger on Bollinger Bands*.

The VW-MACD is a straightforward amendment to Gerald Appel's original Moving Average Convergence Divergence (MACD) indicator developed in 1979 (see Figure 16.9). Appel's MACD plots the difference between a short-term exponential average and a long-term exponential average. When the difference, called the MACD line, is positive (above zero) and rising, it suggests the price trend is up and moving higher. When the MACD line is negative (below zero) and falling, the opposite is true. A smooth exponential average of this difference is calculated to form the MACD signal line. When the MACD line is above the MACD signal line, it illustrates that the momentum of MACD is rising. Likewise, when the MACD is below the MACD signal line, the momentum of the MACD falls. This difference between the MACD line and the MACD signal line is frequently plotted as a histogram to highlight the spread between the two lines. Appel's MACD is widely used to provide indications of the underlying instrument's trend and momentum.

(Chart [or data] produced by TeleChart 2007® or StockFinder®, which is a registered trademark of Worden Brothers, Inc., Five Oaks Office Park, 4905 Pine Cone Drive, Durham, NC 27707. Ph. (800) 776-4940 or (919) 408-0542. www.Worden.com.)

Figure 16.9   VW-MACD source Worden's StockFinder.

One way to add volume weighting to this mix is to substitute the two exponential moving averages used to calculate the MACD differential with two corresponding volume-weighted averages. Thus, the VW-MACD contrasts a volume-weighted short-term trend from the volume-weighted longer term trend. The signal line is traditionally left as an exponential moving average without additional volume weighting. This is because the VW-MACD line is already volume weighted by the inclusion of volume in the MACD differential formula. Changing the signal line an exponentially volume-weighted moving average additionally highlights the volume, causing the signal to move faster and away from the MACD differential when recent volume is greater and slower and toward the MACD differential when volume is lighter. This action is most likely counterproductive to the technical analyst.

As Appel's MACD represents the convergence and divergence of price trends, the VW-MACD represents the convergence and divergence of volume-weighted price trends. Through the volume-weighted modification, the same kind of general improvements are seen in Appel's MACD that were achieved by injecting volume into simple moving averages. The inclusion of volume allows the VW-MACD to be generally more responsive and reliable than the traditional MACD.

Trend Thrust Indicator

"Adaptive approaches will add tremendous value to the investment process; after all that's what this is all about, making money."

—*John Bollinger, CFA, CMT Bollinger Capital Management*

The Trend Thrust Indicator (TTI) is an enhanced version of the VW-MACD. The TTI takes its design from the VW-MACD indicator, but uses a volume multiplier in unique ways to exaggerate volume's impact on the volume-weighted moving averages. Like the VW-MACD indicator, the TTI uses volume-weighted moving averages as opposed to exponential moving averages. Volume-weighted averages weight closing prices proportionally to the volume traded during each time period, so the TTI gives greater emphasis to those price trends with greater volume and less emphasis to time periods with lighter volume. Earlier in this chapter, I showed that volume-weighted moving averages (Buff Averages or VWMAs) improve responsiveness while simultaneously increasing reliability of simple moving averages. Like the MACD and VW-MACD indicators, the TTI calculates a spread through the subtraction of the short (fast) average from the long (slow) average. This spread combined with a volume multiplier creates the Buff Spread (see Figure 16.10).

Adding a volume multiplier further enhances the impact of volume changes to the Buff Spread. The volume multiple is computed by dividing the short-term volume average (short-term is defined as the same time period as the shorter volume-weighted price average) by the long-term volume average (long-term is defined by the same time period as the longer volume-weighted price average). This volume multiple is taken to the second power and multiplied by the fast volume-weighted moving average to produce a volume-enhanced fast average. Likewise, the reciprocal of the volume multiple is taken to the second power and multiplied by the slow volume-weighted moving average to produce a volume-enhanced slow average. This causes the fast average to become proportionally larger when volume increases and to become proportionally smaller when volume decreases. Similarly, the slow average becomes proportionally smaller when volume confirms price and proportionally larger when volume diverges from price.

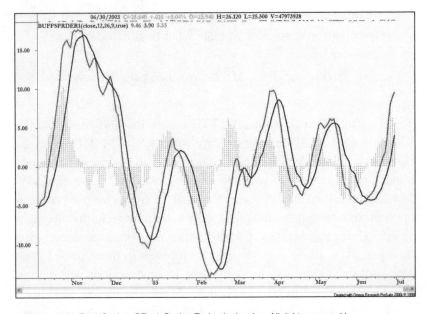

Figure 16.10   TTI trend thrust indicator.

The Buff Spread is then calculated by subtracting the enhanced short average from the enhanced long average. The net effect is a bigger, faster "buffed up" Buff Spread when price and volume confirm each other and a smaller, slower Buff Spread when price and volume diverge.

The calculation of the average Buff Spread or signal line in the TTI is also enhanced with volume information but uses a unique adaptive moving average method. This adaptive average might alter the nine-period length (the standard number of periods used in the computation) of the average TTI signal line. When volume increases, the length of the average spread/signal line becomes longer, creating a smoothing effect. However, when volume decreases, the TTI signal line becomes shorter, emphasizing the more recent momentum. By structuring the adaptive signal line this way, the signal line tracks the Buff Spread more closely and tightly when volume does not confirm price. This should create faster countertrend signals.

However, when volume does confirm price, the average spread/signal line is longer and looser. This widened distance of the average spread/TTI signal line from the Buff Spread delays or negates countertrend actions. When the Buff Spread crosses over the TTI signal line or average spread, this represents accumulation among investors and is a buy signal. Similarly, when the Buff Spread crosses under the TTI signal line (TTI average), this is a sign of distribution, and thus, a sell signal (see Figure 16.11).

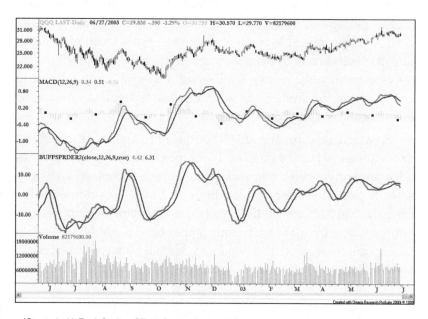

Figure 16.11   MACD and TTI (Buff Spreader).

To prove any hypothesis correct, an accurate and measurable test must be completed. This hypothesis was tested via a trading system comparing two indicators. The first indicator used in the comparison was the traditional MACD developed by Gerald Appel. The second indicator was the TTI indicator. Both indicators use the same price data as the 12-day and 26-day moving averages to generate buy and sell signals. The shorter 12-day moving average is more responsive to current price action and trend changes because it emphasizes more recent price changes. The longer term 26-day moving average contains more information and is more indicative of the longer term trend. Because its scope is broader, the longer term moving average normally lags the signals given by the shorter term moving average. When a moving average curls upward, investors experience positive momentum. The opposite is true when the moving average curls downward.

The difference of the long and short moving averages is the spread. The spread represents an instrument's current momentum. As with the moving average, when the spread curls up, it signals upward momentum in the underlying issue, and when the spread curls down, it expresses downward momentum in the underlying issue. When an average of the spread is created, it represents the trend of momentum. An indication of distribution is given when the spread falls below the average spread, creating a sell signal. Likewise, when the spread crosses above the average spread, it represents accumulation among investors and is a buy signal.

So which indicator, the MACD or the TTI, produced the best signals as measured by the four Rs? If our technical analysis volume theories are correct, then you expect the volume-enhanced system to show improved trading results. Because the TTI is differentiated from the MACD only by the injection and manipulation of volume information, if the TTI significantly outperforms the MACD, it might be logically concluded that volume adds important information in forecasting future price movements.

The Study

Not only did I need to establish a method to objectively tally the results, but I also was concerned about the significance of the sample being studied. A reliable test must be both unbiased and comprehensive, and it must use the scientific method of observable empirical and measurable evidence. To accomplish these goals, the test was broken into several comprehensive parts. Securities were selected across three areas of capitalization: small as measured by the S&P Small Cap Index, medium as measured by the S&P 400 Index, and large as measured by the S&P 100 Index. Equally important were the trading characteristics of each security. Thus, securities were further broken down into the characteristics of volume and volatility. When these seven traits were combined, a total of 12 groups were formed: small cap high volume, small cap low volume, small cap high volatility, small cap low volatility, mid cap high volume, mid cap low volume, mid cap high volatility, mid cap low volatility, large cap high volume, large cap low volume, large cap high volatility, and large cap low volatility (see Table 16.1).

TABLE 16.1   60 Stocks Tested in the Study

60 securities by three sizes of capitalization and four styles selected by the most prominent characteristics

Large Cap Low Volatility	Large Cap High Volatility	Large Cap High Volume	Large Cap Low Volume
PG	EP	CSCO	ATI
HNZ	AES	MSFT	BCC
CL	DAL	INTC	BDK
MMM	ATI	ORCL	ROK
ETR	NSM	GE	CPB
Mid Cap Low Volatility	**Mid Cap High Volatility**	**Mid Cap High Volume**	**Mid Cap Low Volume**
EQT	ACF	ATML	WPO
BOH	BRW	MCHP	BDG
CLI	RSAS	IDPH	TECUA
HE	WIND	GILD	KELYA
NFG	TQNT	ACF	CRS
Small Cap Low Volatility	**Small Cap High Volatility**	**Small Cap High Volume**	**Small Cap Low Volume**
CLP	REGN	PSUN	NPK
CHG	FLOW	ADPT	HGGR
ESS	NOR	KLIC	OXM
GBP	OCA	PCLE	SKY
SHU	CRY	CERN	LAWS

To ensure unbiased results, five securities were back tested in each of these 12 subgroups for a total of 60 securities to ensure a significant sample size. To add credibility, the five securities representing each group were not selected randomly, but through identifying the leaders with the various characteristics being measured. Thus, the five highest-volume and five lowest-volume securities, and the five highest-volatility and five lowest-volatility securities, of each of the three capitalization groups, as identified by Bloomberg on April 8, 2003 (refer to Table 16.1), were used in this study. Any securities that were duplicated (high-volume and high-beta stocks were occasionally duplicated) were used only once. Securities that lacked sufficient history were removed and replaced with the next best suited issue. I used these 60 securities, 12 groups, 4 types, and 3 categories in testing our hypothesis.

To keep the system objective, both long and short system-generated trades were taken into account in our test. A long position was taken when the spread crossed above the average spread. A short position was entered when the spread crossed under the average spread. A $10,000 position was taken with each cross. Commissions were not included. For large caps stocks, the testing period used was October 3, 1991, through June 11, 2003, for a total of 3,000 trading days. Because small and mid cap issues had shorter histories, 3,000 trading days significantly reduced the number of securities eligible when identifying the issues by the characteristics studied. As a solution, 2,000 trading days were substituted for these issues, making the testing period August 3, 1995, through June 11, 2003, for the small and mid cap issues.

Responsiveness

Does volume lead price? In theory, volume increases should precede significant price movements, giving faster downside and upside signals. This basic tenant of technical analysis has been repeated as a mantra since the days of Charles Dow. Through weighting the moving average with a price-leading indicator such as volume, one should not only be able to identify the trend more quickly but also exit sooner when the trend ends. The more signals a system produces, the more responsiveness is demonstrated. In measuring responsiveness, one drawback is the adaptive feature of the TTI signal line. The adaptive features of TTI are designed to increase the responsiveness of sell signals when volume confirms price drops and to expedite buy signals when volume confirms upward price moves. However, when volume diverges from an upward price move, the buy signal given by the moving average of the spread is delayed, or it might possibly negate a buy signal. Likewise, when volume diverges from downward price drops, the adaptive feature slows or possibly negates many sell signals. This feature is designed to reduce the number of "false or bad" signals based on volume theory, and the added reliability could diminish the total number of trades in the TTI.

Yet because volume leads price, the TTI produced more trades across all three areas of capitalization large, mid, and small cap stocks. Across the four styles, the TTI produced more trades in three of the four styles, including the low- and high-volatility issues, and the low-volume issues (see Figure 16.12). However, the MACD produced more trades in the high-volume category.

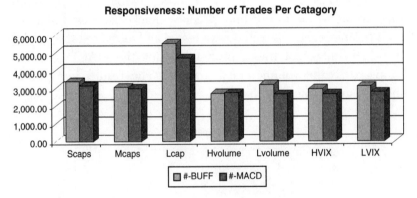

Figure 16.12   Responsiveness of MACD and TTI (Buff).

When examined across the 12 subgroups, the TTI produced more trades in 9 of the 12 subgroups. The mid cap high-volatility issues and the mid and small cap high-volume issues were the exceptions. Overall, of the 60 securities tested, the TTI produced on average 200 trades per security compared with 181 trades per security by the MACD, for an improvement in responsiveness of nearly 10 percent.

Reliability

The capability of an indicator to generate an earlier entry is good, but it is essential for that indication to be reliable. Generally, there is a trade-off between reliability and responsiveness. Short-term moving averages are likely to generate more false signals due to market volatility, but short-term moving averages position a trader in the movement of the trend quicker. Longer term moving averages are commonly more reliable. However, the drawback is that longer term moving averages generally position the trader in and out of the trade later, leaving profits on the table. Technical analysts have explored ways to optimize this trend following trade-off between responsiveness and reliability, by either weighting the average with time or by adding more moving average parameters (multiple moving averages). However, when observed broadly, these modifications have not been found to significantly improve system performance. According to technical analysis theory, volume weighting should improve both for two reasons. First, volume should affirm price movements on heavy volume. Second, volume, when diverging from price, gives later signals, if any at all. Thus, if correct, imputing volume information into price averages should not only produce quicker signals, but much more reliable signals as well. I have tested and measured the reliability by percentage of trades profitable using the MACD indicator compared to the volume-enhanced TTI. The results indisputably support our volume hypothesis

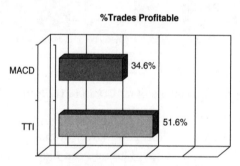

%Trades Profitable

MACD 34.6%

TTI 51.6%

Figure 16.13   Reliability TTI versus MACD all issues.

The TTI produced a higher percentage of trades profitable in all 60 securities (100 percent). To put this into context, of the 60 securities, the highest profitability ratio produced using the MACD indicator was with the security OXM (Oxford Industries). Using the MACD indicator, OXM turned a profit 42.96 percent of the time, which was the best reliability of the securities tested with the MACD. In contrast, with the TTI, the least reliable result produced by any single security was with ATML (Atmel). ATML produced profit 42.18 percent of the time, making it the least reliable of any security tested with the TTI. Overall, the MACD produced an average profitability ratio of 34.67 percent, and the TTI produced an average profitability ratio of 51.61 percent. Thus, using the traditional MACD as a stand-alone indicator, one can expect a little over a third of the signals to be profitable, whereas over 50 percent of the trades produced by the TTI actually produced a profit (see Figure 16.14).

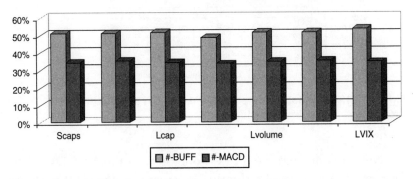

Reliability: Percentage of Trades Profitable

Figure 16.14 Reliability MACD versus TTI by three size groups and four characteristics.

Profitability

A study of this nature is incomplete without including what matters most to any investor: the bottom line; that is, which indicator, MACD or the TTI, made the most money. Next, I review the data again in terms of this most relevant factor to determine the merit of volume information.

Analyzing the results of three capitalization classes, the TTI outperformed the MACD among all three classes (small, mid, and large cap issues). In the small cap category, the TTI outperformed the MACD by $88,400. It also produced greater profits in all four mid-cap subgroup issues (high volume, low volume, high volatility, and low volatility). In the mid cap sector, the TTI produced $35,865 more than the MACD. The TTI was able to outperform the MACD in

three of four mid-cup subgroups, including the low-volume and high-
and low-volatility issues. Among the large capitalization sector, large
cap low-volume stocks were the only subgroup that performed better
with the MACD. Overall, large caps using the volume-enhanced TTI
indicator produced $137,138 more than the MACD indicator. Thus,
the TTI produced more profitable results among all three categories
of capitalization (see Figure 16.15).

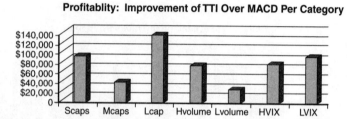

**Figure 16.15   Profitability improvement with TTI across three size
groups and four characteristics.**

Next, I compared the TTI's profitability to the MACDs by the
four styles. Again, as with the three size groups, the TTI produced
more profitable results in all four style groups. The TTI produced
$72,125 more in the high-volume group, $21,199 more with low-
volume issues, amassed a $90,550 improvement with low-volatility
stocks, and bettered the MACD by $77,529 in high-volatility cate-
gory. In total, the TTI made $261,403 more than the MACD indica-
tor. That breaks down to an average improvement of $4,356 per issue
using the TTI indicator (see Figure 16.15).

A way to measure risk-adjusted profitability is through a ratio
known as the profit factor. The profit factor calculates how many dollars a trading strategy made for every dollar it lost. The ratio is calculated by dividing gross profits by gross losses. The MACD was again
outdone in all seven of the major groups, with the TTI registering
higher profit factors across small, mid, and large caps, as well as low-
and high-volume and low- and high-volatility issues. Of the 12 minor
groups, the TTI indicator produced greater average profit factors in 10 of
the 12 subgroups, with mid cap high-volume and large cap low-volume
being the exceptions. Overall, the volume information formulated

via TTI improved the profit factor of the MACD by an average greater than 10 percent.

In conclusion, using volume as the volume manipulated TTI indicator is more effective in identifying the changing perspectives of investors than a price-alone-derived trend indicator. It is apparent through this study that properly analyzed volume information does indeed substantiate price trends. It has been further illustrated that investor accumulation and distribution patterns can indeed be better identified with volume confirmation. Likewise, evidence of trend accumulation and distribution patterns diverging from volume flows should be discounted. As observed through the comparison of the MACD to the TTI indicator, volume consistently increased performance across all major areas measured by this study. An investor appropriately employing volume information would generally enter a winning trade sooner while simultaneously increasing the probability of making a correct investment decision.

17

The Volume Price Confirmation Indicator

"It is arguable that volume does not only depend on whether the market is rising or falling but also on a variety of market conditions. Volume behaves differently in markets characterized by upward trend, downward trend, consolidating movement, continuation rally, counter-trend rally ect. The second caveat is that it is not the sign of the price change but rather the sign of the trading volume that matters."

—*Professor Imad A. Moosa,* Is The Price-Volume Relation Asymmetric? Cross Sectional Evidence From An Emerging Stock Market, *2006*

So far, I have studied several different ways to use volume indicators. As market action unfolds, each indicator has its own unique calculation representing the daily interactions between supply and demand. However, institutional accumulation and distribution patterns are based not so much on these day-to-day movements. Rather, their trading activities are strategically orchestrated through the larger course of market trends. Thus, perceiving volume in this context, the trend is the ideal way to capture the underlying forces being built up within the market. Short-term market actions can be misleading, sometimes deliberately so. Yet over the longer term context of market trends, intuitional behaviors are inevitably revealed. Given these patterns, a volume indicator with the capability to contrast these market trends over time is required.

From rigorous testing, I also confirmed that adding volume information to traditional price moving averages generally achieves faster indications that are concurrently more reliable and decrease risk while increasing return. In light of these discoveries, I wanted a methodology to find the issues experiencing these positive price-volume characteristics over the larger course of the market's larger trends. My pursuit of these investigations led to my innovation of the Volume Price Confirmation Indicator (VPCI).

The Calculation

The VPCI contrasts price trends to volume-weighted price trends. This is accomplished through contrasting the VWMAs (Volume Weighted Moving Avearages) with the corresponding SMAs (Simple Moving Averages). This examination exposes information about the inherent relationship between the price trend and its corresponding volume. Although SMAs exhibit a stock's changing price levels, they do not reflect the amount of investor participation. However, with VWMAs, price emphasis is directly proportional to each day's volume. The asymmetry between these two trend types provides the information harnessed through the VPCI. This information is then analyzed to determine the feasibility of the price trend's capacity to continue in its current path. Hence, the VPCI is an indicator primarily used in confirming or contradicting the price trend.

The VPCI involves three calculations:

- Volume-Price Confirmation/Contradiction (VPC+/–)
- Volume-Price Ratio (VPR)
- Volume Multiplier (VM)

The first step in calculating VPCI is to choose a long-term and short-term time frame. The long-term time frame is used to compute the VPC as a simple and volume-weighted price moving average and again in calculating the VM as a simple, volume-moving average. The short-term time frame is used to compute the VPR as a simple and volume-weighted price moving average and again in calculating the VM as a simple volume-moving average.

The VPC is calculated by subtracting a long-term SMA from the same time frame's VWMA. In essence, this calculation is the otherwise unseen nexus between price and price that has been proportionally weighted to volume. This difference, when positive, is the VPC+ (volume-price confirmation) and, when negative, the VPC– (volume-price contradiction). This computation is a representation of the asymmetry between price and volume expressed over time. The result is quite revealing. For example, a 50-day SMA is 48.5, whereas the 50-day VWMA is 50. The difference of 1.5 represents price-volume confirmation of the uptrend. If the calculation were negative, it would represent price-volume contradiction. This alone provides purely unadorned information about the intrinsic asymmetrical relationship between a price's trend and its volume (see Figure 17.1).

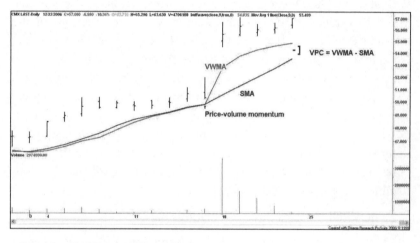

Figure 17.1   VPC = VWMA – SMA.

The next step is to calculate the volume-price ratio. VPR accentuates the VPC+/– relative to the short-term price-volume relationship. The VPR is calculated by dividing the short-term VWMA by the short-term SMA. For example, assume the short-term time frame is 10 days, 10-day VWMA is 25, and the 10-day SMA is 20. The VPR would equal 25/20 or 1.25. This factor is multiplied by the VPC+/– calculated in the first step. Volume-price ratios greater than 1 increase the weight of the VPC+/–. Volume-price ratios below 1 decrease its weight.

The third and final step is to calculate the volume multiplier (VM). The VM objective is to overweight the VPCI when volume is increasing and underweight the VPCI when it is decreasing. This is accomplished by dividing the short-term volume average by the long-term volume average. As an illustration, assume the SMA simple moving average, short-term average volume for 10 days is 1.5 million shares a day, and the long-term volume average for 50 days is 750,000 shares per day. The VM would be 2 (1,500,000 / 750,000).

The result is then multiplied by the VPC+/– after it has been multiplied by the VPR. Now you have all the information necessary to calculate the VPCI. The VPC+ confirmation of +1.5 is multiplied by the VPR of 1.25, yielding 1.875. Then, 1.875 is multiplied by the VM of 2, yielding a VPCI of 3.75. Although this number is indicative of an issue under very strong volume-price confirmation, this information is best used in relation to the price trend and relative to recent VPCI levels. Discussed next is how best to use the VPCI.

VPCI =
c = close
v = volume
s = X # of periods short trend
l = X × 5
vpc = vwma(c, l) – sma(c, l)
vpr = vwma(c, s) / sma(c, s)
vm = sma(v, s) / sma(v, l)
vpci = vpc × vpr × vm
vpcis = vwma(vpci, s)

Using VPCI

Several VPCI signals might be employed with price trends and price indicators. These include a VPCI greater than zero, which illustrates whether the relationship between price trends and volume confirms or contradicts the price trend and by how much. This is the most important indication given by the VPCI indicator. Positive VPCI numbers confirm an uptrend, whereas negative numbers confirm a downtrend and vice versa.

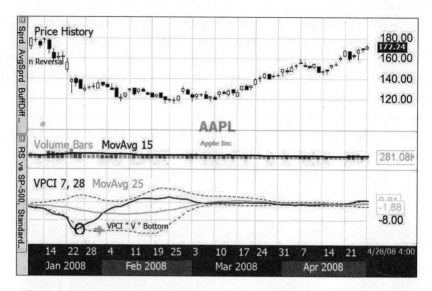

Figure 17.2   VPCI V bottom.

Next in importance is the trend direction of the VPCI, determined by the VPCI rising or falling. This provides the current course
of the VPCI movements, illustrating whether the present direction of
VPCI is converging with or diverging from price.

Finally, a smoothed volume-weighted average of VPCI is created
called VPCI smoothed. VPCI smoothed demonstrates how much
VPCI has changed from previous VPCI levels. This is used as an indication of the VPCI's momentum. A VPCI crossing above or below the
VPCI smoothed might indicate positive momentum and perhaps a
change in or an acceleration of an existing VPCI trend. Bollinger
bands might also be applied to the VPCI, exposing VPCI extremes
(see Figure 17.3).

Fundamentally, VPCI reveals the proportional imbalances
between price trends and volume-adjusted price trends. An uptrend
with increasing volume is a market characterized by greed supported
by the fuel it needs to grow. An uptrend without volume is complacent; greed deprived it of the fuel needed to sustain itself. Investors
without the influx of other investors (volume) will eventually lose
interest, and the uptrend should eventually break down.

TABLE 17.1 Four Divisions of the Price-Volume Relationship

Price Expansion and Volume Expansion		Price Contraction and Volume Contraction	
Trend Up and Volume Rising	Strong Demand	Trend Down and Volume Falling	Weak Supply
Greed with Energy = Invigorated Greed		Fear with Entropy = Apathy	
Phase 1 Phase 2		Phase 1 Phase 2	
Price 10 12		Price 12 10	
Volume 100 300		Volume 300 100	
VWMA = .25 × 10 + .75 × 12		VWMA = .75 × 12 + .25 × 10	
VPC = 11.5 (VWMA) – 11 (SMA)		VPC = 11.5 (VWMA) – 11 (SMA)	
Price Trend +2 (Rising) –VS – VPC = +.5 (Rising)		Price Trend –2 (Falling) –VS – VPC = +.5 (Rising)	
Up Trend		Down Trend	
Bullish	Confirmation	Bullish	Contradiction
Trend Up and Volume Falling	Weak Demand	Trend Down and Volume Rising	Strong Supply
Greed with Entropy = Complacency		Fear with Energy = Fear	
Phase 1 Phase 2		Phase 1 Phase 2	
Price 10 12		Price 12 10	
Volume 300 100		Volume 100 300	
VWMA = .75 × 10 + .25 × 12		VWMA = .25 × 12 + .75 × 10	
VPC = 10.5 (VWMA) – 11 (SMA)		VPC = 10.5 (VWMA) – 11 (SMA)	
Price Trend +2(Rising) –VS- VPC = –.5 (Falling)		Price -2 (Falling) –VS – VPC = –.5 (Falling)	
	Up Trend	Down Trend	
Bearish	Contradiction	Bearish	Confirmation

(Chart [or data] produced by TeleChart 2007® or StockFinder®, which is a registered trademark of Worden Brothers, Inc., Five Oaks Office Park, 4905 Pine Cone Drive, Durham, NC 27707. Ph. (800) 776-4940 or (919) 408-0542. www.Worden.com.)

Figure 17.3   Feb 2003 VPCI V bottom.

A market driven by fear is portrayed by a falling price trend. A falling price trend without volume is apathy, fear without increasing energy. Unlike greed, fear is self-sustaining and can endure for long periods without increasing fuel or energy. Adding energy to fear is likened to adding fuel to a fire and is generally bearish until the VPCI reverses. In such cases, weak-minded investors are overcome by fear, becoming irrationally fearful until the selling climax reaches a state of maximum homogeneity. At this point, the ownership held by the weak investors has been purged, producing a type of heat death. These occurrences might be visualized by the VPCI falling below the lower standard deviation of a Bollinger band of VPCI and then rising above the lower band to form a V bottom. Although V bottoms are rare, since the development of the VPCI in 2002, a VPCI V bottom has marked every true major intermediate term broad market bottom in the S&P 500 since its discovery in 2002 (see Figures 17.3, 17.4, 17.5, and 17.6).

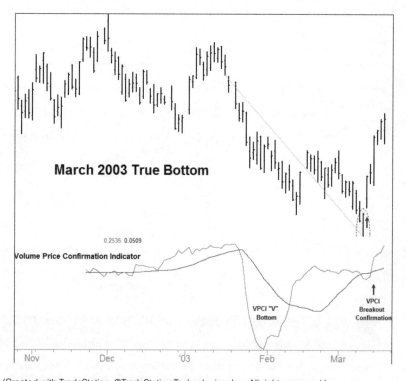

Figure 17.4   March 2003 VPCI "V" bottom double confirmation signal.

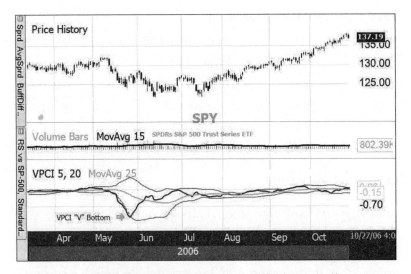

Figure 17.5   June 2006 V VPCI bottom.

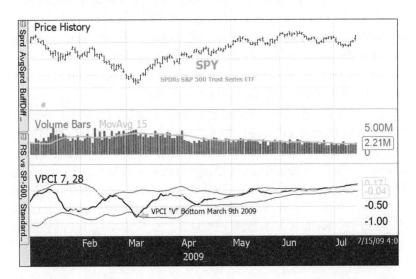

Figure 17.6   March 9, 2009 V bottom marked the end of the devastating bear market.

Note when using VPCI that volume leads or precedes price action. Unlike most indicators, the VPCI often gives indications before price breaks and trend reversals occur. A cheat sheet of the price-volume trend rules is shown in Table 17.2.

TABLE 17.2   VPCI Price Implications

Price	VPCI	Price-Trend Relationship	Implications
Rising	Rising	Confirmation	Bullish
Rising	Declining	Contradiction	Bearish
Declining	Rising	Contradiction	Bullish
Declining	Declining	Confirmation	Bearish

VPCI in Action

Next, we will visit four stock charts, each with different price/volume relationship as noted with the VPCI.

In Figure 17.7, the price trend of SIRI stock is rising, and VPCI is also rising. In this scenario, VPCI is giving three bullish signals. The first signal is VPCI rising. This demonstrates that volume and price are confirming one another, an illustration of strength within the trend. Also VPCI smoothed is rising, and VPCI has crossed above it, indicating momentum within the confirmation. This is a good indication that the existing bullish price trend will continue. Last and most important, both VPCI and VPCI smoothed are above the zero line, indicating a healthy longer term accumulation.

Next, in Figure 17.8, we look at an example of a VPCI giving a bearish contradiction signal. TASR stock price is rising. However, VPCI is falling. This situation cautions that a price correction of significance could be looming. Although price is rising and volume at first glance appears neutral, VPCI is indicating that demand is no longer in control. Here, two bearish signs are given in light of a rising stock price. Both VPCI and VPCI are in downtrends, indicating weakening commitment to the uptrend. Also, both VPCI and VPCI smooth are below zero, which suggests an unhealthy uptrend.

A falling stock price and a rising VPCI is an example of volume-price contradiction. Figure 17.9 shows the S&P 500 stock price is falling, and the VPCI is rising. This illustrates that despite the fall of the market, control is in the hands of buyers. VPCI and VPCI smoothed are in gradual uptrends, contradicting the downward price movement. Eventually, VPCI crosses VPCI smoothed while VPCI rises above zero. The market later breaks out shortly afterward on modest buying pressure.

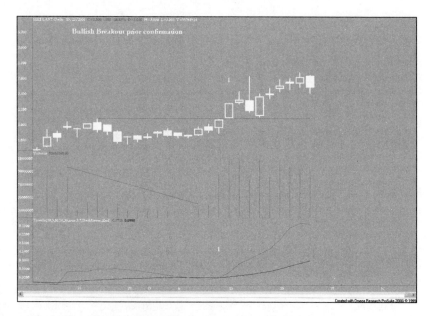

Figure 17.7   VPCI bullish confirmation.

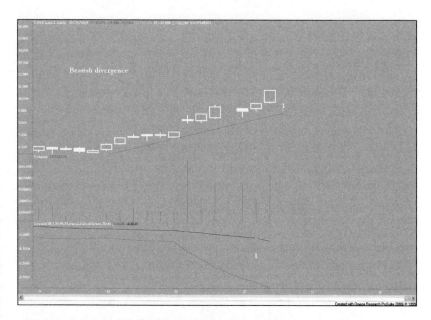

Figure 17.8   VPCI bearish divergence.

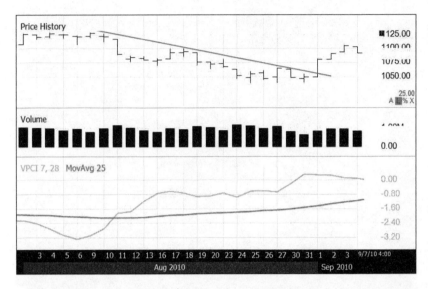

(Chart [or data] produced by TeleChart 2007® or StockFinder®, which is a registered trademark of Worden Brothers, Inc., Five Oaks Office Park, 4905 Pine Cone Drive, Durham, NC 27707. Ph. (800) 776-4940 or (919) 408-0542. www.Worden.com.)

Figure 17.9   VPCI bullish contradiction

An example of a bearish confirmation takes place in RIMM in Figure 17.10. RIMM's price is declining, as is the VPCI. Decreasing VPCI while prices are falling is usually a sign of increasing supply, especially if the stock has previously been in a secular uptrend (as in the case of RIMM). When RIMM begins to break down, the VPCI takes a deeper nosedive, indicating an extended sell-off. After the VPCI bottoms, the bulls regain control of RIMM and the breakdown is reversed. VPCI turns upward, confirming the new price rise. It is common for VPCI to confirm a countertrend. But this example illustrates that if the indicator is giving indications within the context of a countertrend imbedded in a larger major trend, the indications might be quickly reserved.

Putting it all together, let us look at one final example to observe VPCI in action. Something of extreme importance when using VPCI is that volume often leads or is ahead of the price action. Unlike most indicators, VPCI typically gives indications prior to price indications. Thus, when a VPCI signal is given in an unclear price trend, it is best to wait until a clear price trend is evident. This final example in Figure 17.11 is done in a weekly time frame to illustrate VPCI indications in a longer term cycle.

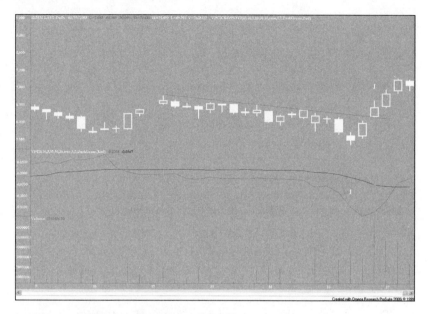

(Created with TradeStation. ©TradeStation Technologies, Inc. All rights reserved.)

Figure 17.10   Bearish confirmation.

We use Figure 17.11 of TM to illustrate the use of the VPCI indicator. At point 1 in Figure 17.11, TM (Toyota Motors) is breaking out of a downtrend, and the VPCI confirms this breakout immediately as it rises crossing over the VPCI smoothed and then the zero line. This is an example of a VPCI's bullish confirmation of the price trend. Later, the VPCI begins to fall during the uptrend, suggesting complacency. By point 2, VPCI crosses under VPCI smoothed, warning of a possible pause within the new uptrend. This is a classic example of a VPCI bearish contradiction. Before reaching point 3, VPCI creates a pattern forming a V bottom. This is a bullish sign, often indicating the sell-off has washed out many of the sellers. Later at point 3, VPCI confirms the earlier bullish V pattern with a bullish crossover leading to a strong bull rally.

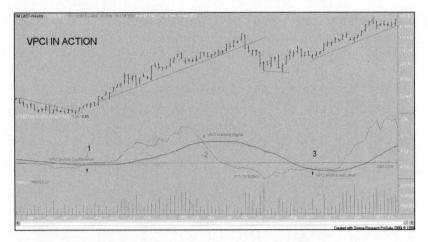

Figure 17.11   VPCI: The only volume indicator to predict the last major market pullback (May 2006) before the market decline.

The Study

Through our volume knowledge and prior testing, it might seem a foregone conclusion that the VPCI is an effective indicator to confirm price trends. However, to prove any hypothesis conclusive, an accurate and measurable test must be completed. The VPCI indicator was tested via a trading system using two moving average systems, similar to how I tested volume-weighted moving averages in Chapter 16, "Volume-Weighted Price Indicators."

In the first study, I back tested the 5- and 20-day crossover system. A long position is taken when the short-term moving average crosses above the long-term moving average. A short position is enacted when the short-term moving average crosses under the long-term moving average. These actions tend to represent short-term changes in momentum and trend. In the second (comparative) study, I also tested using the 5- and 20-day crossover, but I only kept the trades when the VPCI also previously crossed over a smoothed VPCI. This indicates a rising VPCI or price confirmation. The VPCI setting will be the same as the moving averages—20 days for the long-term component and 5 days for the short-term component.

There are a number of limitations to this study, but these settings were deliberately chosen to keep the study simple and uncorrupted. First, the 5-day and 20-day moving average settings are too short to indicate a strong trend. This takes away from the effectiveness of the VPCI as a price trend confirmation and contradiction indicator. However, these settings are quick, provide more trades, and allow for a more significant sample size. Also setting the VPCI at 5 and 20 days when the price data are only 20 days old (length of long-term moving average) is too short. By using these time settings, VPCI might give signals ahead of the price trend or momentum indications given by the moving averages. However, I did not want to change the settings for fear that they might be interpreted as being optimized. To overcome this, I used a 10-day look-back delay on the VPCI and a 5-day look-back delay on the VPCI smoothed. This delay allows the VPCI confirmation signal to be more in tune with the lagging moving average crossover. Ideally, one would use trend lines or other trend indications with the VPCI corresponding to the time frame being invested or traded.

To keep the system objective, both long and short system-generated trades were taken into account in our tests. A $10,000 position was taken with each crossover. Commissions were not included. The testing period used was August 15, 1996, through June 22, 2004, for a total of 2,000 trading days. I measured the results through reliability and profitability.

Not only did I need to establish a method to objectively tally the results, but I also was concerned about the significance of the sample being studied. A reliable test must use the scientific method and be both unbiased and comprehensive. To accomplish this, the test was broken into several comprehensive parts. Securities were selected across three areas of capitalization: small as measured by the S&P Small Cap Index, medium as measured by the S&P 400 Index, and large as measured by the S&P 100 Index. Equally important are the trading characteristics of each security. Thus, securities were further broken down into the characteristics of volume and volatility. When these traits are combined, a total of 12 groups is formed: small cap high volume, small cap low volume, small cap high volatility, small cap low volatility, mid cap high volume, mid cap low volume, mid cap high volatility, mid cap low volatility, large cap high volume, large cap low volume, large cap high volatility, and large cap low volatility.

To ensure unbiased results, 5 securities were back tested in each of these 12 subgroups for a total of 60 securities to ensure a significant sample size. For credibility, the 5 securities representing each group were not selected by random but through identifying the leaders with the various characteristics being measured. Thus, the 5 highest-volume and the five lowest-volume securities and the five highest-volatility and the 5 lowest-volatility securities of each of the three capitalization groups as identified by Bloomberg June 22, 2004, were used in this study. Any securities that were duplicated (high-volume and high-beta stocks were occasionally duplicated) were only used once. Securities that lacked sufficient history were removed and replaced with the next best suitable issue. I used these 60 securities, 12 groups, 4 types, and 3 categories in testing the hypothesis.

Returns/Profitability

To review, profitability was tested using solely a 5- and 20-day moving average crossover and then retested using only those trades also displaying VPCI confirmation signals. The results were quite impressive. Broadly, the VPCI improved profitability in the three size classes small, mid, and large caps and all four style classifications high and low volume, and high and low volatility (see Figure 17.13). In addition, 9 of the 12 subgroups showed improvement. The exceptions were mid cap high-volatility issues, and small and large low-volume issues. Of the 60 issues tested, 39 (65 percent) showed improved results using VPCI. Overall, profitability was boosted by $211,997 with VPCI.

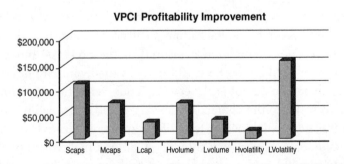

Figure 17.13   VPCI profitability improvement across three size groups and four characteristics.

Reliability

In this study, I measured reliability by looking at the percentage of trades profitable. By employing VPCI in the 5-day/20-day crossover system, overall profitability improved an average of 3.21 percent per issue. Improvement was realized by adding VPCI in all three size groups and all four style groups. Of the 12 subgroups, 10 showed improved reliability when adding VPCI. The large and small cap low-volatility category issues were the only exceptions. Overall, more than 43 of 60 issues (71 percent) showed improvement when including VPCI.

Risk-Adjusted Returns

Another way to look at profitability is through the Sharpe Ratio. The Sharpe Ratio takes the total return subtracted by the risk-free rate of return (U.S. Treasury note) and divides the result by the portfolio's monthly standard deviation. Thus, the Sharpe Ratio gives us a risk-adjusted rate of return. VPCI bettered the results once again across all three size categories and all four style groups VPCI realized improvement in 9 of the 12 subgroups. Mid cap high volatility, large cap low volatility, and large cap low volume were the exceptions. Overall, the Sharpe Ratio showed significant improvement with the addition of VPCI.

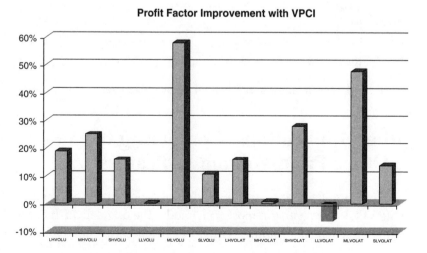

Figure 17.14   Profit factor improvement when using VPCI.

Another way to look at risk-adjusted returns is through the profit factor. The profit factor takes into account how much money can be gained for every dollar lost within the same strategy. The profit factor measures risk by comparing the upside to the downside. The profit factor is calculated by dividing gross profits by gross losses. For instance, one issue might generate $40,000 in losses and $50,000 in gross gains, whereas a second issue might generate $10,000 in losses and $20,000 in gross gains. Both issues generate a $10,000 net profit. However, an investor can expect to make $1.25 for every dollar lost in the first system but $2 for every dollar lost in the second system. The figures of $1.25 and $2 represent the profit factor. VPCI had even more significant improvement in this area (see Figure 17.15). Again, VPCI showed improvements in large, mid, and small cap stock categories, and in all four styles groups: low and high volume and low and high volatility. Among the 12 subgroups, only large cap low-volatility issues did not show improvement with VPCI. Overall, the profit factor was improved by 19 percent, meaning one can expect to earn 19 percent more profit for every dollar put at risk when infusing VPCI in the trading system.

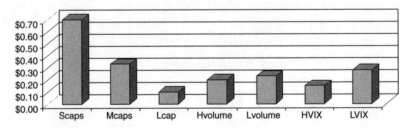

Profit factor improvement VPCI

Figure 17.15   Profit factor improvement across the seven major groups.

Other Applications: Comparing the VPCI to Other Price-Volume Indicators

There are many price-volume indicators one can use to compare to the VPCI. However, the most acclaimed is the original On-Balance Volume. Recognizing volume as the force behind price, Joe Granville created OBV by assigning up days as positive volume (measured by an up close) and then subtracting volume on down days OBV is price-directed volume, the accumulation of +/- volume flows based on price direction. (For more information on Joe Granville's OBV, see Chapter 11, "Interday Volume Accumulation Indicators.") Granville's original objective with OBV was to uncover hidden coils in an otherwise non-eventful, non-trending market. With his OBV indicator, Granville became a renowned market strategist. He also popularized OBV and the wisdom of using volume in securities analysis.

VPCI differs from OBV in that VPCI calculates the proportional imbalances between price trends and volume-weighted price trends. This exposes the influence that volume has on a price trend. Although both OBV and VPCI contain volume-derived data, they convey different information. In composition, VPCI is not an accumulation of history like OBV, but rather a snapshot of the influence of volume on a price trend over a specified period of time. This enables VPCI to give faster signals than an accumulation indicator similar to an oscillator. In contrast to OBV, VPCI's objective is not to uncover hidden coils in trendless markets, but to evaluate the health of existing trends.

To illustrate the effectiveness and proper use of VPCI, a test was conducted comparing VPCI to OBV. The most general VPCI buy signal is the VPCI crossing above the VPCI smoothed in an uptrending market. This indicates VPCI is rising relative to previous VPCI levels. The traditional OBV does not have a lagging trigger like VPCI smoothed, so I amended the OBV by adding an additional eight-period simple moving average of OBV. The net effect gives OBV a corresponding trigger to VPCI smoothed. OBV crossovers of OBV smoothed give indications of OBV rising relative to previous OBV levels. Remember, VPCI is designed to be used in a trending market. Thus, I need two additional tools to complete this test. First, I need an indicator to verify whether the market is trending. A seven-day Average Directional Index (ADX) indicator fulfills this criterion. Next, I need a trend indicator indicating the trend's direction. The MACD with the traditional (12, 26, 9) settings was used for this test.

Finally, I need a test subject that illustrates how these indicators work across a broad market. I can think of no broader or more popular vehicle for this experiment than the SPDR S&P 500 exchange-traded fund. The testing period was from inception in February 1993 until the end of 2006. Results were not optimized in any way, shape, or form. In this system, long positions are taken only when the above conditions are met when accompanied by OBV crossovers in the first test and VPCI crossovers in the second test. Long positions are exited with crossunders of OBV smoothed in the first test or with VPCI crossunders in the second study (see Figure 17.16). Although this test was created rather simplistically and traditionally for both observational and credibility purposes, the results are stunning (see Figure 17.17 and Figure 17.18).

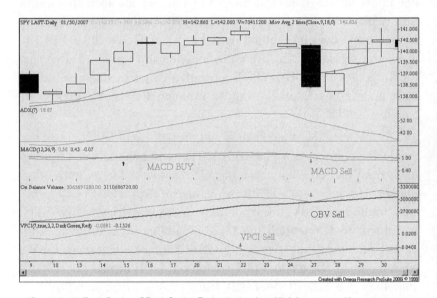

(Created with TradeStation. ©TradeStation Technologies, Inc. All rights reserved.)

Figure 17.16   MACD OBV VPCI setup TradeStation.

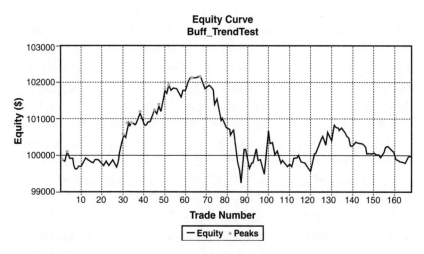

Figure 17.17 SPY (S&P 500 ETF): On-balance volume equity curve.

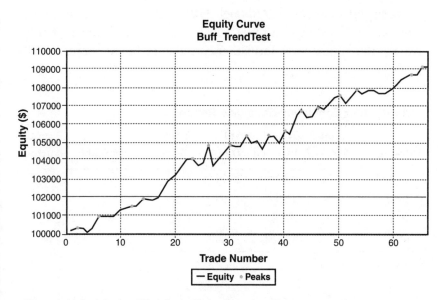

Figure 17.18 SPY: VPCI equity curve.

Excluding dividends and interest, OBV's annualized rate of return in the system was −1.57 percent, whereas VPCI's annualized return was 8.11 percent, an outperformance of over 9.5 percent annualized. VPCI improved reliability, giving profitable signals over 65 percent of the time compared to OBV at only 42.86 percent. Another consideration in evaluating performance is risk. VPCI had less than half the risk as measured by volatility, and it has 7.42 standard deviations compared to OBV with 17.4 standard deviations from the mean. It is not surprising then that VPCI had much better risk-adjusted rates of return. VPCI's Sharpe ratio from inception was .70 and had a profit factor of 2.47 compared to OBV with a −0.09 Sharpe ratio and a profit factor less than 1 (see Table 17.3). Admittedly, this testing environment is uneven. VPCI uses information from volume-weighted prices to gauge the health of existing trends. In contrast, OBV accumulates volume flows as directed by price changes to uncover hidden coils. Thus, the conditions set up in this system, a trending market with apparent price direction, is one in which VPCI is designed to succeed. Although OBV was not necessarily set up for failure, this study illustrates how less savvy practitioners often fail to use the indicators' information correctly or fail to coordinate the indicators properly.

TABLE 17.3   Comparing Strategies' Returns

Strategy*	Annual Return	Time Invested	Std Dev	5-Year Sharpe	% Profitable	Profit Factor
Buy Hold	9.94%	100.00%	17.75%	0.10	N/A	N/A
MACD	-3.88%	24.79%	13.03%	0.27	41.79%	0.97
VPCI	8.11%	35.63%	7.42%	0.74	65.15%	2.47
OBV	-1.57%	27.02%	17.40%	0.05	42.86%	1.00

*Dividends not included.

What if an investor had just used the MACD buy and sell signals within this same system, without using the VPCI information? This investor would have lost out on a nearly 12 percent annualized return, the difference between VPCI's positive 8.11 percent versus MACD's negative 3.88 percent, while significantly increasing risk. What if this investor had just employed a buy-and-hold approach? Although this investor would have realized a slightly higher return, he or she would have endured much greater risks. The VPCI strategy returned nearly 90 percent of the buy-and-hold strategy with about 60 percent less risk as measured by the standard deviation. Looking at risk-adjusted returns another way, the five-year Sharpe ratio for the S&P 500 SPY ETF was only .1 compared to the VPCI system of .74. Additionally, the VPCI investor would have been invested only 35 percent of the time, giving the investor the opportunity to invest in other investments. During the 65 percent of the time not invested, an investor would have only needed a 1.84 percent money market yield to exceed the buy-and-hold strategy. Moreover, an investor would have experienced much smoother performance without nearly as steep capital drawdowns. The VPCI worst annualized return was only a measly –2.71 percent compared to the underlying investments' worst year of –22.81 percent, over a 20 percent difference in the rate of return (see Table 17.4)! If an investor had simply invested in a money market instrument during times not invested in the SPDR S&P 500, using this strategy would have resulted in not even one single down year.

TABLE 17.4   Results Year Over Year

Strategy*	1993	1994	1995	1996	1997	1998	1999
Buy Hold	3.61	–2.21	34.95	20.1	31.44	27.04	19.11
MACD	0.31	5.42	0.88	12.63	14.72	–12.93	–30.6
VPCI	2.93	6.42	6.12	19.83	19.09	8.9	3.17
OBV	–1.03	–1.24	0	18.81	7.3	12.4	–12.43
Strategy*	2000	2001	2002	2003	2004	2005	2006
Buy Hold	–10.68	–12.87	–22.81	26.12	8.62	3.01	13.74
MACD	9.27	11.12	0.9	1.34	1.8	1.69	–11.32
VPCI	–2.71	21.28	–0.65	10.4	4.27	4.8	9.29
OBV	–26.55	–28.34	12.45	–12.79	33.32	–15.58	–8.33

*Annual rates of return without dividends.

Other Applications

The raw VPCI calculation might be used as a multiplier or divider with other indicators, such as moving averages, momentum indicators, or price and volume data. For example, if an investor has a trailing stop loss order set at the five-week moving average of the lows, he or she can divide the stop price by the VPCI calculation. This would lower the price stop when price and volume are in confirmation, increasing the probability of keeping an issue under accumulation. However, when price and volume are in contradiction, dividing the stop loss by the VPCI would raise the stop price, preserving more capital. Similarly, using VPCI as a multiplier to other price, volume, and momentum indicators might not only improve reliability but also increase responsiveness.

In summary, the VPCI reconciles volume and price as determined by each of their proportional weights. This information can be used to confirm or deny the likelihood of a current price trend continuing. These studies clearly demonstrate that adding the VPCI indicator to a trend-following system results in consistently improved performance across all major areas measured by the studies. An investor using VPCI information properly would likely increase profits, reduce risk, and increase reliability. It is apparent through this study that properly analyzed price and volume information might be used to substantiate or refute price trends. Like a maestro's baton in the hands of a proficient investor, the VPCI is a tool capable of substantially accelerating profits, reducing risk, and empowering the investor to make more reliable investment decisions.

Volume Indicators Table

Name	Type	Developer
Money Flow AKA Tick Volume	Tick Volume	Don Worden
Volume Weighted Average Price (VWAP)	Tick Volume	Unknown
The MIDAS Method	Tick Volume	Dr. Paul Levine
Intraday Volume Breakout (IVBO)	Tick Volume	Hamzei Analytics
Wave Charts	Tick Volume*	Richard D. Wyckoff
Time Segmented Volume	Tick Volume*	Don Worden
Cumulative Delta Indicator	Tick Volume	Steve Decker
Tick Volume Indicator	Tick Volume	William Blau
Volume Breakdown Indicator	Tick Volume	Unknown
Relative Dollar Volume Flow Indicator	Tick Volume	Dr. Brett Steenbarger
Trade Volume Index	Tick Volume	Unknown
Trendographs	Volume-Price Range	Edwin S. Quinn
Equivolume	Volume-Price Range	Richard W. Arms, Jr.
Ease of Movement	Volume-Price Range	Richard W. Arms, Jr.
Market Facilitation Index	Volume-Price Range	Bill Williams
Volume Adjusted Moving Averages	Volume-Price Range	Richard W. Arms, Jr.
Better Volume Indicator	Volume-Price Range	Unknown
The Force Index	Volume-Price Range	Dr. Alexander Elder
Density Charts	Volume-Price Range	Unknown

Name	Type	Developer
On-Balance Volume	Interday Volume	Joseph E. Granville/Paul Clay
Volume Flow Indicator (VFI)	Interday Volume	Markos Katsanos
Volume Zone Oscillator	Interday Volume	Waleed Aly Khalil
Price Volume Trend	Interday Volume	David L. Markstein
Volume-Weighted Relative Strength (VWRSI)	Interday Volume	Russell Minor
Demand Index	Interday Volume	James Sibbett
Up Down Volume Ratio	Interday Volume	Unknown
V/D Volume	Interday Volume	Unknown
PVI Positive Volume Index	Price Accumulation	Paul L. Dysart, Jr./Norman Fosback
NVI Negative Volume Index	Price Accumulation	Paul L. Dysart, Jr./Norman Fosback
Effective Volume	Intraday Volume	Pascal Willain
Effective Volume Ration	Intraday Volume	Pascal Willain
Intraday Intensity Index/ Chaikin Money Flow	Intraday Volume	David Bostonian
Twiggs Money Flow	Intraday Volume	Colin Twiggs
Williams Accumulation Distribution	Intraday Volume	Larry Williams
Williams Variable Accumulation Distribution	Intraday Volume	Larry Williams
Klinger Volume Oscillator	Intraday Volume	Stephen Klinger
Modified Price Volume Trend	Intraday Volume	David G. Hawkins
Chaikin Accumulation/ Distribution Oscillator	Intraday Volume	Marc Chaikin
Chaikin 21-Day Money Flow	Intraday Volume	Marc Chaikin

continues

Name	Type	Developer
Balance of Power	Intraday Volume	Don Worden
Money Stream	Intraday Volume	Don Worden
% B	Intraday Volume	Joseph Barics
Finite Volume Elements (FVE)	Intraday Volume	Mark Katsanos
Price Volume Threshold	Intraday Volume	Matt Blackman
Enhanced Williams % R	Intraday Volume	Robert Kinder, Jr.
Volume Oscillator	Volume Only	Unknown
Percentage Volume Oscillator	Volume Only	Unknown
Normalized Volume Oscillator	Volume Only	Unknown
Williams Capitulation Index	Volume Only	Larry Williams and Matt Blackman
Volume Rate of Change	Volume Only	Unknown
Money Flow Index	Volume-Weighted Price	Gene Quong/Avrum Soudack
Weighted On-Balance Volume (WOBV)		Unknown
Volume-Weighted Moving Averages (VWMA)	Volume-Weighted Price	Buff Dormeier
Volume-Weighted MACD	Volume-Weighted Price	Buff Dormeier
Trend Thrust Indicator	Volume-Weighted Price	Buff Dormeier
VPCI	Volume-Weighted Price	Buff Dormeier
VPCI Stochastics	Volume-Weighted Price	Buff Dormeier
Anti-Volume Stop Loss	Volume-Weighted Price	Buff Dormeier

Name	Type	Developer
	Others	
On-Balance Volume Reflex	Open Interest Volume	Fred Purifoy
Woods Cumulative-Volume Float Indicator WCVFI	Volume Float Analysis	Steve Woods

*Other applications

18

A Compendium of Breadth Indicators

"I began trying, first of all, to gauge what the key elements of bull and bear markets are, because no matter what stock you buy, it's the market you're in that will probably dictate how successful you are in any specific stock purchase."

—*Jeffrey S. Weiss, CMT*

Market breadth is a close cousin to volume. Both volume and breadth are concerned about one primary piece of information: participation. Like volume, market breadth has everything to do with quantities. Whereas volume indicates the number of shares traded, market breadth gets even more specific by indicating the number of securities traded that meet a specific set of market statistics. The term *breadth* usually refers to width, or broadness. *Market breadth* refers to how broad or wide the market is, not as a whole, but rather as groups of individual issues. By perceiving the market as a market of markets, you can gain a much better understanding of the depth of the market's overall trend. This information might be useful in gauging the internal strength of the market. Numerous methods are used to measure market breadth.

Market/Breadth Statistics

Market statistics are studies of market behavior that are derived from the performance of groups of individual securities. In this way, this "market of markets" methodology might be used to contrast the investors driven by optimism (bulls) to those investors driven by pessimism (bears).

Popular breadth studies include

- Number of issues advancing, which is the number of stocks that closed above their previous day's close (or the most recent close for the specified period of time).

- Number of issues declining, which is the number of stocks that closed below their previous day's close (or the most recent close for the specified period of time).

- Number of issues unchanged, which is the number of stocks that close at the same price as the previous day's close (or the most recent close for the specified period of time).

- Number of issues reaching new highs, which is the number of stocks that reach a new high during a specified period of time (typically 52 weeks).

- Number of issues reaching new lows, which is the number of stocks that reach a new low during a specified period of time (typically 52 weeks).

- Number of issues or percentage of stocks above or below a moving average (typically 50 or 200 days).

- Points gained, which is the price change for all issues that close higher during the specified period of time.

- Points lost, which is the price change for all issues that close lower during the specified period of time.

- Total volume of stocks trading higher, which is the sum of the volume totals of all issues closing higher than they did on the previous period (typically one day).

- Total volume of stocks trading lower, which is the sum of the volume totals of all issues closing lower than they did on the previous period (typically one day).

Breadth Statistics: A Source of Market Information

Of the items discussed in this work, market breadth statistics are the only forms of information that are not derived directly through simple observation of the price and volume data derived from the chart. Breadth information cannot be overemphasized as a valuable tool in determining the state of the market's overall condition. Like volume, we use breadth statistics to validate and confirm the price action. For example, let's say you were going to place a sports bet. You might choose between two teams, the Bulls or the Bears. Your desire is to pick the stronger of these two teams to win the bet. A variety of factors can influence your opinion as to which is the stronger team. Wouldn't a statistic about who has been winning the recent matchups be helpful in making such a determination? In the securities industry, these statistics are called *market breadth*.

The market's breadth might tell us such things as how many shares of issues are advancing higher or declining lower. Through these internal statistics, you can measure the broad-based support of the buyers and sellers as they position their portfolios. Market breadth interpretation is similar to volume analysis. When more issues are advancing than declining, the implication is bullish. When more issues are declining than advancing, the implication is bearish.

Likewise, when the number of shares of stocks trading lower (down volume) is greater than the number of shares trading higher (up volume), the implication is bearish and vice versa. The further the extremes between the measures of the ratios of bulls and bears, the stronger the market breadth's implication. Thus, the more issues (or shares of issues) moving higher, the wider the support among the bulls. And, the more issues (or number of shares of issues) moving lower, the broader the support among the bears.

Breadth might be used as a gauge of the market's mood or psychological sentiment and can help indicate whether investors are acting in bold confidence or if they are riveted in fear. In sideways markets or trading ranges, the market's breadth might hold a key to determining the direction of the next trend. However, market breath is often more prominently used as a warning sign that the existing price trend could be under pressure. Generally, a market's breadth should reflect the same shape and essence of its market composite, mirroring the actions of its underlying index. When the breadth reflects the market composite, the breadth is said to confirm the composite. However, should the market composite trend higher, and fewer and fewer issues confirm that direction, you might then conclude that the market has "bad breadth," or is diverging.

This divergence often occurs when the price of large caps stocks, which have a high cap weighted influence on a price index, continue to move in the direction of the existing trend. However, fewer issues in the overall composite might actually move in the same direction. Often, institutions begin their distribution operations with smaller stocks because they are often the least liquid.

An institution looking to decrease its equity exposure often reduces its exposure of less liquid smaller capitalized stocks first. This is because if the markets should decline suddenly, these smaller less liquid issues are the most difficult to liquidate. Therefore, large institutions gradually reduce their positions in the bull market to avoid a situation where their own operations drive prices down. Meanwhile, individual investors become overly comfortable with these large "brand name" stocks. Professional investors, through a shallow yet influential group of influential stocks, are able to drive the composite higher or lower, whereas the less closely watched small cap issues are either removed or significantly underweighted in the broad indexes. This behavior is also seen among the new high and lows, usually creating a high before the market index makes it high. In 1997, the new 52 weeks high peeked two years before the board market peek in 2000. A more recent example is the divergence of dwindling new highs in the 2007 market top and the confirmation of expanding new highs in the 2009 market rally (see Figure 18.1).

Hence, the composite maintains its existing trend while market breadth takes on a divergent path. This is known as breadth divergence, indicating that the move of the market composite is not widely supported by its members (see Figure 18.2). According to the fore-most expert on market breadth, Tom McClellan

"the key value of examining breadth data is that it tells you about liquidity. It is possible to keep the DJIA, SP500, or Nasdaq Composite going higher in an illiquid market environment if the available liquidity is channeled into the right stocks. That is what we saw in 1999–2000, as the tech bubble was narrowing into a small handful of winners. But the A-D Line had peaked back in 1998, and the majority of issues were not joining in the party because there was not enough money to go around to lift the majority of stocks. That was a message of illiquidity, and that illiquidity eventually came around to bite even the best and brightest of the tech bubble. It is only possible to lift the broad list when there is a whole lot of money available to spread out into lots of places. So when we see the broad list doing well, it is a sign that liquidity is plentiful."

(Source: Howard Spieler.)

Figure 18.1   Divergence S&P 500 and new highs.

These data statistics are useful in and of themselves, or they can be used in combinations and formulas to create breadth indicators. The statistics were first used independently and then were combined to form market breadth statistics and simple formulas and ratios. It is believed that economist Leonard P. Ayers was the first practitioner of breadth statistics. Ayers kept a running total of the difference between advancing issues and declining issues back in 1926. This indicator is known today as the advance-decline line, first published in *Barron's* in 1931. This work was later validated and expanded by Harold M. Gartley in his course "Profits in the Stock Market." The NYSE A-D Line peaked May 1928 over a year before the great crash of 1929.

(Source: Tom McClellan, McClellan Financial Publications, Mcoscillator.com.)

Figure 18.2   NASDAQ advancers minus decliners diverging.

Warning Construction Ahead: Breadth Data Pit Falls

Like price and volume data, breadth data can be used and manipulated to create market breadth indicators. Before I engage in a discussion on these indicators, note that breadth analysis it not without problems. Just as volume index data can be misrepresented, breadth index/exchange data are also a bit tainted with a variety of issues. The first problem is the breadth indicator's construction, stemming from the fact that many breadth indicators are cumulative. This means they are calculated based on prior historical readings. This proposes a problem with the advance-decline line. Issues are continually being added and removed in the indexes and exchanges. When a stock is removed, it is usually because it cannot meet the listing requirement. This generally occurs because the company is failing and on its way out of business. This might lead to an unintended downward bias in the data. Mergers also occur, causing the acquired stock to advance higher. Usually, this advance is offset by the decline of the acquirer.

A company's stock that is on its way out of business is going to add to the decline line's numbers. Once a company is out of business, its stock has no influence upon the index. It cannot affect the present index because it no longer exists on an exchange or as an index member component. However, because the advance-decline line is a cumulative history, the stock's prior performance can still be reflected in the advance-decline line, even though the company no longer exists. This results in a downward bias on the line. Analysts compensate for this pitfall by focusing on the present time period's data in analyzing confirmation or divergent patterns.

A similar problem you should be aware of with market breadth analysis is the varying number of issues traded on the exchanges. Over long periods of time, there is a significant upward bias in the number of member firms on the exchange, which leads to issues of scale. One solution to this problem, advocated by Tom McClellan, is to use the ratios as opposed to raw values. As an example, an advance-decline ratio can be used instead of the advance-decline line. To calculate the ratio, subtract the advancing issues from the declining issue, and then divide that calculation by the total number of issues, both advance and declining:

$$\text{Advance Decline Ratio} = (\text{Advancers} - \text{Decliners})/ (\text{Advancers} + \text{Decliners})$$

In this way, ratio data removes the distortions from the raw data allowing for better evaluation of longer time frames. Other breadth ratios can also be constructed in the same manner from other breadth data, such as new highs, new lows, or up and down volume. Also, another added benefit of expressing the data as a ratio is that they allow for more suitable comparisons between rival exchanges and indexes. Thus, you can competently compare the NYSE to the NASDAQ composite or the S&P 500 index.

Another issue with the advance-decline line is decimalization. When the lines were originally constructed, it took at least a ⅛th point to move a stock either up or down and thus be included as an advance or decline. This means that a stock would have to be up or down by at least 12.5 cents to "count" as a change in an equation. In 1997, the rules of the game changed, allowing stocks to trade in

⅟₁₆ths. In 2001, the rule changed again to allow decimalization, meaning stocks began trading in pennies. Today, with decimalization, it takes only a one-cent move or less to count as an advance or decline. The obvious result is that there are more issues changed and fewer issues unchanged. The deeper implication is that it takes less supply or demand to drive a market higher or lower. Before decimalization, it took six times as much buying or selling pressure to move a security than it does now. Many argue that this change has led to the market being more susceptible to manipulation. With that in mind, the vast majority of securities advancing or declining during the course of a day move more than six cents.

Because of decimalization, know that the breadth component data is a bit skewed, at least minimally. It is still quite difficult to discern how much actual impact decimalization has on the advance-decline statistics. To help determine the impact of decimalization, Tom McClellan conducted a test study comparing the NYSE composite to those members of the composite that only traded with less than a ⅟₁₆th change, and to those issues trading with a change greater than a ⅟₁₆th. His results showed that the issues that have changed less than a ⅟₁₆th of a point tend to mirror the overall advance-decline line. This study confirms my instincts that the effects of decimalization on breadth statistics are minimal.

The last potential issue I discuss concerning breadth statistics has to do with the makeup of a stock exchange's internal composition. Originally, the exchanges were comprised solely of operating companies. In time, other instruments were added to the composition of the exchange. These include exchange-traded funds, closed-end funds, equity-linked securities, real estate investment trusts (REITS), and preferred stock. Many of the ETFs, equity-linked securities, and closed-end funds are made up of equities, which can lead to double counting. Other issues listed on the exchange are hedged or inversed and can have the opposite impact. Many issues are comprised of bonds, meaning these index members reflect the behavior of bonds, not stocks. Likewise, preferred stocks tend to mirror activity in the bond market rather than the stock market. Similarly, REITs echo the sentiments of the real estate market as opposed to the equity markets. Presently, fewer than 60 percent of the issues traded on the NYSE are domestic common stocks. As of the date of this writing, 58.8 percent of the issues traded on the NYSE were "common stocks;" 8.86 percent were closed end bond funds; 20.94 percent were preferred stocks; and 11.37 percent were categorized as "specialty" (rights, warrants, structured produces, and other odds and ends).

Because of these significant "impurities" on the equity exchanges, renowned market strategist Paul F. Desmond of Lowery Research Corporation advocates using operating company only breadth statistics. In doing so, he eliminates the nonoperating companies from the statistics. In this, he was able to avoid such adverse markets like the Fall of 2001. Although, the traditional exchange breadth statistics were giving bullish indications, the purified operating company breath statistics warned of a potential decline. Other technicians, I being one myself, have primarily utilized breadth statistics using the index data as opposed to exchange data. Another more recent example was in 2010 with the cumulative advance decline line data. The NYSE advance-decline made a new mark in August 2010 when neither the broad markets nor the Up–Down Volume Line were not even close to doing so (see Figure 18.3). The problem of potential impurities solely rests in the composition of exchanges, not the indexes, because equity indexes generally are made up only of operating companies.

(Source: Tom McClellan, McClellan Financial Publications, Mcoscillator.com.)

Figure 18.3   Divergence NYSE advancers and decliners.

Neither Richard Arms nor Tom McClellan, both foremost experts in breadth analysis, believes these nonoperating companies are heavily polluting the data. When breadth statistics were first used in market analysis, common stocks paid a much higher dividend yield, causing stocks to be much more interest rate sensitive than they are presently. Mr. McClellan has theorized that because most of the nonoperating securities are interest rate sensitive, their inclusion might actually add some predictive power to the breadth statistics. McClellan has further suggested that many of these nonoperating instruments, like preferred stocks are more heavily owned and traded by institutions. Thus, these preferred shares might be a better gauge of liquidity than their operating-company-only brothers. Because of these findings, Tom McClellan has kept an "uncommon" advance-decline line for issues that are not common stocks. He has found that by adding this non-common issuer as the data input in his work, it acts similarly to the advance-decline data but with fewer whipsaws.

Breadth-Based Indicators

The next logical step is to conform breadth statistics into a logical and useable format. This is the rise of breadth-based indicators that employ breadth data in their composition. These indicators vary from the simple to the more complex. They might include data from exchanges, indexes, or any other composition of securities. These indicators might be expressed through a variety of mathematical techniques, including but not limited to simple addition or subtraction, cumulative sums, ratios, logs, simple or advanced moving averages, stochastics, and oscillators.

An example of a simply constructed breadth indicator is the advance-decline line. Similarly, contrasting the new highs versus the new lows creates the high-low index. Like the advance-decline line, net volume is calculated from the difference of up and down volume. Net points gained is calculated from the disparity of points up versus points down.

Positive and Negative Volume Index

The next innovation in breadth statistics was the combination of breadth statistics with market data. In 1936, Paul F. Dysart, Jr. began using the Positive Volume Index (PVI) and the Negative Volume Index (NVI). PVI is the cumulative running sum of the total advancers minus the decliners on a given day, calculated only when the exchange volume is higher than the previous day; otherwise, PVI is unchanged. Conversely, NVI is the cumulative sum of total advancing issues minus declining issues on given day when the exchange volume is lower than the previous day; otherwise, NVI remains unchanged.

PVI = Rising Volume Periods Sum of Advancing – Declining Issues

NVI = Falling Volume Periods Is the Sum of Decliners – the Advancers

According to market historian George A. Schade, Jr. CMT, Dysart believed "if volume advances and prices move up or down in accordance [with volume], the move is assumed to be a good movement—if it is sustained when the volume subsides." Conversely, should the market "hold its own on negative volume days after advancing on positive volume, the market is in a strong position." A bull market signal is generated when the NVI rises above prior highs while the market is trending up (see Figure 18.4). When NVI falls below a previous low while the market is in a downtrend, this constitutes a bear market signal. However, not all movements above or below a prior NVI or PVI level generate signals, as Dysart also designated "bullish" and "bearish penetrations." Originally, Dysart believed PVI would be the more valuable indicator. However, two years prior to his death in 1969, Dysart wrote that NVI had "proved to be the most valuable of all breadth indexes."

According to Schade, Dysart acknowledged that although very accurate early in its implementation, NVI lost its effectiveness in the mid-1960s. Norman G. Fosback attributed the loss of NVI effectiveness to the significant increase in the number of issues added to the

(Chart provided by George A. Schade, Jr., CMT)

Figure 18.4   The NVI of Dow Jones Industrials.

exchange over time. To help overcome this issue, John A. Carder, CMT substituted the exchange volume with the volume of the Dow Jones Industrial Average. Using the data from the average seemed to rectify the issue. Today, I suggest you might employ cap-weighted index volume for the purest results of the computation. You can learn more about this innovation in Chapter 19, "Buff Up Your Volume: Introducing Capital Weighted Volume."

Arms Index/TRIN

Next, as computers made the mathematics easier to compute, different types of breadth statistics were calculated as ratios, allowing market technicians to further glean additional information about the internal health of the market. By far the most popular of such ratios is the Arms Index, named after its innovative developer, Richard Arms. It may also be known as the short-term timing index or the TRIN (its quotron symbol comes from TR for trade and IN for index).

The Arms index is not an index per say but a ratio of two ratios. The first ratio is the number of issues up divided by the number of issues down. That ratio is then divided by the volume in those rising issues versus the volume in the falling issues, thus forming the Arms Index ratio.

Arms Index = [Advances/Decliners] / [Up Volume/Down Volume]

Originally, Arms designed the index to forecast intraday movements of the market. Arms realized early in his career that although some stocks diverge from the primary trend of the market, most stocks generally follow the market. Thus, to Richard Arms, buying at the right time was more important than buying the right stocks. Arms' goal was to identify the market's direction and identify intraday buying points. To do so, Arms believed that if the market was to move higher, the stocks presently moving higher should receive the majority of the volume. Likewise, should the market move lower, the falling stocks should receive the higher volume. Overall, healthy markets should be accompanied by volume increasing at a stronger rate than the index components. An Arms ratio of 1 indicates a state of equilibrium, whereas, an Arms ratio of 0.5 reveals that the stocks rising have double the volume of the decliners. A ratio of 2 means the stocks declining are receiving twice the volume of those declining. Thus, the indicator differs from most other indicators in that it is bullish when it is low or falling and bearish when high or rising.

Used as an intraday tool, the Arms index is a useful ratio. With the click of the Arms' ticker symbol, you can obtain a continuous and dynamic read on the present flow of assets into and out of the market. You could also then chart the intraday movements of the ratio to detect any changes in the Arms' trend and compare them to those of the underlying index or exchange. This information might be useful in spotting intraday purchase and sale points. A market could be declining while the Arms index is falling, confirming the bearish trend. However, if the declining trend persists and the Arms index begins to fall, you might conclude the declining issues no longer receive their share of volume. Such a divergence can be a signal of a potential turn in the market's direction. These divergences are of particular importance when the ratio is at extremes.

Although the Arms index was designed as a shorter-term timing tool, it did not take long for others to find other applications. It appeared rational to use the data in the same manner as the breadth statistics. Richard Russell extended the data into longer time frames and used a 21-day moving average. Martin E. Zweig popularized a method of identifying extremes using a 10-day average all designed to look at different scales of trin. Other popular uses include a 4- or 5-day moving average and a 55-day moving average. A variety of bands are placed upon the Arms index readings may vary upon the time scale to identify overbought and oversold extremes.

However, it is the opinion of this analyst that the Arms index is best utilized for what Mr. Arms originally had intended, a short-term, intra-day indicator. This opinion is not based on the Arms Index daily informational readings, but rather on how the information is composed and manipulated. The Arms index is a ratio computed logarithmically, not arithmetically. This method of computation by definition creates an issue of scale. The ratio can be infinitely high, but only so low.

This methodology becomes a crucial issue when combining the data with other techniques, such as moving averages. To illustrate this point, let us go back to a prior Arms Index example and compose a two-day moving average. An Arms index of .5 indicates that twice as much volume flowed into the advancing issues as declining issues. An Arms index of 2 indicates that twice as much volume flowed into the declining issues compared to the advancing issues. An Arms Index of 1 indicates equilibrium; however, the average between the two days is 1.25 ([(.5 + 2) / 2]), imparting a downward bias.

I believe the first person to address the need for a better smoothing issue was market technician John R. McGinley, CMT in 1978. McGinley proposed a mathematical solution of using anti-logs (exponents) to turn the Arms Index ratio back into a number. Since then, there have been a variety of Arms Index knockoffs, such as The Open Arms Index developed by Harvey Wilbur and popularized by Peter G. Eliades, and the modified Arms Index.

There are a countless number of combinations you can devise to build breadth indicators, so I cannot discuss them all, but I highlight a few that may be of value.

The McClellan Oscillator

In the 1960s, the Advance-Decline Line saw a big rise in its popularity after chartists like Richard Russell and Joseph E. Granville had pointed out the divergence it showed in 1961, just ahead of the big bear market of 1962. One of the people who embraced this tool was the late Peter N. Haurlan, publisher of the "Trade Levels Report." Prior to publishing his newsletter, Haurlan worked as rocket scientist for the Jet Propulsion Laboratories in Pasadena, CA, helping to plan unmanned space probe missions to the outer planets.

At night, when the JPL computer was not in use, Haurlan was able to track the stock market using spacecraft tracking techniques, including the use of exponential moving averages (EMAs). EMAs were used in missile guidance systems as a way of filtering position and heading inputs to adjust flight controls. The advantage of an EMA is that the signal processor needs to keep track of only two variables: the input data and the prior EMA value. The new EMA value changes based on how far the input variable is away from the old EMA value, and it moves fast or slow depending on the "smoothing constant." A 10 percent smoothing constant, for example, produces a 19-period EMA.

A simple moving average, by comparison, requires the calculation based on keeping track of all of the values contained in the lookback period. For a 50-period moving average, that means keeping track of 50 different numbers, which was hard for the old analog computers to deal with.

In his newsletter, Haurlan featured A-D statistics and included values for the 10 percent Trend (19-day EMA) of the daily A-D difference and the 5 percent Trend (39-day EMA). Haurlan liked to look at those independently.

Sherman and Marian McClellan developed a key insight in 1968 when they wondered what it would mean to look at the difference between the 10 percent Trend and 5 percent Trend of the daily advance-decline difference. Finding the answer was not easy considering personal computers did not exist in the 1960s, making historical data difficult to obtain. All of the calculations had to be done by hand and then plotted with a pencil on graph paper. They announced their findings to the world in 1969 on Gene Morgan's television show

"Charting the Market," which appeared in Los Angeles on KWHY. The appearance led to Peter Haurlan publishing the book *Patterns For Profit* in 1970. It was Gene Morgan who coined the term McClellan Oscillator to describe the difference between those two EMAs.

The McClellan Oscillator is a useful indicator because it describes the acceleration that takes place in the breadth numbers. A positive or negative value gives a simplistic bullish or bearish statement about the short-term trend of the market, but there is much more information available. Very low readings show oversold conditions that are usually conclusive at the end of a decline. Very high readings show over-bought conditions but also signal the strength needed to continue a new up move. Divergences are also important to look for as a sign that the strength of a trend is waning.

A companion tool to the McClellan Oscillator is the Summation Index. Anyone who took calculus may remember integrating the area underneath a curve, and that is what the Summation Index does to the plot of the McClellan Oscillator. The Summation Index changes each day by the value of the McClellan Oscillator, either positive or negative. It rises and falls with the market's overall trend and has been adopted as a primary tool by many technical analysts.

One of the problems that the McClellans did not foresee back in the 1960s was an expansion in the number of issues traded on the NYSE. To grapple with that change, and its effects on the amplitudes of the McClellan Oscillator and Summation Index, the McClellans implemented a "ratio-adjusted" calculation technique to factor out the number of issues traded. You can get more details about the specific math involved at their web site www.mcoscillator.com.

The Ratio Adjusted Summation Index (RASI) is a particularly useful indicator for intermediate term market trend following (see Figure 18.5).

When it gets down below –500 and turns up, it gives a nice low risk entry point for the next advance. And if it is able to climb up above +500, then it shows sufficient strength to continue the advance. The McClellans refer to this as "escape velocity," in a nod to Peter Haurlan's work with rockets back in the 1960s. Failing to climb up above +500 is a sign that the rally is weak and that the prior lows are likely to be retested or even exceeded.

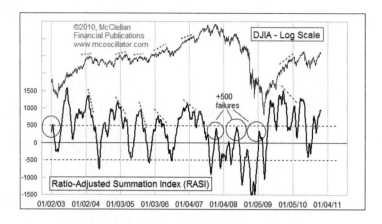

(Source: Tom McClellan, McClellan Financial Publications, Mcoscillator.com.)

Figure 18.5   RASI (Ratio Adjusted Summation Index).

The McClellans also like to calculate these same indicators using the difference between Up Volume and Down Volume (UV-DV), to create the McClellan Volume Oscillator and McClellan Volume Summation Index. Sherman and Marian McClellan's son Tom, editor of the *McClellan Market Report* and *Daily Edition* says that watching the volume versions of these indicators can help to confirm or refute what is happening in the A-D versions. For example, if the McClellan A-D Oscillator goes up through zero but the Volume Oscillator does not, then that is a warning sign that the apparent rally might not be genuine (see Figure 18.6).

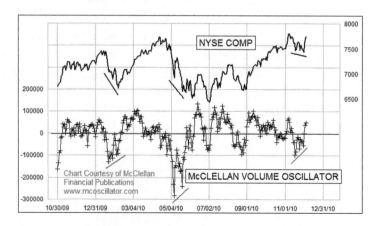

(Source: Tom McClellan, McClellan Financial Publications, Mcoscillator.com.)

Figure 18.6   McClellan Volume Oscillator.

19

Buff Up Your Volume: Introducing Capital Weighted Volume

"The significant problems we face cannot be solved at the same level of thinking we were at when we created them."
—*Albert Einstein*

It's Time to Buff Up Your Volume

Whether an investor listens to the news, reads the paper, or digitally retrieves financial information, the major headline is the price change of the major indexes. The price of the index is the headline; the volume of the index is fortunate to be included in the footnotes. Yet, for those of us digging deeper into these data sets, there exists a more basic problem with the indexes and exchanges of volume data in that it is terribly misleading. Yet every major data provider—Dow Jones, Reuters, Thomson—provides the same virtually worthless volume data. This deceptive index data is distributed to brokerage firms, news providers, and Internet users. This data issue is so significant that I have not used volume data from indexes in my analyses in more than a decade.

Traditional Volume: Price Volume Relationship Disconnect

"As the stock market student progresses in his learning, he finds that relative figures are almost always more useful than raw data (actual figures). The more advance observers thus study, not only actual volume of trading in stock, for a given period, but also the ratio or per cent which that volume represents of the total volume."

—*Harold M. Gartley, 1935*

So what's wrong with the volume data of indexes and exchanges? There is a significant disconnect between the relationship of the price index to the index's volume totals. Yet the central theme conveyed throughout this book is that volume is best understood in relationship to price. With this perspective in mind, it is important to understand the differences between how price indexes and volume totals are compiled. Prices indexes are calculated through summing the individual performance of each component member in accordance with its weighting within the index. Many methods exist to determine this weighting, including capitalization, equal weighting, revenue, dividend weighting, and an endless array of other possibilities. Typically, though, weighting is done by market capitalization—how much each company is proportionally worth to the collective whole. A company's capitalization is calculated by multiplying the number of shares available for sale (shares outstanding) times the stock's price. As a result, in a cap-weighted index, the companies that are worth more have a larger pro rata influence on the index. Likewise, the companies with lower values have a smaller pro rata influence on the index.

The corresponding index volume, on the other hand, is not weighted or even indexed. Rather, index volume is a grand total of all the shares traded within the index. This means that the index's price relationship is not proportional to its volume totals. Using an equal-weighted price index does not solve the problem either—not by a long shot. Although each member has an equal price weight, each member does not have an equal volume weight. For example, let's examine two stocks equal in capitalization. Stock 1 trades at $10 per share, and stock 2 at $100 per share. Assuming the two stocks generate equal interest, the lower priced stock should have 10 times the volume of the higher priced stock. A good illustration of this principle is the 2:1 stock split. What happens to the volume? Typically, it doubles.

Herein lies the main issue. The data between index volume totals and price indexes are not homogeneous. Take, for example, a stock in an equal-weighted index that has a 2 percent price increase. This 2 percent change in the equal-weight S&P 500 Index accounts for a .00004 (.02 × 1/500) change in the price index. However, a similar change in volume doubtfully has the same effect. Continuing with the prior example, let's say the volume of the stock increases by 2 percent. Thus, the stock price and volume have both increased by 2 percent. However, it is highly unlikely that the 2 percent proportional increase in stock volume is equally proportional in the S&P 500 Index's total volume computations. This is because the S&P 500 Index volume is a simple tally of all 500 individual components' volume added together. What is even worse, typically the displayed S&P 500 volume is not the S&P 500 volume at all but actually the volume of all NYSE listed issues.

Keeping with our example, if the stock with the 2 percent change in price and volume is a high-volume, low-price stock, a tiny bopper, the stock's daily volume could represent a disproportionably large percentage of the total volume of the index. If this stock represents 1 percent of the index's total volume, the stock's 2 percent change in volume would equate to a .0002 (.02 * .01) effect on the total volume. That compares to the same 2 percent price move accounting for only a .00004 change in the price index. Thus, the 2 percent change in price and volume in the stock accounts for a five times greater effect on the index's volume than the index's price change. In this way, the equal-weighted index is equally weighted with regard to price but not proportionally weighted with regard to volume. Thus, what one ends up with in equal-weighted price indexes is an unequal representation in volume. Whether the price index is equal or cap-weighted, or any other form of price weighted, generally the lower priced stocks with larger volume have an unrepresentative higher influence on the volume totals, whereas the higher priced stocks with lower volume have a significantly lower and unrepresentative proportional influence.

Dollar volume, the share price multiplied by the volume, somewhat assists low-priced stock issues but does nothing to address the weighting discrepancies.

Blue Chips to Cow Chips

Nowhere has this index volume problem been more obvious than in the effects of the credit crisis of 2008. Some have coined this crisis the blue-chip-to-cow-chip phenomenon because some formerly large blue chip stocks have fallen to relative obscurity through the events of the credit crisis. Obvious examples are Fannie Mae, Freddie Mac, Bank of America, American International Group, and Citigroup. Formerly, these stocks had a huge capital-weighted influence on the price movements of the indexes. However, at the time of this writing, these stocks trade at a small fraction of their pre-credit crisis levels. Typical cow chip stocks lost 90 percent of their value. Yet, what has happened to their market volume? Because of their shrinking size and new share issuance, these issues' volume has soared by 500 percent or more.

An example of the blue-chip-to-cow chip phenomenon is seen in the effects of the credit crisis on Citigroup versus Exxon. In 2007, Exxon traded at $90 and represented 3.8 percent of the S&P 500 based on its capitalization. At the same time, Citigroup traded at $50 and represented 1.72 percent of the S&P 500. However, on May 25, 2010, Exxon traded at $60 while its capital weighting had dropped to 3 percent of the S&P 500. Thus, Exxon's influence on the S&P 500 price index dropped by 21 percent. In contrast, Citigroup traded at $3.65 and only represented .792 percent of the S&P 500 price index, and its price influence on the index dropped by nearly 54 percent.

Now let's contrast the volume of these two prominent stocks after the credit crisis. In a typical 2007 pre-credit crisis day, the S&P 500 components traded about 3 billion shares per day, of which 27 million were Citigroup shares exchanging hands. In contrast, Exxon typically traded 18 million shares a day in 2007. At the time of this writing, Exxon traded 50 million shares and closed at 59.71. Thus, Exxon's volume was up 177 percent from pre-credit crisis average levels, while its stock price was down 33.6 percent from the same point. Citigroup traded a whopping 238 million shares, and its price adjusted for splits was down 90 percent. However, Citigroup's volume was up 881 percent from typical 2007 levels!

Figure 19.1   Cow chips happen.

At the time, Exxon's S&P 500 Index weighting represented 3 percent; thus, its price change represented a 3 percent contribution to the price index. However, 7.3 billion shares traded in the S&P 500 component stocks on this date, which made Exxon's representation only .68 percent of the S&P 500 total volume. Therefore, Exxon—the second largest price component of the S&P 500—represented only a small fraction of the volume totals. In contrast, Citigroup's price accounted for only a .792 percent weighting in the S&P 500 Index. Yet its volume accounted for 3.26 percent of the S&P 500's volume totals. Thus, Citigroup's price change represented less than 1 percent of the price index, whereas its volume represented over 3 percent of the index's volume totals. Thus, Citigroup's volume data had nearly five times the influence on total volume data as Exxon's. But Exxon's price influence was nearly four times as large as Citigroup's! Through this example, you can easily see how the present volume-tallying methods present an unequal and completely distorted picture!

"Do you deal in red or blue chips?"

"Mostly brown."

Figure 19.2   Brown chips.

Although this illustration is of the S&P 500 capital-weighted index, the same issue occurs in all the volume data being reported on every index. In addition, this same problem with volume data exists in all exchange volumes, including NYSE, AMEX, and Nasdaq. This is because the traditional way to report volume is through total volume tallies.

Index Volume Analysis Alternatives

Because of the severely distorted data, I have not used exchange or index volume in my broad market analysis in more than a decade.

Instead, I formerly used the exchange-traded fund (ETF) data of the broad market and major sectors and industry groups in my volume analysis. Although this represents a major improvement, it is far from perfect. It is better because each unit traded in the ETF represents a buyer and seller exchanging a weighted and proportionally adjusted unit of the index, thereby avoiding the problem of smaller high-volume, low cap-weighted stocks overweighting the larger low-volume, high cap-weighted issues. I used only the major, most active ETFs to avoid misrepresentations that frequently occur in the less liquid ETFs.

However, using ETF volume data was far from a perfect solution. One problem is that many indexes have multiple ETF alternatives. The larger problem, however, is that this method assumes the activity in the components' underlying shares is being replicated in the ETF trading. Although this is typically preferred over the total volume method of analysis in indexes and exchanges, it is not an accurate assumption. In addition, this method also lacks visibility in that you cannot observe from the origin of the volume flow. Is it from the higher weighted price components or the lower? More important, is the volume coming from stocks moving up or moving down? This is impossible to ascertain from the ETF volume alone. However, such information is vital in breadth analysis.

Cap-Weighted Volume

"The reasonable man adapts himself to the world; the unreasonable one persists in trying to adapt the world to himself. Therefore, all progress depends on the unreasonable man."

—*George Bernard Shaw*

So what's a market analyst to do? The solution I have devised is capital-weighted volume. Cap-weighted volume weights each individual issue's volume according to the issue's price-capital weighting in the underlying index or exchange. Thus, if a company is a larger, more influential component, then its corresponding volume is reflected pro rata in accordance with the component member's larger size. Likewise, a small insignificant company's volume is also reflected pro rata in accordance with its smaller size. In this way, a component's volume is equally represented with respect to its cap-weighted price influence on the index or exchange. The following six steps will allow you to buff up your index volume:

Capital-Weighted Volume

Step 1: Calculate market capital.

Market Capital = Stock's Price (Close or Current Price) × Number of Shares Outstanding

Step 2: Calculate index/exchange total market capital.

Index or Exchange Total Market Capital = Sum of All Members' Market Capital

Step 3: Calculate each stock's capital weighting.

Individual Stock's Capital Weighting = Stock's Market Capital / Total Market Capital Index or Exchange

Step 4: Calculate stock's capital-weighted volume.

Individual Stock's Capital Weighting × Volume (Closing or Current)

Step 5: Calculate index/exchange capital-weighted volume.

Index or Exchange Capital-Weighted Volume = Sum of All Individual Stock's Capital Weightings

Step 6: Recalculate index or exchange capital-weighted volume with price index change backed out.

Capital-Weighted Volume Index × –1 × (Index's price change)

Comparing Traditional Volume Tallies to Cap-Weighted Volume

"And this is important—the percentage relationship provides a means of recognizing instantly any unusual activity (volume) in a stock."

—*Edwin S. Quinn, 1935*

"You never said your 50,000 shares were penny ones!"

Figure 19.3   Don't be fooled by the penny ones.

Let's return to the previous example of Citigroup and Exxon. To review, pre-credit crisis, Exxon's price represented 3.8 percent of the S&P 500 Index's price movement. Exxon's volume represented only .6 percent of the index's total volume. Similarly, Citigroup's price represented 1.7 percent of the price index and .9 percent of the total volume. At the time, Exxon was the biggest component of the S&P 500, but its volume only accounted for .6 percent of the volume total. Citigroup was the fifth biggest S&P 500 component but represented only .9 percent of the volume total. However, with cap-weighted volume, Exxon's typical volume of 18 million shares would have a cap-weighted proportional influence on the index of 3.8 percent. If Exxon's volume soared or fell by 50 percent, its volume change would be reflected by its 3.8 percent capitalization weighting in the index in the same way as price component changes. Citigroup's capital-weighting volume would be equal to its equity capital weighting of 1.7 percent of the S&P 500 Index. In this way, the cap-weighting method proportionally harmonizes each index's volume contributions with its respective capital price weightings.

Let's return to our example of Exxon and Citigroup for comparison purposes. This time, we look at the post-credit crisis date of May 25, 2010. On this day, Exxon represented 3 percent of the S&P 500 Index and traded 50.5 million shares. That compares to its average volume of 28 million shares during the previous several months. So on that day, Exxon had a strong volume surge of 77 percent. Likewise, on the same day, Citigroup's volume surged by 40 percent to 238 million shares from a normalized 170 million shares.

However, using the archaic total-volume method, Exxon's influence on the volume tallies that day was a mere .7 percent of the total S&P 500 volume. Using the improved cap-weighted volume data restored Exxon's full cap weighting of 3 percent. Thus, Exxon's cap-weighted volume represented 3 percent of the total cap-weighted volume as compared to only .7 percent of traditional index volume—more than a 400 percent improvement! Citigroup's volume of 238 million shares represented 3.3 percent of the traditional volume totals. However, using cap-weighted volume harmonized Citigroup's volume relative to its small .792 cap weighting—this time reducing Citigroup's volume influence by more than 400 percent from traditional volume tallies of the S&P 500! The total volume of all the S&P 500 components was 7.2 billion shares on that day as compared to an average volume of 6.3 billion shares, up 15 percent. However, calculating the relative index volume change on a cap-weighted volume basis revealed that volume was up more than 25 percent!

Flash Crash: Cap-Weighted Volume in Action

> "Remember that the relative changes in volume are far more important than the actual changes, because all during an active period, the trading in almost every stock is increased."
>
> —*Harold M. Gartley and Edwin S. Quinn, 1935*

Not only does cap-weighted data offer a more accurate representation, but it also allows us to track the actions of institutions better. Large institutions have difficultly trading smaller stock because of their influence on price when establishing or exiting a position. If an institution wants to liquidate or accumulate, it might first unload big liquid stocks to avoid spooking the market. A perfect example of cap-weighted volume in action comes from the days leading up to the "Flash Crash." On May 6, 2010, the market made history: The Dow Jones Industrial Average plunged nearly 1,000 points and sent the market into chaos as the biggest one-day point loss ever. However, cap-weighted volume gave strong hints that something was suspicious prior to the market's dislocation. Using traditional data, April 16, 2010, was a typical down day. The S&P 500 was down 19.5 points (–1.6 percent) with NYSE shares trading 1.75 billion shares, the Nasdaq composite losing 34.4 points (–1.35 percent) on shares of 2.89 billion. The volume change represented an increase from the 30-day exponential average of the NYSE of +36.5 percent and on the Nasdaq composite of 17 percent. Overall, it was a slow news day with commentators struggling to find headlines.

However, the cap-weighted volume cast a completely different picture. On April 16, the S&P 500 cap-weighted volume set an all-time volume record. Viewing volume from this cap-weighted perspective, volume increased by a whopping 45 percent from the 30-day cap-weighted volume exponential average, a record held to this day. To put that into context, the total volume (not cap-weighted) of the NYSE during the Flash Crash was the second highest volume day ever, up 47 percent from its 30-day exponential average volume. However, cap-weighted volume was up only 43 percent during the Flash Crash. The cap-weighted volume on the Nasdaq composite was up 53 percent compared to 17 percent with traditional Nasdaq volume, and the Nasdaq 100 changed even more, up 55 percent from its 30-day exponential moving average. These activities on April 16 were a shot across the bow, warning that big institutions were aggressively selling their largest and most highly liquid holdings (see Figures 19.4, 19.5, and 19.6).

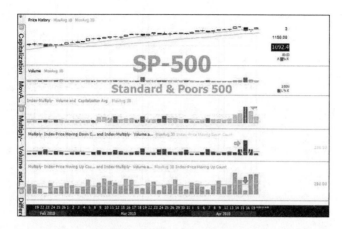

(Chart [or data] produced by TeleChart 2007® or StockFinder®, which is a registered trademark of Worden Brothers, Inc., Five Oaks Office Park, 4905 Pine Cone Drive, Durham, NC 27707. Ph. (800) 776-4940 or (919) 408-0542. www.Worden.com.)

Figure 19.4   S&P 500 cap-weighted volume versus NYSE traditional volume tallies.

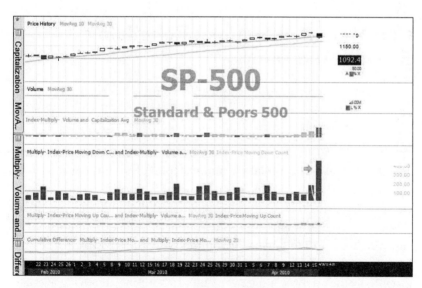

(Chart [or data] produced by TeleChart 2007® or StockFinder®, which is a registered trademark of Worden Brothers, Inc., Five Oaks Office Park, 4905 Pine Cone Drive, Durham, NC 27707. Ph. (800) 776-4940 or (919) 408-0542. www.Worden.com.)

Figure 19.5   Total Nasdaq cap-weighted volume versus total volume April 16, 2010.

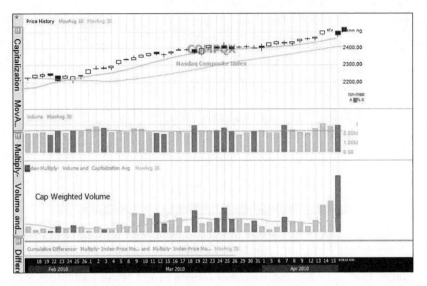

Figure 19.6   S&P 500 cap-weighted volume on April 16 versus Flash Crash on May 6 (2010).

Cap-Weighted Volume: Rebuilding Breadth Indicators

Like total volume, capital-weighted volume can be used to form any variety of market breadth indicators. Using April 16 again as an example, downside volume was more than 90 percent of upside volume (see Figure 19.7).

One can also accumulate a running total of upside versus downside volume. If the upside/downside ratio is positive, more volume comes into stocks that appreciate, whereas if the number is negative, there is stronger volume in the stocks that depreciate. An uptrend of cap-weighted upside/downside volume reveals a growth of the volume of stocks appreciating, whereas a downtrend exposes the volume growth of stock depreciating over time. In addition, a moving average can be applied to provide indications of momentum and suggest changes in trend. Using the prior example of the Flash Crash, cap-weighted upside/downside volume crossed under its 19-day and 29-day exponential moving averages on Monday, May 3, three days before the Flash Crash. The 19 and 29 days represent a modified McClellan oscillator of cap-weighted upside/downside volume. That indicator gave a warning signal on May 5, one day before the event (see Figure 19.8).

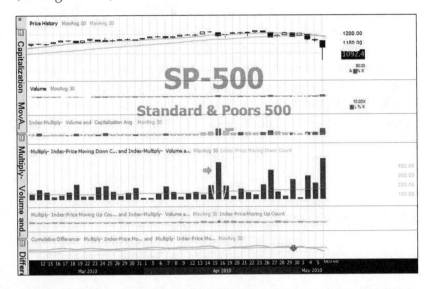

(Chart [or data] produced by TeleChart 2007® or StockFinder®, which is a registered trademark of Worden Brothers, Inc., Five Oaks Office Park, 4905 Pine Cone Drive, Durham, NC 27707. Ph. (800) 776-4940 or (919) 408-0542. www.Worden.com.)

Figure 19.7   Cap-weighted volume upside versus downside volume on April 16, 2010.

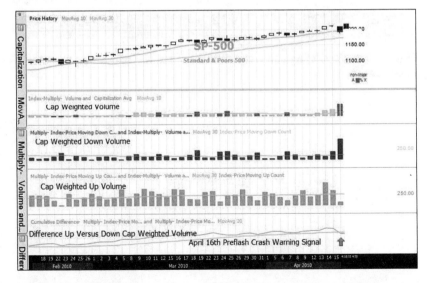

Figure 19.8   Pre Flash Crash warning subtracting cap weighted up versus down volume.

As you can surmise, any combination using index volume totals can be effective with cap-weighted volume. For equity indexes containing operating companies only, the methodology is perfect. However, exchange composites likely to contain preferreds, closed-end funds, tracking stocks, and multiclass issues are subject to similar distortion issues associated with nonoperating companies. In keeping longer term cap-weighted volume tallies, I suggest keeping the running totals accumulated one year or less as the secular growth in volume can distort the data during longer periods of time.

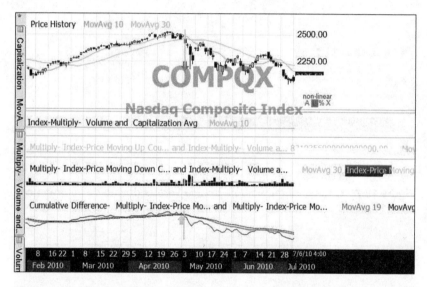

Figure 19.9   McClellan cap weighted volume of Nasdaq warns prior to Flash Crash.

20

Risky Business

"Every bet that we make involves a trade-off based on a decision to pay or risk something of value for the uncertain prospect of gain. Placing winning bets in investing, as in life, therefore, requires the development of a strategic ability to make better bets between and among financial and non-financial outcomes. Where most of us tend to trip up, often unwittingly, is when we fail to grasp the complete extent and true nature of tradeoffs implicit in what always comes down to choices."

—*Larry Hite, Hedge fund manager Market Wizards*

The Best Offense Is a Good Defense

Throughout this text, I have equipped you with the training and tools to prepare for battle. Now it is time to discuss our opponent. The market has been crowned the eternal heavyweight champion of the world by the advocates of efficient market theory, random walkers, academia, and the media. This is not without good reason. In going up against the market, you are going up against some stiff competition. If you do not respect the market, you'll likely end up on the canvas. The best offense against this juggernaut is a good defense. In this chapter, I discuss the two pillars of establishing a prevent defense: money and risk management.

I once attended a conference/ski trip in Breckenridge, Colorado. Because I am from the Midwest, my ski experiences were limited to the cool summer waters of the northern Indiana lakes. I was inexperienced at snow skiing and overly confident as an athlete—not a good combination when you're a mile high on a mountain range.

There were plenty of courses from which to choose. At first, I chose a beginners course. It was nice and easy and, by the time I navigated to the bottom, I was an expert skier, or so I thought. My next choice of courses was the black diamond; it just sounded like fun! As the lift took me up and up the mountain, I became less confident of my slope selection. But once I was up there, there was only one way down. So I started down the mountain. It was extremely steep, which allowed me to gain considerable speed. As I flew down the mountain, I saw another skier not going down the mountain vertically as I was, but across the mountain horizontally. Going laterally across such a steep mountain slope was a skill I was not even aware was attainable. This brought up a significant problem. I needed not be a market technician to see our two trend lines were about to align. Although I thought of myself as a good skier, I had one glaring weakness that was quite evident even on the beginners slope—I had not learned how to stop. Traveling at a high rate of speed, I decided to just fall down. Unfortunately, all that did was slow me down, and not much.

Now on the ground and rapidly falling down the mountain, I intersected the other skier. Fortunately for her, she skied right over me as if I were just another mogul. Still traveling at a high speed, I hit some sort of natural rock ramp and flew into the air. I landed and rolled down the mountain until I eventually stopped. I may have been knocked out for a short while. When I looked up, four men were standing over me. I saw the snow was red. I surmised the red snow came from the blood flowing from my forehead. As circumstances would have it, these men were all surgeons. "Wow, that was quite a spill," said one of the doctors. Another advised me, "You'd better get some stitches." Another said, "No, that one's going to require staples." The third doc said, "I'd use this new glue technique." Then the fourth doctor told me, "You'll be alright; just go to the medical tent and get yourself checked out." I intended to take the fourth doctor's advice, but when I arrived at the medical tent, I received an enormous stack of disclaimers to fill out, as opposed to treatment. I spent the next 10 minutes bleeding out while making only a small dent in the paperwork. By this time, I had figured out that I'd better stop the bleeding myself and get checked out later. I did the first part, but I never returned to the medical tent or to the black diamond.

Investors are all too familiar with disasters of a similar nature. Following the bull market of the 1980s and '90s, the market hit its own bump, wiping out millions of overly optimistic investors who took too much risk without an exit plan. Many investors are making the same mistakes I did on the mountain. They are biting off more than they can chew. In other words, they lack money-management skills. Also, they do not know how or when to stop; they lack risk-management skills. These investors headed down the big market mountain of 2000 unprepared and unaware of the lurking dangers. As they progressed down their black diamond path, they found they couldn't stop. Without money or risk-management skills, they too got knocked out.

The Best and the Worst of It

"When you think that a company is too good and the earning are too strong for it to go down, that's when you'll have your head handed to you."

—*Dan Zanger, Chartpatterns.com*

How did investors find themselves on the edge of the black diamond called Investors' Leap? In the wake of the 1990s' secular bull market, investors were advised not to miss out. Many experts pointed out that if you miss the best days in the market, your returns will drop substantially. As a result, time in the market was advocated over cautiously gauging of the market.

"Investor's leap? That's further up!"

Figure 20.1   Investor's leap.

Let's take this idea to task. We'll start with the idea that time in the market is better than timing the market. In a 1999 article, "Missing the Ten Best," Paul J. Gire, CFP pointed to the common practice of the mutual fund industry to encourage buy-and-hold investing. Through a message of "don't miss the 10 best days," advisors and mutual funds reminded investors that the market from 1984 through 1998 realized an annualized rate of return of 17.89 percent. However, if investors missed the top 10 best days, performance fell to only 14.24 percent. If they missed the best 20, performance return fell to 11.99 percent. Missing the best 30 resulted in a return of 10.01 percent, and missing the best 40 meant a yield of only 8.23 percent. However, these numbers tell only half the story. Mr. Gire pointed out that excluding the best days while not including missing the worst days "could be construed as an ethical violation of the CFP Board's Code of Ethics." So what are these unreported findings? If investors missed both the 10, 20, 30, and 40 best and the 10, 20, 30, and 40 worst days, performance jumps to slightly over 20 percent during all the time periods cited in the study (see Figure 20.2).

So is the conventional wisdom of discounting the decision of when to buy reliable? If you had invested in the Nasdaq on the close of business December 31, 1999, and held until December 31, 2009, your cumulative return would have been –44.23 percent. To break even by 2015, you would need to average a gain of 8.84 percent per year. However, if you bailed and reinvested in a Treasury note paying 2.95 percent, you would not break even until 2025. If you were one of the unfortunate investors to buy the Dow in September 1929, you would have waited 25 years (November 1954) to see the Dow reach its 1929 peaks. Now, these examples contrast diversified groups of stocks. When you consider individual stock selection, the stakes are significantly higher. An investor who bought Cisco on January 1, 1998, and held to January 1, 2000, would have experienced a 64 percent gain. On the other hand, an investor who bought Cisco on January 1, 2000, and held to January 1, 2002, would have experienced a 65 percent loss. Any investor with just a bit of experience investing over the past decade can list many more such examples.

# Of Trading Days Missed	Best	Worst	Both
10 days	14.24%	24.17%	20.31%
20 days	11.99%	27.04%	20.68%
30 days	10.01%	29.45%	20.80%
40 days	8.23%	31.66%	20.87%

(Source: Missing the Ten Best.)

Figure 20.2   Missing the best, worst, and both.

The Buy and Hope Strategy

Professor Jeremy J. Segal, in his 1994 book *Stocks for the Long Run,* correctly states that equities have the highest returns and are the only major asset class that has not lost money over a 30-year cycle. Others who believe in the efficient market theory and random walk promoted the idea of abandoning active management for "low-expense" index funds and exchange-traded funds (ETF). Thus, according to many experts, the best an investor can do is concentrate investments in low-cost equity index funds and ride the rollercoaster with their seatbelt tightly fastened. In other words, the popular strategy was to avoid both money and risk management.

"The market was very volatile today."

Figure 20.3   Volatile markets.

Believing that over the long term equities generate somewhere between 8 percent and 10 percent return, it was widely assumed that an investor could live relatively safely off a 5 percent draw from his or her investments. How this investment turns out largely depends on the investor's need for income. Take an example of two investors looking to retire. Both investors have saved $1 million for retirement and invest in the same S&P 500 index fund. However, one investor decides he is ready for retirement in 2000, whereas the other targets 2010 as a retirement goal. The first investor retired on January 1, 2000, and took a 5 percent draw off his original $1 million investment. This created an income stream of $50k per year for our retired investor. When the second investor reaches his retirement date of June 30, 2010, the previously retired investor would only have $297,040 left of his original million. This represents a cumulative time-weighted return of negative 24.47 percent or negative 2.64 percent annualized. At this rate, the retired investor will be broke in less than six years. If the retired investor decided to recalibrate his 5 percent draw based on his present balance, it would reduce his income from $50k per year to just $15k per year.

"A small investor to see you. He says you know
him, he use to be a large investor."

Figure 20.4   Be defensive.

Meanwhile, the unretired investor who began with a $1 million
portfolio on January 1, 2000, and then dollar cost averaged an additional
$50,000 a year into the index fund until June 30, 2010, would have
invested a total of $1.525 million. As of June 30, this investor would
have $1.319 million for retirement. This equates to only a 16.24 percent
cumulative time-weighted loss, or –1.67 percent annualized return.
Why the difference? The working investor was able to dollar cost average into the market, buying more shares while the market was down.
However, the retired investor was doing the opposite. To meet his
income needs, the investor had to sell more shares at lower values.
Although the buy-and-hold approach might work better for those not
needing income, those who view their portfolios as an income source or
a supplement to income might not be able to afford such risks.

One way to approach this problem is money management. In
1990, Harry Markowitz won the Nobel Prize in economics for his
work with asset allocation. Markowitz's work proved that the simultaneous rebalancing of a portfolio of high-risk assets with inverse correlations increased return while reducing risk. This discovery refuted
the long-held belief that high-risk assets can only increase the risk
inherent in a portfolio. Although I am not holding my breath for any
calls from Oslo, I have also demonstrated that volume analysis allevi-
ates this same paradox. By combining both asset allocation and

volume analysis, we can hope to build a money management system capable of better managing the inherent risks of a portfolio.

Dynamic Asset Allocation

"Every gambler knows that the secret to surviving is knowing what to throw away and knowing what to keep."
—*Kenny Rogers*

As a risk-averse money manager, I use and advocate a dynamic, active asset allocation process. For my portfolios, diversification is accomplished through a four-dimensional strategic allocation process.

The first diversification dimension is position allocation. Position allocation is the most basic form of portfolio allocation—diversifying between different issuers. The most important part of position allocation is position sizing. An investor can "put all his eggs in one basket" or diversify into a multiple of individual issues. Position size should be determined on a percentage of one's capital basis.

People have different views about luck. I know only one thing about luck; mine is bad. For example, this past year, McDonald's had a Final Four scratch-off game on each large cup of unsweetened iced tea. You could choose to scratch one of two basketballs. One of the balls had a prize, the other had "Sorry, try again." Thus, there was a 50/50 chance of winning. I lost six times in a row. The odds of that are 1 in 64. The seventh time, I won, but only because I had given my ticket to my wife to scratch. I have learned not to participate in gambling, lotteries, and raffles, and I refuse to draw straws. I lose. But don't get me wrong, I am extremely blessed. It is as if the good Lord is telling me that he has given me enough wisdom that I am not to leave anything to chance. As a portfolio manager, bad luck can become a serious drawback. I might have 10 stocks all equally meeting my rigorous buy criteria, but only room for 5 stocks in the allowable 2 percent position size. Given my bad luck, what will I do? I'll buy all 10 stocks with a 1 percent position size. I believe it is not so much the securities you pick that will make you rich or poor, but the process you employ. The more you invest in any one company, the more you place your faith in that particular investment and the less you place your faith in your process for investing.

"You're annoyed aren't you that I made more at bingo last year than you did on the stock market."

Figure 20.5   Bingo cartoon.

Rarely, though, do securities appear to be 100 percent equal in their potential. If I have a higher or lower conviction level, then position size might be increased or decreased to allow the over- and underweighting of securities. Equity strategist Doug Sandler sees position allocation the same way he sees managing a professional sports team. Like an investor, a professional sports team has only so much money to spend, a salary cap. The team consists of all-stars, starters, rookies, and a disabled list. An important decision in money management is deciding how much to "spend" in each of these categories. For instance, you might choose to allocate 40 percent of your portfolio to all-stars, stocks that embody your best and most reliable investments ideas. Thirty percent might be dedicated to starters, your core holding. Another 15 percent might be appropriated to rookies, stocks that have potential but are unproven. The final 15 percent might be allocated to the disabled list, stocks that are currently underperforming. The next decision is to determine the position size of issues in each category. As all-stars garner more attention, they might represent a larger position size, such as 5 percent. Thus, such a portfolio would contain 8 all-stars, meeting the 40 percent (5x8) weighting of the category. A 3 percent position size for stars allows for 10 core holdings to meet the 30 percent target. A 1.5 percent position size allows for 10 disabled stocks and 10 new positions, each meeting the 10 percent. In this way, you can overweight the stocks in which you have more confidence while maintaining the discipline of a balanced and diversified portfolio.

The second diversification dimension to be further applied is horizontal allocation, investing among different market sectors. Although many believe it is appropriate to have exposure in each of the 10 major S&P sectors (energy, industrials, financials, and so on), equity investors might seek to produce excess returns through over- or underweighting equity sectors. A top-down approach to investing would set up target ranges for each sector of the market. Thus, you might choose to have between 10 percent and 15 percent of your portfolio dedicated to industrial issues, while allocating 3 percent to 5 percent toward financials. This approach can be enhanced by further allocating the sector weighting across geographic regions, such as domestic, internationally developed, and developing markets.

A third way of enhancing our diversification dimension is through vertical allocation, allocating our investments among various market capitalizations. Securities can be further diversified among the large mega caps down to small micro caps. Like horizontal diversification, vertical allocation might be accomplished through a conscience top-down effort. If mid caps appear more attractive and large caps appear more vulnerable, you might choose to take 10 percent of the allocation of large caps and add it to the allocation of mid caps.

The fourth diversification dimension of our allocation process is the fusion of multiple performance drivers. Performance drivers are the catalysts that make an individual issue attractive. For a fundamentalist, this might include style, such as biases toward specialized growth or value. For a technician, this might encompass perspectives such as trending or nontrending, as well as other technical approaches. A portfolio should be diversified to minimize the impact of any one performance driver. By employing a multilayer process of performance drivers, you gain exposure to a wider variety of reasons why any one particular issue might outperform. As an example, I use a proprietary tool called VARSITI (Volume Adjusted Relative Strength Increasing Thrust Indicator) to find issues and sectors experiencing relative strength with the volume needed to support the price movement. I can combine this relative strength tool with another tool that looks for issues that are being oversold on weak volume. By combining two catalysts, I hope to minimize the impact of either one going into a prolonged slump.

Through such a multilayer money management approach, you can be assured that your performance is indeed based on your ability to analyze and discern rather than the movements of concentrated positions. Assigning layers of diversification also provides the portfolio manager with more clarity in determining performance factors. However, the main benefit of such hyper diversification is the reduction of risk and more consistent returns.

Risk Management

"I got every license relevant, I took courses from the International Association of Financial Planners. Then I found out none of that taught me to trade."

—*Robert Deel, CEO Tradingschool.com*

Good investors are good winners, while great investors are great losers. This means winning the war sometimes entails losing some battles, retreating, and surviving to reinvest another day. Too often, investors, including professionals, have only a one-sided investment formula that solely focuses on what to buy. However, I believe investment success is much more than making good buy decisions. I see another, equally effective path to investment success. This is through risk management or attempting to minimize the impact of poor decisions.

Risk management might sound complicated; however, the concept is something we all engage in every day. Buying insurance, going to the dentist, locking the doors, getting a tune-up, being polite to the police officer who just unjustly pulled you over are all types of risk management. We endure these sometimes expensive and tedious processes because we recognize that these temporary costs generally lead to fewer headaches and greater prosperity in the long run. These same principles might apply to the risk management of investment portfolios.

When I skied down the black diamond, I made several mistakes: First, I did not know how to stop. Second, I got scared and just fell down. And third, I chose the wrong slope and had no way off. Likewise, risk management discipline should neutralize these same investing issues by first, knowing when to sell; second, controlling your emotions; and third, being aware of opportunity costs.

There are two important parts of investing: the fun part, determining what to buy, and the hard part, determining when to sell. However, knowing when to sell is essential because exits, not entries, determine the outcome of investments. Look at Figure 20.6. Point A is the entry point, and points B through F are possible exit points. Was the investment made at point A a good decision?

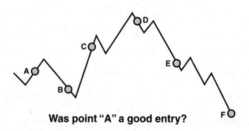

Was point "A" a good entry?

Figure 20.6   Exits determine the outcome of a trade.

It depends on your point of exit. Investors spend much time and effort deciding what stocks to buy, overemphasizing the buy decision, while they underemphasize the sell decision. However, once they decide to purchase, control is no longer in their hands, but in the hands of the market. This lack of control often leads to a lack of discipline. Many investors are happy only when they sell at the very top and enter near the bottom. By nature, people are conservative with winning positions and aggressive with losing positions. In other words, they cut their winners short and allow their losers to run. However, this goes against the laws of compounding (see Table 20.1).

TABLE 20.1   Power of Compounding Lower

If an investor loses ___,	An investor needs approximately ___ to break even.
10%	11%
20%	15%
25%	35%
35%	50%
50%	100%

In contrasting the downward laws of multiplication in Table 20.1 to the laws of compounding in Table 20.2, it is easy to see why savvy investors believe that "winners take care of themselves, losers never do."

TABLE 20.2   Power of Compounding Higher

However, if an investor makes ___, he or she only needs to make approximately ___ to make ___.		
10%	9%	20%
20%	8%	30%
30%	7%	40%
40%	6%	50%

The Anti-Volume Stop Loss

"If I am not in control, I'm always under stress, and I am only in control when I have a stop in the market."

—*Walter Bressert, Publisher HAL Commodity Cycles*

It is important in any risk-management process to predetermine an objective decision point level (a stop loss) to exit, thereby protecting principal in case you are wrong. My objective sell point is determined by using a quantitative formula I refer to as Anti-Volume Stop Loss (AVSL). Having a quantitative, yet intelligent sell point eliminates the emotional struggles involved in deciding when to exit a position. AVSL is a technical methodology that incorporates the concepts of support, volatility, and, most importantly, the inverse relationship between price and volume. The AVSL combines the concepts of the VPCI (Volume Price Confirmation Indicator) and John Bollinger's Bollinger Bands to create a trailing stop loss.

> AVSL = Lower Bollinger Band – (Price, Length, Standard Deviation)

Where:

> Length = Round (3 + VPCI)
>
> Price = Average (Lows × 1 / VPC × 1 / VPR, Length)
>
> Standard Deviation = 2 × (VPCI × VM)

One of the most difficult decisions is determining what one's maximum loss threshold should be. Some say 2 percent; others say 20 percent. I believe the more volatile a security, the looser the stop should be. A nonvolatile security, such as Coca-Cola, might move 7 percent a year, while a volatile security such as Google might move 7 percent in a day. If you use a 7 percent stop for Coca-Cola, it might take a year to be stopped out while the security underperforms. However, if you use 7 percent for Google, you can be stopped out intraday, not allowing the investment an opportunity to develop. By using the lower Bollinger Band of the securities lows, the AVSL considers each individual security's own volatility. Thus, a volatile security would be granted more room of the stocks low while a stable security would have a tighter leash (see Figure 20.7).

The next important step is employing the price-volume relationship into the calculation. Volume gauges the power behind price moves. In accounting for this, when a security is in an uptrend and has positive volume characteristics, it is given more room. However, if the security exhibits contracting volume characteristics, then the stop is tightened. In this way, if a negative news event affects an unhealthy security, the stop is tighter, thus preserving more of your profits. However, if the negative news event affects a security whose price-volume relationship is healthy, the stop has been loosened, avoiding the temporary whipsaw of an otherwise strong position. In these ways, AVSL lets the market decide when to exit your position (see Figure 20.8).

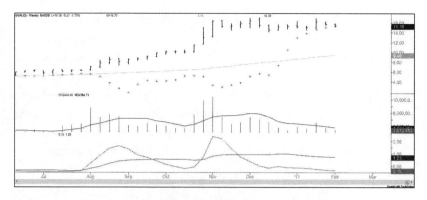

Figure 20.7   AVSL trailing stop. The white dots are the stop points.

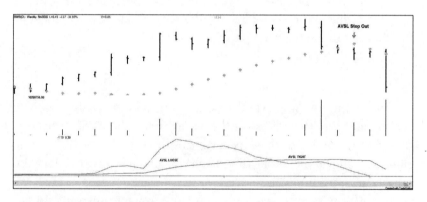

Figure 20.8   Security is stopped out when it closes below the AVSL (white dot).

AVSL tailors each security for support, volatility, and the price-volume relationship based on an investor's time frame as calculated from the chart data. For example, my portfolio positions are continually re-evaluated with this AVSL methodology, which yields the possibility of raising the decision point threshold periodically based on the time frame of my investment objective. With my short-term Giddy-up portfolios, I use daily chart data and seek to raise my maximum loss stop on a daily basis. My intermediate ETF and stock positions are calculated off of weekly data and then re-evaluated weekly. With my longer term stock portfolios, the decision point is calculated off data revised monthly. This analytical approach that uses measurable facts over emotion or gut instincts allows me to maintain my objectivity. Thus objectivity, not emotion, informs my investment decisions.

The Best Mistakes Are the Realized Ones

"A loss never bothers me after I take it. I forget it overnight. But being wrong—not taking the loss—that is what does damage to the pocketbook and to the soul."

—*Jesse L. Livermore*

Inevitably, investors will decide to prune a losing position only to realize later that they did so at the wrong time. The AVSL process is designed to minimize these occurrences; however, over time, occasionally selling at the wrong time is unavoidable. However, selling also creates an opportunity to reinvest. As a risk-averse manager, I will sell underperformers to reinvest in potentially stronger prospects. In this way, building a portfolio can be compared to growing a fruitful garden. A gardener begins by sowing seeds. As the season unfolds, the gardener picks the weeds and waters flowers just as the savvy investor sells losers and reinvests in winning positions.

Finally, some common thoughts and emotions keep investors from admitting their mistakes. These are usually excuses in need of rebuttal, as illustrated in Table 20.3 and Figure 20.9.

It has been said that the difference between a long-term investor and a short-term trader is that a long-term investor is just a short-term trader still holding a long-term loss. The best mistakes are small and quickly realized. The worst mistakes are large and unrealized.

Thus, the key to money management is developing a good investment plan and having the convictions to stick with it. In this, we can take a lesson from Abraham Lincoln. In 1832, Lincoln was defeated for state legislator; in 1833, he failed in business; in 1834, he was elected to Congress; in 1835, he lost his girlfriend; in 1836, he suffered a nervous breakdown; in 1838, he was defeated for speaker; in 1843, he was defeated for Congress; in 1846, he was elected again; in 1848, he lost renomination; in 1854, he was defeated for U.S. Senate; in 1856, he was defeated for Vice President; in 1858, he was defeated for U.S. Senate again; but, in 1860, he was elected President of the United States. Abraham Lincoln started as a lieutenant in the army, but finished as a private. Yet he became one of our nation's greatest leaders because he did not let any of his failures become big enough to bring him down, and he had the courage to maintain his convictions.

TABLE 20.3 Excuses in Need of Rebuttal

Excuse	Rebuttal
One day, it will come back.	You might be down, but not out; stay in the game.
It's only a paper loss.	Whether realized or unrealized, losses are real.
I am down now 20%.	Does the market care about your cost basis?
I might be selling at the wrong time.	Are the reasons you bought still in force?
It can't get any worse.	Preserve your capital; it is precious and hard earned.

(Source: Doug Sandler, Wachovia Securities.)

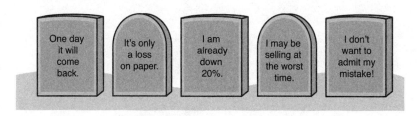

Figure 20.9 Famous last words.

Ty Cobb and Babe Ruth were two of the all time greatest baseball players. Ty Cobb was known for his setting the record in stolen bases. Babe Ruth was known for hitting a record number of home runs. What you may not know is that Ty Cobb was also thrown out more than any other player trying to steal those bases. And Babe Ruth struck out more than any other player trying to hit those home runs. These fellows did not let failure stop them, and neither should you. Learn from your mistakes, protect your capital, and failure will not be final.

21

Putting It All Together: Volume-Dictated Strategies

"Curly: 'You know what the secret of life is?'
Mitch: 'No, what?'
Curly: 'One thing. Just one thing.'
Mitch: 'That's great, but what's the one thing?'
Curly: 'That's what you've got to figure out.'"
—*City Slickers*

Thus far, we have reviewed the fundamentals of volume analysis, mastered the art of chart reading, uncovered the old and discovered some new volume and breadth indicators, and learned the principles of risk and money management. After spending the time to learn, it is only natural to want to put these concepts into quick practice. Yet learning technical analysis is a bit like learning martial arts. When someone first begins to learn martial arts, she is actually more vulnerable than before. This is because a beginner has not developed experience in applying martial arts techniques. As a consequence, when people first begin practicing, they often find themselves in awkward positions. The same can be true for technical analysis. A little academic knowledge without practical experience can hit an investor where it really hurts—the pocketbook!

Investors often spend time understanding and practicing a certain technique or indicator, but this knowledge is built in isolation; thus, the inexperienced analyst might exclude other important considerations. In such cases, investors lack the ability to use their information to form a big-picture perspective. Technical analysis should not be performed in a vacuum; it is a process of analyzing interrelationships and objectively assessing the probabilities of various outcomes.

Employing Volume-Based Strategies

A technical analyst might be able to tell you that if a stock breaks through a certain point it can find resistance here or support there, but this information is built on ifs, not certainties. One of the most common mistakes is to use your technical insight to look too far ahead. In doing so, you risk benefiting from the rewards of the present. Forecasting is for economists and weathercasters, not technical market analysts. The work of the market analyst is to understand where the market is and to discern the driving factors that propel it forward. This is where strategy comes into play. Having a strategy enables you to apply your knowledge to the more significant whole. Employing a consistent method to gauge the market strategically is what market analysis is truly about. Gauging the market involves assessing the probabilities of various market outcomes—the risks as well as the possible rewards. In this chapter, we discuss some of my own scaleddown methods, which might allow you to put your newly acquired knowledge into a simple yet useful framework to map the market.

Understanding the Market: Supply and Demand

The approach I employ begins by identifying the factors that drive the market through supply and demand. A technical analyst should understand these five important aspects of the market before investing:

- What is the direction of the secular primary trend of the broad market—up, down, or sideways?
- Is the volume confirming or contradicting the primary trend?
- Does market breadth confirm or contradict the primary trend?
- Which market sectors illustrate leadership on a price and volume momentum basis?
- Which individual securities show the strongest patterns of accumulation?

Step 1: Direction of Trend

The first and primary objective of the technical analyst is to identify the direction of the broad market's primary trend. By understanding the primary market trend, the analyst might perceive what the market and its investors are actually doing.

Step 2: Trend Sustainability

"Volume is naturally closely correlated to price change. The most intelligent and productive studies are correlations of the two."

—*Harold M. Gartley*

After the direction of the primary trend is determined, the technical analyst must decide whether the trend is sustainable. To draw such a conclusion, the analyst must develop a deeper understanding of the forces at work that create the trend. This is where volume analysis comes into play.

You can use a variety of volume indicators to assess volume's contribution to the trend of the broad market. However, the broad market's trend is a compilation of many individual stocks. Each security within an index has its own individual trend, each being supported or unsupported by volume. We can observe the broad market's price-volume relationship as a collection of individual issues through the volume-price confirmation indicator (VPCI) Index (see Figure 21.1). The VPCI Index is the collective VPCI of each individual stock comprising the broad market's membership. Understanding how each individual issue performs reveals how well the board market performs as a whole. The broad market may move up or down on higher or lower volume. However, sometimes the broad market moves higher, but the relationship between an individual stock's trend and volume might move another way. Therefore, using the broad index and the index's volume, or even cap-weighted volume, could distort the purposes of the VPCI calculation. However, by calculating each member's VPCI independently, the VPCI index might be more effective in measuring volume's influence on each individual price trend comprising the broad market's trend.

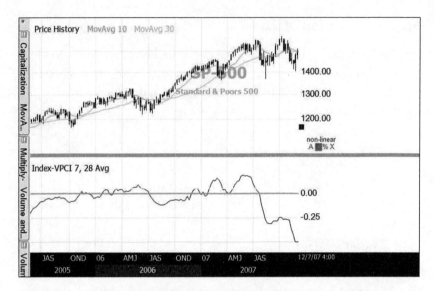

(Chart [or data] produced by TeleChart 2007® or StockFinder®, which is a registered trademark of Worden Brothers, Inc., Five Oaks Office Park, 4905 Pine Cone Drive, Durham, NC 27707. Ph. (800) 776-4940 or (919) 408-0542. www.Worden.com.)

Figure 21.1   VPCI Index forewarns the 2007 market top.

The VPCI index is used to interpret the broad market in the same way the VPCI is used to analyze individual stocks. When the broad equity market advances, the VPCI index should also be moving higher, confirming the trend. However, if the VPCI moves downward while the broad market moves higher, then the VPCI index contradicts the price trend. When the broad equity market moves downward, a VPCI index moving downward confirms the trend. However, if the VPCI index rises, it contradicts a downward price trend. If the market consolidates sideways, the direction of the VPCI index might indicate the next direction of the broad market.

Step 3: Market Breadth

After you have subjectively identified the broad market's price trend and the price-volume relationship within the trend, you can begin exploring other peripheral factors such as market breadth. One such market breadth indicator is the advance-decline. As an example, an advance-decline line of the S&P 500 illustrates how many issues within the S&P 500 composite moved up versus down during the last 252 trading days. This gives you perspective about the breadth of market participation. Next, you can review this information with respect to how much volume flows into and out of those stocks. The cap-weighted up volume versus cap-weighted down volume yields an enhanced view of this information. Through these two pieces of information—market breadth of issues and market breadth of volume—you can begin building a map of the market.

Building a Market Positioning System

Recently, a financial advisor stepped into my office to show off his new iPhone. The phone's global positioning system showed us exactly where we were even within the larger context of the office building. Cute, but useful? What would be useful for investors would be a market positioning system (MPS). By using market breadth data, advance-declines, and cap-weighted up or down volume as coordinates, we can build an MPS to evaluate the position and direction of the market.

To build an MPS map, we must first establish the x and y axes. The x axis, going horizontally left to right or west to east, represents the price trend coordinates of market breadth through the advance-decline line. The coordinates of the y axis moving vertically up and down or north and south represents the cap-weighted up or down trend line (see Figure 21.2).

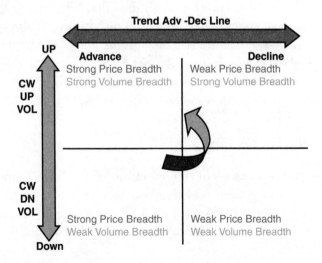

Figure 21.2   Market breadth positioning system.

Comparing our MPS map to the globe, the vertical center crosshair represents the prime meridian, a net cap-weighted volume of zero. The horizontal crosshair would be analogous to the equator, a net advance-decline of zero. The center point of the crosshairs would then represent perfect equilibrium between buying pressure (demand) and selling pressure (supply). As our market breadth coordinates move to the left of center, there are more advancers than decliners, indicating a bullish advance-decline line. As the coordinates move to the right of center, decliners outweigh advancers, indicating a bearish advance-decline line. As the coordinates move higher, it illustrates that cap-weighted advancing volume exceeds cap-weighted declining volume. As the market breadth coordinates move lower, it reveals that cap-weighted down volume surpasses up volume.

The optimal location for a bull market scenario is the upper-left corner as this represents both bullish volume and bullish price breadth. Excluding oversold extremes, the worst place to be for a bull is the lower right-hand corner as both volume and price breadth readings are bearish. Both the upper right and the lower left quadrants represent a market that is out of sync but at least has some internals working in the bullish direction.

This analysis is even more powerful when it is dynamically tracked by plotting the volume and price trend breadth coordinates and then sequentially connecting the points, as with Crocker charts. As the points move in a northwesterly direction of the upper-left corner, the implications are bullish. Such actions confirm the broad market's upward trend, contradict a downtrend, and suggest a new bull market might develop during sideways consolidation. As the points move in a southeasterly direction of the lower right corner, the implications are bearish and interpreted in the reverse.

Step 4: Market Sectors

"The proper analysis of the operation of the law of supply and demand within individual stocks serves two essential purposes. Not only does it reveal the trend of public interest; it also discloses whether such interest is favorable or unfavorable."

—*Edwin S. Quinn*

Only after building an assessment of the state of the market should the investor approach the decision of where to invest. However, before we choose individual stocks, it might be helpful to understand how each sector of the market performs.

Market sectors are classifications of investments. The five broadest classifications of assets include stocks, bonds, commodities, real estate, and cash. Although we have focused primarily on the equity market, we can invest in all five major categories through exchange-traded funds (ETF). Asset classes are useful in diversifying portfolios while giving the investor additional options when stocks might not appear to be the most attractive asset class. The stock markets can be broken down into many different sectors. Standard & Poor's has 10 sector classifications, and Morningstar has 31 major industry groups, plus another 209 subindustry groups.

The decision to over- or underweight market sectors depends largely on your investment style. One popular approach is relative strength. Relative strength discerns which stocks, sectors, or asset classes perform the best during a given period of time. Historically, investing in the strongest areas rebalanced over time has led to outperformance. A major reason why the S&P 500 benchmark is difficult to beat is that it is technically rebalanced through relative strength. A study conducted from 1990 through 2008 by Dash and Loggie of Standard and Poor's showed that the S&P 500 beat the relative strength absent the S&P 500 equal-weight index by an annualized amount of 1.5 percent. When referring to relative strength, the vast majority of market participants consider only the relative strength of price. However, my analysis uses the relative strength of price in relation to the relative strength of volume. This might improve the prospects of identifying the leading market sectors and those exhibiting the volume to endure.

My sector analysis consists of such an unbiased account of true market momentum. I want to be in the sectors where the money flows into and moves out of the sectors where the money leaves. This relative strength sector analysis is conducted in a two-part progression. The first part identifies the sectors with the highest relative price-volume momentum. This is accomplished by identifying the market sectors according to the strongest and most dynamic moves of the Volume-Weighted Moving Average Convergence Divergence (VW-MACD) relative to the S&P 500. The second part ranks the top-performing sectors by their persistence in sustaining high performance. The sector that has been in the top quartile for the longest period of time would be ranked at the top. However, if a sector has only just cracked the top quartile, it would be ranked at the bottom among the top quartile stocks. In this way, we can pinpoint not only the relative strength of the price-volume momentum, but also the endurance of the sectors (see Figure 21.4).

Figure 21.3   Market sectors.

The dynamic interactions among the sectors can be visualized by animating the data. In this approach, the values of the sector indices are plotted for a period of time. The recent history of each sector is shown as a tail behind the sector symbol. The length of the tail shows the rate of change of sector values. In the example that follows, two sectors—health services and drugs—are well beyond the 90th percentile but losing momentum. Their rate of change is low and has recently changed direction as evidenced by the inverted U-shaped tail. The sector values then return to the median value over a period of ten days (see Figure 21.5 and Figure 21.6).

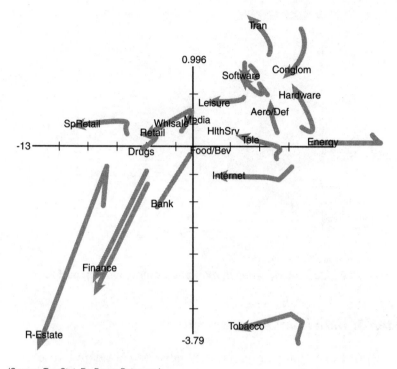

(Source: TeraStat, Dr. Bruce Peterson.)

Figure 21.4   Sectors dynamic market positioning system.

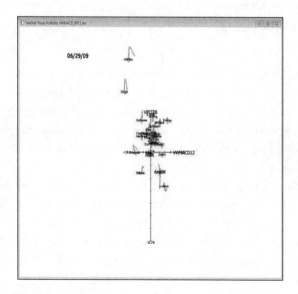

(Source: TeraStat, Dr. Bruce Peterson.)

Figure 21.5   Sectors dynamic market positioning system, part 1.

(Source: TeraStat, Dr. Bruce Peterson.)

Figure 21.6   Sectors dynamic market positioning system, part 2.

Step 5: Individual Stock Selection

"Just as volume in a single stock must be considered in relation to total trading, price movements of individual stocks are
misleading except as they are compared with the trend of the
market as a whole."

—*Edwin S. Quinn*

At this final stage of the investment process, an analyst has predetermined the internal condition of the broad market and identified the external areas of strength within the market sectors. From
this point, investors can begin the process of investigating the selection of individual securities. An objective system should discern what
qualities represent important catalysts that make any particular stock
an attractive candidate and also how to control the risk of the investment. My process begins by evaluating the trend and the market volume of the broad market. In the broad market analysis, I used the
MPS to form a multidimensional perspective of the markets. So we
shall proceed again, but this time in the evaluation of individual
securities.

Building an MPS with Individual Stock Issues

"Harold M. Gartley is impressive in the extent and depth of work he did. His 1935 book (*Profits in the Stock Market*) has chapters that show phenomenal insight, depth and wisdom. Gartley believed in comparing volume and hence, divided volume numbers, did not add, subtract or multiply. I believe he was more oriented toward trading and investing in individual stocks so he asserted that the most useful element of volume is to study its relativeness, to compare a stock's volume fluctuations to the market's volume."

—*George A. Schade, Jr., CMT 2010*

To build an MPS of individual stocks, we must begin by establishing the coordinates. The MPS coordinates used for the individual stock analysis are trend and volume. We measure trend with the Trend Thrust Indicator Index (TTI) and volume with the VPCI index. Trend is plotted on the horizontal axis and volume on the vertical axis, highest to lowest according to the TTI rankings. Through these two coordinates—the TTI Index represents the strength of the trend and the VPCI index the state owf volume—we can chart the movement of securities on our MPS map.

Now that the framework of our MPS map has been established, we can begin the process of tracking the market's components. It is helpful to first define what constitutes the market. If you want to track the broad market, you might choose a broad market index, such as the S&P 500 (or the Wilshire 5000 for a very broad market). You can also choose a narrower market sector, such as financials or technology, or you can chart the course of a market style index, such as the S&P 500 Growth Index or S&P 500 Value Index. If your focus is on industries rather than individual issues, you can also plot the Morningstar industry groups or other industry composites. The possibilities are nearly endless, but our focus here is on individual security selection within the broad market.

To track the components of the S&P 500 with the MPS, each individual security of the S&P 500 is plotted according to its position relative to the VPCI and TTI Index. In our MPS map, the equator is the horizontal center where a security's volume is neither bullish nor bearish when compared to other market components. Securities above the equator experience bullish volume relative to their peers and vice versa. The vertical center position, or the prime meridian, represents the vertical center of the price trend. Stocks to the left of the prime meridian have stronger upward trends relative to the market. Stocks to the right of the prime meridian illustrate that their price trend is relatively weaker or down in relation to the average member of the composite.

The Four Phases of Volume Analysis

From the crosshairs of these two points come four quadrants. Securities in the upper-left corner are in a relatively high state of upward trend with confirming volume. Securities in the lower-left corner are in a high state of upward trend but have contradicting volume. Securities in the lower-right corner are in a downward trend with confirming volume. Securities in the upper-right corner trend down on contradictory volume. Through this simple MPS, every security, including sectors and ETFs, can be mapped and dynamically charted according to its relative position in the VPCI and TTI indexes (see Figure 21.7).

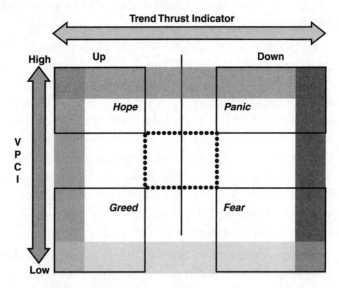

Figure 21.7   MPS VPCI and TTI.

Where a stock is located on the map can have an impact on its performance. The following results represent how components in the S&P 500 performed while entering a location on the map. This test was performed on individual stocks of the S&P 500 from January 1, 2010, through April 30, 2010. Excluding dividends, the S&P 500 benchmark was down 2.04 percent during the testing period. In our test model, once a stock entered and closed the week within a zone, its performance was tracked until the stock closed the week significantly out of the zone. The following zones were tracked:

- **Most bullish volume index.** This represents the stocks in the VPCI index with the top 10 percent highest VPCI readings. The bull volume index comprises the stocks containing the top 10 percent highest weekly VPCI readings. The stocks are purchased when they make the top 10 percent list and are held until they fall out of the top 50 percent of VPCI scores. The return of the most bullish volume index was 10.41 percent for the period (see Figure 21.8).

- **Most bearish volume index.** This represents stocks in the bottom 10 percent of the VPCI index. The most bearish volume index is comprised of stocks with the lowest weekly VPCI readings. The stocks are purchased when they enter the bottom 10 percent of VPCI index issues and are sold when they reach the top 50 percent. The most bearish volume index return was 2.62 percent during the period.

- **Most overbought index.** This represents the issues in the top 10 percent of the TTI Index. The most overbought index is comprised of the stocks making up the highest 10 percent weekly TTI readings within the TTI Index. These stocks are purchased when they reach the highest 10 percent and are sold when they reach the bottom 50 percent of the TTI Index. The return of the most overbought index was 0.62 percent during the course of the testing period.

- **Most oversold index.** This represents the issues in the bottom 10 percent of the TTI Index. The most oversold index comprises the stocks with the lowest 10% weekly TTI readings within the underlying index. These stocks are purchased when they reach the bottom 10 percent and are sold when they reach the top 50 percent of the TTI index. The most oversold index returned 0.99 percent during the course of the testing period.

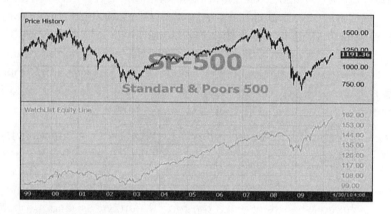

(Chart [or data] produced by TeleChart 2007® or StockFinder®, which is a registered trademark of Worden Brothers, Inc., Five Oaks Office Park, 4905 Pine Cone Drive, Durham, NC 27707. Ph. (800) 776-4940 or (919) 408-0542. www.Worden.com.).

Figure 21.8   S&P 500 compared to VPCI most bullish volume index.

From this, we can glean that the extreme edges, especially volume extremes, tended to outperform the broader market. As further discerned from the test results, the optimal place for stock investment was at the top with the issues in the mostly bullish volume index. However, analysis consists of gaining an understanding of how these smaller parts interact within the larger whole. This understanding is crucial in building an investment strategy. To advance this understanding, we might glean information from how these indexes perform with respect to each other as they overlap. These overlaps are the extreme corners of the MPS map where the most overbought and oversold trend indexes collide with the most bullish and bearish volume indexes. Additionally, stocks don't enter a quadrant and stay there. They move. Our map consists of moving targets. Thus, the important information on our MPS map is not only the location but also the direction in which the securities moves.

An issue whose coordinates move up vertically across the MPS plane indicates that the issue's volume is becoming increasingly more bullish, whereas if an issue's VPCI coordinates move lower over time, it indicates the price trend is becoming increasingly more bearish on volume. Likewise, an issue moving from left to right is an issue losing momentum, becoming relatively more oversold. An issue moving from right to left gains relative momentum and becomes more over-bought. In my MPS analysis, we will track the issues from their locations and movements across the MPS plane.

We begin in the upper-left quadrant where stocks are overbought with bullish volume (see Figure 21.9). This most overbought, bullish volume quadrant consists of stocks above the equator and to the left of the prime meridian. The uppermost-left corner consists of the stocks overlapping the most overbought and most bullish volume index. The stocks in this corner, which were held until they left the larger overbought, bullish volume quadrant by falling below the equator (the bottom half of the VPCI index) while also moving to the left of the prime meridian (the oversold side of TTI), experienced a 9.4 percent return. The stocks originating in the upper-left corner that fell downward via a relatively falling VPCI ranking experienced a 7.48 percent average return. However, when these upper-left corner stocks moved horizontally to the right, losing price momentum, they returned only an average of 1.06 percent. From this, we learn that the stocks originating in the upper-left corner that continued moving up and to the left experienced better returns. However, issues moving to the right from a weakening trend were less profitable than issues that experienced downward movements with loss of volume.

Moving downward, the next quadrant in our MPS map is the lower-left quadrant where stocks are overbought but with bearish volume (see Figure 21.10). This is identified on the MPS map by the stocks to the right of the prime meridian and beneath the equator. In the very lower-left corner are the stocks overlapping the most over-bought index with the most bearish volume index. Stocks purchased upon first reaching this corner and held until moving both above the equator (bullish volume) and to the right of the prime meridian (bearish trend) experienced a gain of 1.57 percent. The stocks originating from this corner that were sold upon moving up (bullish volume) experienced a 1.65 percent return. However, stocks moving to the right on a weakening trend experienced a 0.56 percent loss. This further demonstrates that stocks moving to the right during the study tended to be more bearish than those moving up or to the left.

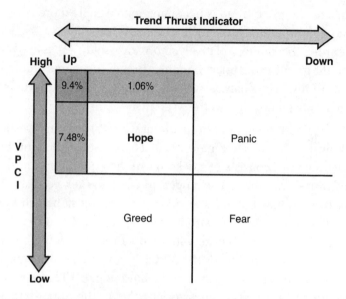

Figure 21.9   High VPCI high upward trend.

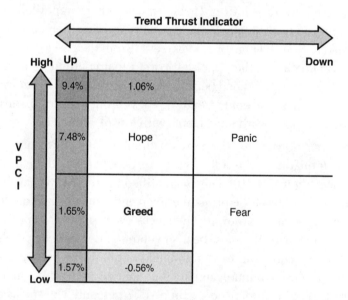

Figure 21.10   Low VPCI high upward trend.

Moving to the right on the MPS map is the lower-right quadrant containing stocks that are oversold on bearish volume (see Figure 21.11). The outermost-right corner is where the most oversold and

most bearish volume indexes overlap. Stocks purchased upon entering this corner and held until leaving the lower-right quadrant by
moving both higher across the prime meridian and up across the
equator averaged 4.54 percent, the third best-performing corner on
the map. This might come as a shock because this corner is seemingly
the most bearish location on our MPS map. However, earlier we discussed the VPCI V bottom where stocks become oversold on a price
and volume basis and quickly rebound on subtle volume declines. No
doubt many of the stocks deep in this corner are soon to be V-bottom
candidates. Stocks in this corner that moved to the left (improving
price trend without volume) averaged 1.57 percent. Stocks moving up
to the equator on more bullish volume than trend improvement averaged 1.86 percent.

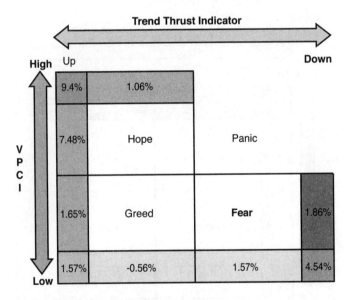

Figure 21.11   Low VPCI downtrend.

We can gain some insights from these observations. A stock that is
deeply oversold on bearish volume should experience both trend and
volume reversals. An improvement of trend without bullish volume
and an improvement in volume without corresponding trend
improvement will produce inferior results as compared to situations
in which both elements are present.

Finally, moving upward to the upper-right quadrant, we find stocks that are oversold but have bullish volume characteristics (see Figure 21.12). The upper-right corner of this quadrant is where stocks reside that have the most bullish volume while simultaneously are the most oversold. Stocks purchased when they first entered this corner and held until becoming overbought (crossing the prime meridian) and weakening volume (crossing the equator) experienced a 5.11 percent gain. Stocks that crossed the prime meridian, demonstrating weakening volume while remaining oversold, returned 0.56 percent. Stocks that crossed the equator, maintaining strong volume but never gaining strong price trend through being overbought, returned 1.21 percent. This tells us that the preponderance of the bullish volume returns came from holding the stocks after the trend had moved into overbought territory.

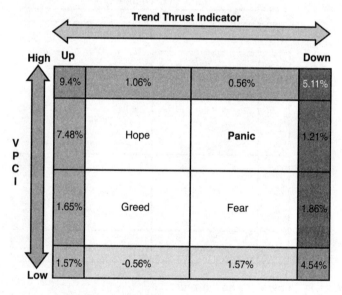

Figure 21.12   High VPCI downtrend.

Price Volume Extremes

"If the market is balanced, basically equal amounts of buying and selling are present. The market has brought in an opposite response. The market is moving rotating because it has found a fair price around which it can distribute. If the market is imbalanced, either buying or selling is predominant. The market is moving higher or lower in order to find an opposite response. The market is moving directionally because it is seeking a fair price around which it can distribute. In brief, a balanced market has found a fair price. An imbalanced market is seeking a fair price."

—*Market Profile, Chicago Board of Trade*

Not only can we gain insights into the movement of the overlapping extremes, but we might also learn something as stocks travel from one quadrant to the opposite quadrant. The first such movement we explore is stock beginning in the most bullish quadrant of high trend and bullish volume that were sold upon reaching the opposite quadrant. These stocks in the upper-left quadrant, when held until they lost both trend and volume, as measured by moving into the lower-right corner, gained on average 11.43 percent. Stocks originating in the lower-left quadrant with high trend and bearish volume held until they moved to the opposite quadrant of bullish volume and bearish trend experienced a 3.11 percent gain. Oversold stocks with bearish volume in the lower-right quadrant held until they reached the opposite quadrant of overbought with bullish volume produced a 2.45 percent return. Stocks originating in the bullish volume negative trend quadrant held until reaching the lower-right corner of the bullish trend quadrant and weakening volume returned 8.91 percent (see Figure 21.13).

Market Equilibrium

The previous examples illustrated purchasing stocks as they enter various extremes. However, most of the time, stocks are not at extremes but somewhere in the middle. By isolating the stocks in the center of the map, we can test how these stocks perform. The vertical middle was defined by stocks with a VPCI index above 30 and below 70, thus corresponding to the Tropic of Cancer and the Tropic of Capricorn. Likewise, the horizontal middle was defined by a TTI

Index of above 30 and below 70. Stocks located in both middle groups made up the center of the MPS map. This center represents stocks nearing equilibrium in the price-volume relationship (see Figure 21.14).

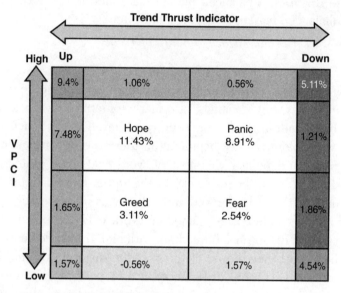

Figure 21.13   VPCI trend extremes.

For the test, I purchased stocks when they entered the center and sold them when they exited the center. On average, these stocks returned 1.01 percent. Thus, purchasing the center stocks resulted in underperformance compared to purchasing stocks at any of the extremes; however, purchasing the center stocks resulted in slight outperformance compared to the buy-and-hold approach. My experience suggested that this slight relative outperformance could likely be attributed to active management on the sell side rather than purchase location on the buy side. Selling stocks as they move down fulfills the money management principle of cutting losses short, while selling stocks as they become overbought is generally prudent in sideways markets. Stocks at the equilibrium or moving toward equilibrium should be viewed with caution.

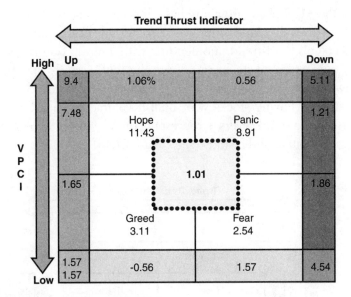

Figure 21.14   Market equilibrium.

Based on these test results, one can infer that stocks originating with bullish volume as measured by the VPCI index tend to significantly outperform stocks purchased on bearish volume as measured by the same index. When upward trend is combined with bullish volume, the results are magnified further. However, bullish-volume stocks need some upward-trend momentum as performance was significantly reduced when upward-trend momentum was absent. The worst-performing extreme to begin was stocks overbought but lacking volume confirmation. This was especially so when trend momentum was later lost.

Direction Trumps Location

Furthermore, stocks in extreme positions, the outermost corners of the MPS map, outperformed other nonoverlapping extremes, whereas stocks in the center represented stocks nearing equilibrium, which generally underperformed those stocks purchased through using other strategies. Overall, the location on the MPS map where the security was originally purchased was the most significant factor in investment returns. However, the direction that the stock moved across the MPS plane after purchase also had a major effect on the results. Generally, stocks moving the northwesterly direction of increasing upward-trend momentum with bullish volume significantly outperformed stocks moving in the southeasterly direction of downward trend momentum and bearish volume. Thus, this study suggests that buying stocks with bullish volume and holding them until the price trend reverses represents the most profitable strategy during the course of the study (see Figure 21.15).

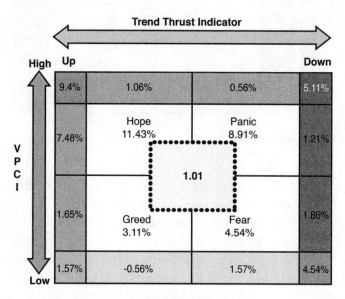

Figure 21.15   VPCI and trend direction.

22

Modern Day Volume Issues

"There is a certain relief in change, even though it be from bad to worse; as I have found in traveling stagecoach, that it is often a comfort to change one's position and be bruised in a new place."

—*Washington Irving*

Over the past few decades, the structure of the financial markets has undergone significant change. The market has been transformed from a quasi manually operated exchange into a highly competitive computerized network. These dramatic changes in trading practices and changes in regulations have resulted in soaring trading volumes. This, in turn, has caused considerable confusion over the use of volume as an analytical tool. Some have even gone so far as to say that volume data is no longer relevant. The Flash Crash only inflamed such suspicions.

However, there is no need to be discouraged. Many concerns about volume's validity are misunderstandings, while others are legitimate and need to be taken into account. Most misconceptions originate from a failure to understand what volume analysis is and from ignorance of how the markets presently function. In this final chapter, I address these concerns while explaining the structure of modern-day market mechanics.

How Trading Volume Has Changed

The average daily market volume in 1999 was 970 million shares. By 2005, it had quadrupled to 4.1 billion, and by 2009, it had more than doubled again to 12 billion shares per day. Recently volume has returned to trade 8 billion shares per day as many investors and traders have been disenchanted by the volatile drops associated with the secular bear market.

Daily U.S. Equity Share Volume

(Source: Barclays Capital Equity Research.)

Figure 22.1   Market volume growth.

Over the course of time, trading volume has incurred a secular growth originating from developments in the economy, investment products, information technologies, and regulations.

Economic Reasons Causing a Secular Growth of Volume

Market capital has significantly grown over the past century. As the markets and economy grow, so does the quantity of shares available for sale. Just as the price averages have risen over the past century, so too has the market volume of the New York Stock Exchange (NYSE) and other exchanges seen a steady uptrend. As the economy grows, market prices rise, and new capital is formed. This leads to increased share volume through new offerings and stock splits.

Inflationary pressures might be another economic reason for increased share volume. More dollars being circulated causes inflation. All things being equal, equity assets tend to rise with inflation, eventually leading to more shares available to trade. Again, this process is largely manifested through new offerings and stock splits.

Since the 1950s, the public has grown increasingly interested in the equity markets. Not only has the number of investors increased, but investor involvement has increased, too. One reason for this is a result of the development of employer-sponsored retirement plans. In the past, many American workers were the beneficiaries of employer-sponsored pensions. More recently, however, employers have deferred the responsibility of retirement planning to the worker through 401(k) plans. Today, most Americans participate in the market at least indirectly through mutual funds largely offered via their employers' retirement plans.

Additionally, as the American economy has grown, so too has the average American become more affluent. As wealth grows, many more of these individuals become involved with the market either directly via individual stocks or indirectly through mutual funds, exchange-traded funds (ETF), or variable market-based insurance products. Typically, these investment products have higher turnover, which is higher volume per the number of shares outstanding.

New investment products have promoted the secular growth of volume by attracting more public interest in products and services with historically higher turnover. According to respected technical analyst Philip J. Roth, CMT of Miller Tabak + Co. LLC., the average turnover was only 24 percent in the 1970s, but by 2010, it was 210 percent down from 244 percent in 2009.

Mutual funds have been available since the 1920s. However, they have become increasingly more popular over the past several decades. Through mutual funds, investors can defer the selection of individual equity issues by hiring a professional manager to manage the investments. Today, there are more mutual funds available to the public than there are publicly traded stocks listed on the major exchanges. Not only has the availability of mutual funds increased interest in the marketplace, the active management styles provided by professional managers has led to more shares being traded through higher turnover.

The early 1990s introduced the concept of ETFs. With ETFs, an investor can easily participate in the performance of an index with minimal expense. Via specialized granted tax treatment through ETF investment, most ETFs can avoid the capital gains associated with mutual funds.

ETFs accomplish their mission of efficiently tracking the index through creating and redeeming ETF shares. If there is significantly more demand for an ETF, the ETF sponsor can create new ETF shares for the purchaser. Likewise, if there is significantly more supply than demand, the ETF participants can redeem shares. Because an ETF is a composite of an index, creating and redeeming shares involves buying and selling all of the index member shares in proportion to the underlying index.

Similarly, should the price of the ETF move too far away from the sum net asset value of ETF components, arbitrageurs will buy the ETF shares and redeem them for the underlying shares of the components for profit. This is called index arbitrage. Index arbitrage occurs when a spread arises between the index and the sum of ETF parts. Several analysts have estimated that activities related to ETFs account for as much as 30 percent of the total market volume. Thus, it is not only the volume of the 800 plus publicly traded ETF shares, but more so the trading activities from the underlying components continually being redeemed and re-created that causes total market volume to increase.

Hedge funds and hedging strategies are again not new, but, like mutual funds, have gained acceptance among the public during recent years. A significant growth of volume has come from high-tech tactics that hedge funds might employ. Algorithmic trading uses computers to initiate trading strategies. Computers can identify potential opportunities faster than their human programmers and then quickly route orders or baskets of orders for execution. This is known as program trading.

One such example is statistical arbitrage. *Statistical arbitrage* is a high-frequency trading strategy that uses correlations between like/similar securities or baskets of individual like/similar securities. With this strategy, computers identify a security moving in a specific direction. A computer then verifies that like securities are moving in tandem. If not, the computer places orders in anticipation that like securities will trade back to statistical correlation. The faster the high-frequency fund can identify and execute these potential opportunities, the more potential for profit. Therefore, these statistical arbitrage strategies are implemented at lightning speeds with razor-thin spreads, resulting in the manufacturing of significant trading volumes.

Changed Regulations and New Technologies Encourage Growth of Trading Volume

On May 1, 1975, the Securities and Exchange Commission (SEC) deregulated the fixed costs of brokerage commissions, allowing brokerages to compete on value as well as service. In addition, the brokerage firms no longer have a virtual monopoly on information. Since the birth of the Internet, information has become widely available, and the Internet provides an efficient means for placing orders. Since the mid-1970s, brokerage commissions have dropped from an average of approximately 15 cents per share to nearly 3 cents a share today. As commissions have fallen, individual investors have assumed more responsibility for security research and the risks associated with placing their own orders. The traditional broker's role has been transformed into that of a financial advisor providing advice, financial planning, and educated opinions. As information has become more accessible and the costs of trading has fallen, substantially more individuals have invested in equities while their trading activity has increased significantly. With time, these developments have encouraged growth within the trading volumes of stocks.

Undoubtedly, decimalization has had the largest influence on volume growth throughout the last decade. Prior to April 9, 2001, stocks traded in fractions. In the early and mid 1990s, stock mostly traded in eighths or, in other words, units of 12.5 cents. The intent of these large spreads was to ensure plenty of depth behind the quotations to aid in maintaining an orderly market. In 1997, the Nasdaq permitted stocks to be traded in sixteenths, cutting the spread between the bid and the ask in half. New York followed, and the SEC mandated that all stocks be permitted to trade in penny increments by April 9, 2001.

Today, as opposed to fractions, all stocks trading above one dollar are allowed to trade in decimals—penny increments. Stocks under a dollar can trade below penny increments. Trading in pennies creates tighter, more competitive spreads, thereby significantly lowering trading costs while promoting significantly higher trading volume.

These narrow spreads allow other participants to come in between the bid and the offer. This practice of trading between the bid and the ask has traditionally been called scalping. For example, a stock might trade at a $25.00 bid and a $25.08 offer. A scalper may offer to buy the stock at \$25.02 with the hope of selling it back at \$25.03 or higher. Effectively, the scalper is acting as a pseudo market maker, buying stock in inventory only to sell it quickly at a higher price. Such actions actually help keep the spreads lower and the market more efficient. With the scalper's bid of \$25.02, a seller can sell the stock 2 cents higher than the former bid of \$25.00. If the scalper then offers to sell the stock at \$25.05, a buyer could purchase the stock 3 cents lower than the former offer of \$25.08. Should those trades come off in such a fashion, the activities would provide the scalper with a 3-cent profit.

A 3-cent profit might not seem worthy of Wall Street's time and efforts. That is, of course, unless you can scalp frequently and often with high trading volumes. In essence, that is what the SEC Act of 1998 and the National Market System (NMS) allow firms to do.

The SEC's Regulation ATS (Alternative Trading System) allows equity execution markets to operate without being a national securities exchange. This regulation allows for and governs nonexchange markets. ECNs and other alternative trading systems become subject to more security and transparency after their volume exceeds a 5 percent threshold of total trading volume for any given security they trade. At that point, they must display quotations publicly and abide by fair access rules.

Presently, this rule applies only if the quotation is displayed to more than one participant. If a dark pool does not display quotes to any participant, all participants are excluded from the rule regardless of volume. Such quotes are referred to as indications of interest (IOI). Not all dark pools even use IOIs. In fact, most do not. Overall, this infrastructure keeps the competition of trades between the bid and the ask high, leading to narrower spreads and higher volume.

Regulation NMS (National Market System) mandates uniform execution rules for all exchanges and alternative trading systems. Based on the framework of these regulations, essentially one only needs a computerized matching engine to compete with the exchanges. The spirit of the rule is to foster increased competition by ensuring that orders occur at the best prices. This rule, combined with decimalization and the speed and access provided by technology, has greatly benefited the expansion of computerized automation of order executions.

However, prior to August 3, 2009, there was some confusion about the exact reporting responsibilities among ATS participants. It was suspected that some of the methods used by ATS could have led to double counting of trades and therefore volume. U.S. Senator Charles E. Schumer shared these concerns. In an inquiry to the SEC, Schumer wrote,

> Presently ATS are required to report trades to the Consolidated Tape on a 90 second delay. They also report aggregate trade volume to the Commission on a quarterly basis. This trade volume data is not standardized—for example, some ATS 'double count' by counting a matched order as two trades, while others treat a matched order as only one trade. I am very concerned that nobody seems to know the precise amount of trading volume that occurs in the nondisplayed markets.

As a result of this possible double counting, trade volume from some venues, such as dark pools, might have been overstated. On November 5, 2008, the SEC approved a proposal from the Financial Industry Regulatory Authority (FINRA) to clarify the reporting requirements effective August 3, 2009.

Public concerns are offered in two popular forms: high-frequency trading and the aforementioned dark pools.

High-Frequency Trading

Because there are numerous high-frequency trading strategies, they might be best described by the attributes they share:

- In Texas, there are large billboards posted all along the highways stating "Speed Kills." Along the Internet highways of high-frequency trading, the signposts read "Speed Wins." As the name implies, *high-frequency traders trade at exceptionally high speeds*. High-frequency trading is an *ultra fast-turnover* trading strategy. I am not referring to day traders here. A day is an eternity to the high-frequency trader. A high-frequency trader never holds a position overnight. Even a minute is a heck of a long time to a high-frequency trader. In fact, the *International Economy* reported that one of the high-frequency CEOs said his company's record duration of holding a position was 11 seconds, which in his words was "unacceptably long." Ideally, these traders operate in the realm of milliseconds.

- A high-frequency trading strategy typically consists of a multitude of small orders to establish and liquidate securities very quickly. Generally, high-frequency traders do not trade directionally. Their primary purpose is to identify *very small but numerous scalping opportunities* or earn rebates paid by the exchanges for posting liquidity.

- To accomplish this, high-frequency traders send numerous orders knowing that *most orders will not be filled* and, if not filled, might be subject to immediate cancellation by the high frequency trading firm.

- To achieve the highest speeds, not only do high-frequency traders *employ the fastest computers and routers*, but they also want to be as close to the market as possible. Co-location is a practice where high-frequency traders place their hardware adjacent to the market matching engine. According to the Nasdaq, this can improve speed by up to 4.6 milliseconds.

In general terms, high-frequency traders are typically proprietary trading shops that use their own capital with some limited intraday leverage. They operate by injecting temporary liquidity within tiny market inefficiencies offered between the bid and the ask. Because of their high turnover, just a few million dollars can generate millions of shares in trading volume. It is estimated that between 50 percent and 70 percent of the total market volume results from high-frequency traders. With that information, you might correctly conclude that these activities have grossly exaggerated the volume data on the market indexes. However, since the introduction of decimalization, the volume increases from high-frequency trading have been worked in over a period of years. This growth represents the vast majority of secular volume growth across the last decade. It has been brought about by the increased opportunities to scalp created by these changes in regulations and advancements in technology.

When considering how high-frequency trading has affected volume analyses, you must consider that these actives have not occurred overnight but rather have accumulated over the last decade and now represent the new reality. Because these high-frequency trading activities had an impact on volume growth, the volume analyst generally need not be overly concerned that current volume flows are misrepresented by high-frequency trading. There can be special situations in which high-frequency traders are attracted in or out of a certain security, but this is the exception not the rule.

Volume analysis primarily concerns how much volume it takes to push a stock so far relative to previous volume levels. Yet high-frequency trading has a negligible impact on price movement. True demand comes from investors accumulating shares over and above the availability of supply at a given price. Likewise, true supply is created by more shares being distributed than those demanded at a given price. Therefore, high-frequency traders have little if any direct impact on price because the shares traded are typically immediately redistributed to the public at or between the best bid and offer. An investor engaging in such activities who begins the day flat and ends the day flat is not materially affecting price. Although this has created higher volume, the volume growth has been worked in slowly over a period of several years. In volume analysis, volume surges are the most significant sign in identifying developing new trends, breakouts, and reversals. However, the secular growth trends of volume over the short and intermediate time frames are a negligible factor in short- and intermediate-term volume analysis.

Dark Pools

Another form of ATS is the dark pool. The name itself sounds mysterious if not downright sinister. And like high-frequency trading, dark pools have been the subject of much scrutiny.

Originally, dark pools were created as a vehicle for institutions to conduct large block trades with one another to mitigate the adverse effects on price associated with trading large blocks. Even an extremely liquid stock, when met with a large one-sided order, can be moved significantly. Dark pools were designed to match one party with an unbalanced trade to another party. This matchmaking minimizes the impact of block trades and thereby reduces volatility of the markets. In this way, dark pools provide a source of liquidity for large order flows that might otherwise move the markets. Matching large block order flows between buyers and sellers is nothing new to the markets.

Traditionally, though, this task has been handled by floor brokers who bring the buyer and seller together.

Dark pools are considered dark because they protect the buyer and seller from being identified and keep their clients' intentions to trade unknown. They can accomplish this by not providing the proposed bid or offer to the consolidated tape. This is important. If other market participants catch wind that a large institution is a buyer or seller, they can run the stock up or down based on this knowledge.

Dark pools can protect their participants through Regulation ATS, which has looser reporting requirements for ATS firms processing less than 5 percent of the trading volume within a given security. A dark pool meeting these requirements need not report orders or IOIs on its order books. This benefits the dark pool participants by keeping their orders and their order size undisclosed to the public. Although their orders are undisclosed to the public, their executions are not. Dark pools must follow the rules required of the consolidated tape. This means the price must conform to the best bid offer at the time of the trade. It also means the price and the volume must be reported within 90 seconds of trade completion. What is ambiguous about dark pool trade executions is where they originate. Dark pools report their trades to either of two Trade Reporting Facilities (TRF). One is run for the NYSE and one for Nasdaq. The trades are reported to either Tape A (NYSE-listed), Tape B (NYSE Amex and NYSE Arca listed), or Tape C (Nasdaq listed), depending on where the stock is listed. Per regulations, nothing else needs to be reported about where the trade originates. This rule differs from that of the exchanges that must also report the venue from which the trade took place. It is believed that dark pools make up 15 percent of the volume of the OTC tape and about 10 percent of the total market volume.

Although dark pools were created to provide liquidity to large institutional traders, they might have drifted from this original purpose. These dark markets have opened up to all types of order flows, including those of the high-frequency traders. Today, many dark pools are used as tools through which high-frequency traders route their algorithmic trading strategies. Today, the average trade size originating from most dark pools order are no larger than those originating from the exchanges.

Concerns About High-Frequency Trading and Dark Pools

Flash Trading

Flash trading is a form of trading where an exchange "flashes" an order to a preferred high-frequency trader a few seconds before the rest of the market is allowed to view it. This allows the high-frequency trader an opportunity to improve upon the quoted price. When flash trading is combined with dark pools, some believe the combination has the potential to create an unfair advantage over the competition.

The Growth of Dark Pool Volume

Dark pool pricing is based off the consolidated tape, thereby preventing trades from occurring outside the bounds of the best bid and offer. This works so long as the vast majority of the market depth is behind that of the consolidated tape. As the market share of dark pools grows, it essentially drives away the depth and volume behind that of the consolidate tape. This causes the information behind the public's consolidated tape to become more and more erroneous as the private privileged market volume avoids displaying its quotes to the consolidated tape. As liquidity is siphoned off the exchange, the information behind the public's consolidated tape becomes more and more erroneous as the private privileged market volume avoids displaying its quotes to the consolidated tape.

Quote Flickering

Since 2003, the percentage of quotes canceled per execution has gone up threefold (see Figure 22.2). Through posting their bid and offers, high-frequency traders provide liquidity. However, although they execute many orders, they pull or cancel many orders, too. Providing such uncommitted liquidity is called quote flickering. Such practices can create uncertainty regarding market depth, thereby undermining investor confidence.

Gaming

High-frequency traders understand that often their stiffest competition is one another. Each high-frequency trader has its own complex proprietary algorithms measuring every subtle movement in the depths of the market's profile. This is the first level of the algorithm.

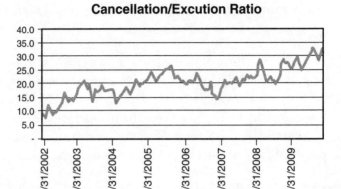

Cancellation/Excution Ratio

(Source: NASDAQ ITCH data provided by Knight Capital Group.)

Figure 22.2   Cancellation ratio.

However, to compete, it also may be helpful to anticipate the competition's reactions to the trader's operations as well. This deeper level of the algorithm allows the high-frequency trader to make adjustments based on the anticipated actions of its competitors. Taking into account that much of the market's depth is created by high-frequency traders' own activities, a high-frequency trader might attempt to change the complexion of the market's profile by creating bogus orders. Such actions create a false appearance of buying and selling pressure. The appearance of these ingenious orders may cause other competitors to readjust or hesitate. Thus, through misleading or slowing down the competition, the high-frequency trader creating the "noise" is well positioned to reap the benefits. This practice is called quote stuffing. With this stated, it's likely the vast majority of quote changes are due to legitimate business practices (see Figure 22.3).

Other forms of gaming might occur within dark pools. Investors might be aware of or suspect that a large dark pool can place a smaller order on the visible market driving prices against the dark pool participant. Either side of the dark pool can participate in this "gaming" to affect price. For example, a dark pool might indicate it wants to trade a large amount of a specific stock. With this knowledge, a trader can then offer to buy a small amount of the stock. If the order fills, then the trader can infer that there is a big sell order for a lot of shares. If the order does not fill, then the trader can infer there is a big buy order. With such information, a trader can attempt to anticipate a large trade anticipating that the forthcoming trade volume will drive the stock price higher if a buy or lower if a sale.

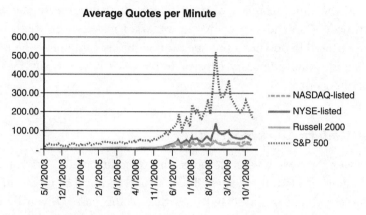

(Source: Knight Capital Group.)

Figure 22.3 Average quotes per minute.

In attempts to derail such practices, some dark pools employ algorithms to prevent executions on low volume-high volatility swings. Others keep the practice at bay through exclusive memberships, forcing out members suspected of using such tactics.

Contrasting Market Ages

Based on the depiction of unseen high-tech computerized trading systems trading across high-speed networks in milliseconds, you can deduce that this is not your grandfather's stock market or, for that matter, it is not even your older sibling's! In this regard, it might help to understand what the structure of today's market looks like compared to that of the past.

The Market Structure of the Past

In the 1990s, there were 10 stock exchanges with more than 25 member firms accounting for over 80 percent of the total volume. With the help of an electronic order book, the market's mechanics were conducted manually through floor brokers on the trading floor while market makers competed for order flow on the Nasdaq. The knowledge and insights of these market specialists were thought to be impossible to replicate in automated processes. Each market special-ist had the same mandate of operating a "fair and orderly market." With wide ⅛ spreads, specialists and market makers were both well compensated in providing the necessary liquidity to stabilize the mar-ket should any temporary gaps or imbalances between supply and demand occur.

The Modern Market Structure

Over the past several decades, the structure of the market has undergone profound changes. Today's market is substantially more complicated and sophisticated than that of the past. Driven by the reforms of Regulation NMS and empowered by modern technologies, the present market is divided into multiple distinct markets, each operating independently via its own proprietary trading systems. Thus, the markets do not operate off of a single order book. To avoid frag-mentation, these markets are linked together through a common net-work and regulation. Order flow is directed through this network, upholding the trade-through rule for proper execution. The quotes provided by each independent market are reported to the consolidated tape that supplies brokerage firms with the best national best bid and offer quotes. In effect, the modern market has become an open archi-tecture structure that is both exceptionally fast and extremely efficient.

Today, there are 13 exchanges, accounting for approximately 70 percent of total market volume. This compares to prior to Regulation NMS, when dark pools, internalization, and ECNs represented a much smaller share of market trading. There are now more than 70 ATSs, which includes dark pools and internalizers. Internalized vol-ume is primarily produced through discount brokerages who might execute trades against the brokerage firm's internal order flow. At the same time, due to this fragmentation, classic exchange market makers have become a much smaller part of the picture, as high-frequency traders have become the de facto market makers in this electronic age (see Figure 22.4).

The high-frequency traders provide short-term liquidity, which keeps spreads tight. These tight spreads allow for low trading costs.

For example, the effective bid-ask spread is an estimate of the costs investors incur from the spread. The effective bid-ask spread has dropped from 7 cents to less than 2 cents on NYSE-listed securities. Such efficiencies are believed to have saved long-term index-type investors 0.5 percent per year and the saving is much more for investors using high-turnover strategies.

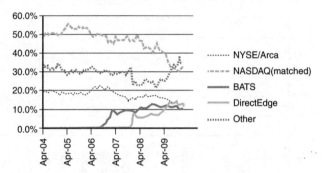

(Source: Barclays Capital Equity Research.)

Figure 22.4   Trading volume market shares.

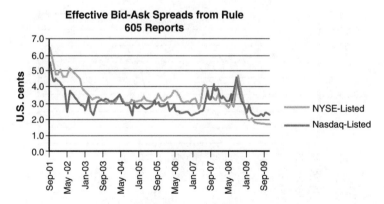

(Source: Public Rule 605 Reports from Thomson, Market orders 100-9999 shares.)

Figure 22.5   Effective bid-ask spreads.

The effective bid-ask spread is calculated as twice the difference between the actual trade price and the midpoint of the quoted National Best Bid Offer at the time of order receipt.

The efficiencies brought about by the modern market are more apparent in large-cap actively traded issues than in smaller less active issues. Spreads on actively traded large caps, such as those in the S&P 500, have dropped from nearly 2.5 cents in 2003 to less than 1.5 cents by 2009. However, less actively traded small-cap stocks have not reaped as much benefit (see Figure 22.6).

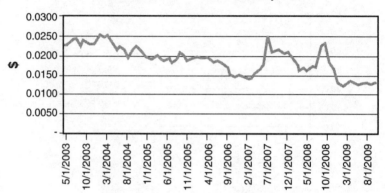

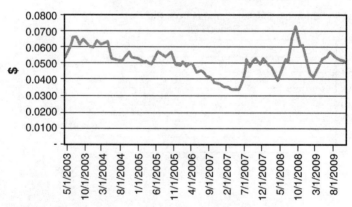

Figure 22.6   S&P 500 bid-ask spread and Russell 2000 bid-ask spread.

The contrast between the modern market structure and the past structure brings up a relevant and sometimes controversial question: Are investors better off now than they were in the good old days?

Much of life involves a little give and take. I suppose the markets are not much different in this regard. On one hand, the traditional roles and expertise provided by the specialists and market makers in providing stable markets have been significantly limited. On the other, we enjoy the efficiencies offered through the speed of electronic markets. Today, we benefit from generally tighter spreads leading to lower costs. The give-up might be a loss in confidence in the market's stability and perhaps some loss in the depth of liquidity in the less actively traded issues relative to the higher volume levels.

Although higher volume in the market should imply higher liquidity, this has not necessarily been the case for all issues in the high-frequency age. High volume insinuates that many want to transact over a specified period of time. Liquidity, on the other hand, is the viability of the markets to arrange a match between those investors who seek to exchange. The changes in the structure of the market have had an indirect effect on volume, causing it to soar. But these same changes in market structure have had a direct effect on the market's liquidity (its capability to orchestrate an exchange).

The most predominant way to measure liquidity is through market depth. Market depth shows how many shares are backing the best bid and/or offer. Since 2003, large actively traded stocks in the S&P 500 have experienced a significant growth in market depth leading to better liquidity. However, smaller less actively traded stocks have not experienced as much of this benefit.

Perhaps a better way to determine liquidity is to look deeper into the levels behind market depth. Deeper levels of market depth can be established by calculating how many shares are behind the best bid and offer should the best bid offer be filled or canceled. Examining 6 cents behind the best bid-ask since 2003 shows that the large-cap active stocks of the S&P 500 have experienced significant improvements in market depth. However, when considering all listed stocks 6 cents deep, market depth has had a less drastic improvement. Taking into account that during the study period volume more than doubled, the S&P 500 issues exhibited modest relative market depth improvements, whereas most other stocks experienced minimal improvement (see Figure 22.7).

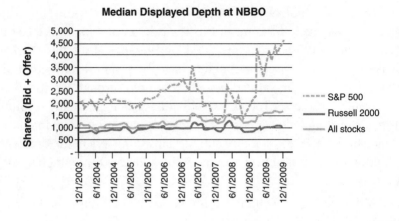

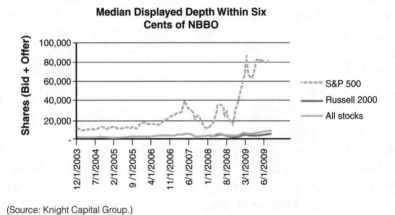

(Source: Knight Capital Group.)

Figure 22.7   Liquidity depth and liquidity 6 cents deep.

The inability to find significant liquidity affects a trader's ability to move large volumes of stock. A trader might try to purchase a large quantity of a certain issue only to find its own trading is significantly moving the market. This is due to a lack of depth on the other side of the trade. Given such an environment, the trader might break the large order into several smaller pieces, making the order more digestible for the market. Today, this is a common practice known as an iceberg order, meaning the displayed order is actually just the tip of the iceberg. There are also dark orders, and a large variety of algorithmic orders, such as Volume Weighted Average Pricing. From 2004 through 2009, the mean average size of a trade fell by half from nearly

800 shares to less than 400 shares per execution (see Figure 22.8). Smaller trades might mean that traders feel that large orders might adversely affect executions, which suggests a loss in market liquidity.

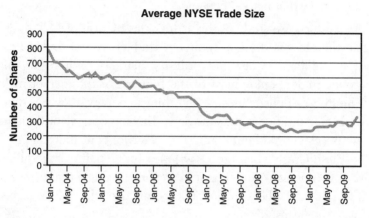

(Source: NYSE-Euronext, nyx.com.)

Figure 22.8   Average NYSE trade size.

Another concern regarding the liquidity of modern markets is the speed of trading. Since decimalization, trading has witnessed a significant improvement in the speed of executions (see Figure 22.9). This reflects the new world of high-frequency trading. Normally, speed might be thought to be liquidity neutral. But considering this is an environment cloaked with cancellations, the question becomes: How certain are quotations whose longevity is measured in microseconds?

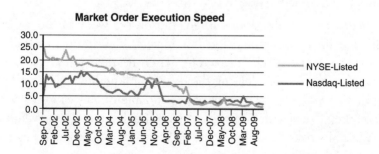

(Source: Rule 605 data from Thomson for all eligible market orders [100-9999 shares].)

Figure 22.9   Market speed of market orders.

The biggest obstacle to a liquid and stable market environment is asymmetric or one-sided markets. This is a double-edged sword as the more liquid a market becomes, the more apt it is to encounter volatile swings and crashes. Thus, the less liquid a market becomes, the more risky that market becomes.

A real-life case study of this is the Flash Crash of May 6, 2010. Unlike the old guard, high-frequency traders are not under a mandate to maintain a "fair and orderly" market. As a result, high-frequency traders enjoy most of the benefits of the market makers with limited responsibilities. When things go awry, they can quickly unwind their positions and shut down their trading algorithms until the smoke clears. Without doubt, this behavior contributed to events of the Flash Crash when the Dow Jones Industrial Average plunged nearly 1,000 points—the biggest loss ever in a single trading session. At 2:42 P.M. EST, the Dow lost 600 points over the course of just 5 minutes, the fastest drop ever!

As stocks crashed, quotes became erroneous. Orders flowed away to the newbies in the electronic markets. And who could blame them? With spreads in penny increments, they were no longer being compensated to step in and bite the bullet associated with one-sided markets. Nor in this age of speed trading do the specialists and market makers have the level of visibility they once had to gauge potential supply or demand and to judge such risks. In a September 2010 *Bloomberg* article, Nina Mehta asked former Bear Stearns trading executive Patrick Healy about the ramifications of such actions to specialists and market markers in the past: "In the old days, the specialist obligation was quite stringent. If he didn't meet it, he got canned, and someone else traded the stock."

With the old obligations lifted, the orders went to the ECNs. With too many sellers and too few buyers, high-frequency traders shut down. Senator Schumer wrote, "High-frequency traders pulled out during the freefall, leaving the dearth of liquidity and exacerbating market volatility." The lack of dependable quotes caused severe decoupling issues with ETFs that seek to track the real-time value of a basket of stocks. It seems in the ETF world, one dropped egg can threaten to break the whole basket.

At first glance, the crash was thought to be the result of an enormous trading error. Soon, however, it became evident that the cause could not be attributed to a single mistake, malfunction, or erroneous order. Many believed the crisis was exacerbated by market orders and stop losses.

In this regard, the Flash Crash was reminiscent of the Market Break of May 28, 1962. On that day, the Dow fell sharply over a 20-minute span closing the day down 5.7 percent, the second largest single-day point drop on record at the time. Volume was so heavy that the reporting was not completed until nearly two and a half hours after the market closed. Contrasting the 1962 Market Break to 2010's Flash Crash, Ian Domowitz, Managing Director at Investment Technologies Group, stated in *Advanced Trading*: "A sharp market dislocation is not necessarily due to fragmentation or electronic market structure. Market fragmentation was non-existent back then. Trading occurred on a physical floor. Dark liquidity referred to tickets in the pockets of floor traders."

In a memo to the SEC, the Managed Funds Association drew a similar conclusion:

Both "market breaks" in 1962 and 2010 happened suddenly and erratically, and in both cases liquidity seemed to evaporate for a brief period of time. Just as electronic market makers are said to have retreated on May 6th, 2010, New York Stock Exchange specialists shifted to selling on May 28th, 1962 and did not intervene in the decline.

Similar market dislocations occurred in 1997, 1989, and twice in 1987 with the October 19th crash being the most notable. In these instances, the markets went down despite human efforts to intervene. Because the modern market was moving faster than it ever had, it created the fastest drop. However, in that case, you must also give the market structure credit in creating the fastest recovery ever. Most of the 600 points lost in 5 minutes was recouped in the next 10 minutes.

Given that like events unfolded similarly in different structures, you could conclude that the cause of such events is not necessarily due to or prevented by the market's structure or mechanisms. The 1963 SEC study of the Market Break concludes: "The history of the May 28 market break reveals complex interactions of cause and effects—including rational and emotional motivations... might suddenly create a downward spiral of great velocity and force." Thus, crashes are due to investors being temporarily overwhelmed with fear. In such cases, a bearish herd mentality develops. Investors acting on fear drive stocks down wiping out all the available demand. In the midst of the selling stampede, bulls unsure about what is "spooking the herd" delay purchases for fear of getting trampled. As a result, new buyers are unwilling to step in, which results in a one-sided market.

This brings us back full circle. Whether rational or emotional, identifying such patterns of behavior is what volume analysis is all about. Low volume is the market led astray. High volume is the good shepherd leading the way. By measuring the level of participation by investors at various levels and directions, volume analysis is intended to gauge the velocity and force of supply and demand within the market.

The Effect of Changes in Market Structure on Volume Analysis

High-frequency traders generally do not take positions. They are in effect 21st century light-speed scalpers. To the extent a high-frequency trader takes a position, its actions are reflected on the tape just like anyone else's actions. Non-directional trading does not directly affect volume analysis. High-frequency scalping activities have created higher volume levels and a new form of liquidity. However, these activities have been worked in slowly over the course of years and are now considered routine practice. So as long as computers become faster, costs lower, and spreads narrower, a secular growth of volume will exist. This hardly affects short- and intermediate-term analysis at all. Previous volume growth might need to be accounted for in some forms of long-term analysis.

Neither do dark pools take positions. They match orders. Although dark pools do not post quotes, that is immaterial to volume analysis, because they still must report trade executions to the tape following the 90-second rule. With a relatively small market share (10–15 percent), dark pools should have little impact on the market's efficiencies. However, if the market share grows so that dark pool order flow rivals that of the consolidated tape, then dark pools can jeopardize the trade through rules. Dark pools work fairly only because they cannot break the bid ask of the consolidated tape. However, the more dark pool volume grows, the less validity the consolidated quotes may hold.

One needs to recognize that secular volume growth brought about by the modern market structure exists and is here to stay. There is no need to back out or purify the data. This is just a natural cycle of tighter spreads resulting from decimalization and open competition.

Volume Data Reliability

The bigger issue within volume analysis is the reliability of the data. This reliability is especially problematic in the computation of index data.

The first misunderstanding an investor might encounter is differentiating between the confusing arrays of volume sources for equity trading data. Although there are 13 stock exchanges, and more than 70 ATSes, only four exchanges are currently actively list stocks nationally. These are the New York Stock Exchange (NYSE), NYSE Amex (formerly the American Stock Exchange), NYSE Arca (formerly the Archipelago ECN, which bought the Pacific Stock Exchange), and the Nasdaq Stock Market. NYSE Euronext is the parent company of the NYSE, NYSE Amex, and NYSE Arca. Nasdaq OMX is the parent company of the Nasdaq Stock Market. There are also several other stock exchanges, some of which remain independent; others are owned by Nasdaq OMX and others are partially owned by brokerage firms.

The NYSE and NYSE Amex list several kinds of equity products but generally not Exchange Traded Funds (ETFs). NYSE Arca focuses solely on ETFs, whereas Nasdaq lists all types of issues. Volume is reported based on the listing venue. The Consolidated Tape Association reports trades and quotes for two tapes: one for NYSE-listed issues (Tape A) and one for issues listed on the regional (NYSE Arca & other non-Nasdaq) exchanges (Tape B). The CTA is run by SIAC's Security Information Processor (SIP). Nasdaq-listed stock volumes and quotes are reported by the Nasdaq SIP, also known as the Unlisted Trading Privileges Plan, or Tape C.

It is important to understand that trade reporting is based upon the location of where the stock is listed. For example, Nasdaq trades stocks that are listed on the NYSE. That activity is reported on Tape A. Similarly, NYSE Arca trades stocks that are listed on the NYSE, NYSE Arca, NYSE Amex, and Nasdaq. The NYSE listed activity is reported by NYSE Arca to Tape A, whereas the NYSE Arca and NYSE Amex activity are reported to Tape B. NYSE Arca's trading and quoting in Nasdaq-listed issues are reported to Tape C.

As noted earlier, stocks do not just trade on exchanges. Dark pools and brokerage internalizers must also report their volume to one of the tapes based on where the stock executed is listed. There are two trade reporting facilities (TRF), controlled by FINRA. One is commonly called the Nasdaq TRF and one is called the NYSE TRF. However, the TRFs report executions to any of the three tapes, depending on the stock's underlying listing. Thus, all NYSE volume is on Tape A, all regional exchanges on Tape B, and all Nasdaq volume is on Tape C, regardless of where the trade is executed.

Another problem with volume data involves data collection. Stocks can trade from 4 A.M. until 8 P.M. However, trading session hours are from 9:30 A.M. until 4:00 P.M. The CTA issues the adjusted market summary at 4:15 P.M., even though after-hours trading can still occur. Those trades are reported with a special modifier identifying them as after-hours trades. These might be considered part of the next day's trading session if not reported in a later summary. However, not all vendors use the CTA's market summary. A data vendor might report data as they stand at a different point in time.

An analyst can take several steps to effectively deal with these issues. First, the analyst can be consistent. The reason variations in the data exist is that different sources are not uniform in their procedures. However, the analyst studying the data must be consistent. The first step in achieving consistency is to choose one data provider. Flipping from one data provider to another can easily impair the data as different providers might use different tapes or tape combinations and/or report data at different times. For example, *The Wall Street Journal* might use only tape A in its volume totals. However, Yahoo! Finance might use a combination of all three tapes in reporting the total volume.

Next, the trader must be consistent in the time when he obtains the data. Retrieving the data before 4:15 is not wise because the data might be subject to revision. If the source of the data is vendors using after-hours trades, then the final statistics also change in the after hours. This becomes a problem if the analyst also collects the data at different times in after-hours trading.

A better solution might be to manually not obtain the data at all, but to maintain an automatic and self-correcting feed from one consistent source. Various analytical and trading platforms maintain these data automatically. Some even allow the user to choose the tape (Tape A, B, C, or consolidated) to download the data. The ideal solution, though, is to choose one data source and consistently keep your own cap-weighted volume on the price index or indexes you are analyzing as discussed in Chapter 19, "Buff Up Your Volume: Introducing Capital Weighted Volume." In this way, one is comparing "apples to apples" (for instance, the stocks in the price index against the capital weight volume of those same index issues). Again, even with this advanced method, you must be consistent about when you compile the data.

Congratulations on finishing *Investing with Volume Analysis*. I hope you found these concepts about market volume enlightening. Please keep in touch with me and other volume practitioners at www.VolumeAnalysis.com. Here, you will find many useful resources in applying the tools and indicators discussed throughout this book. Farewell my friends, and may the force be with you!

Bibliography

"The Early Chartists: Schabacker, Edwards, Magee." James Maccaro (2002). http://www.visionbooksindia.com/details.asp?isbn=8170947081.

"The Empirical Investigation of Relationship Between Return, Volume, and Volatility Dynamics in Indian Stock Market." Sarika Mahajan and Balwinder Singh (2009), *Eurasian Journal of Business and Economics 2009*, 2 (4), Pgs. 113–129.

Alfred Cowles. http://en.wikipedia.org/wiki/Alfred_Cowles.

"The History of the Dow Theory." Richard Russell. http://ww2.dowtheoryletters. com/dtlol.nsf.

"Forecasting Methods Successfully Used Since 1928." Willford I. King (1932), *Journal of the American Statistical Association*, Volume 27, Issue 179 (September 1932), Pgs. 316:317.

"Technical Methods of Forecasting Stock Prices." Willford I. King (1932), *Journal of the American Statistical Association*, Volume 27, Issue 179 (September 1932), Pgs. 323–325.

Trader Vic—Methods of a Wall Street Master. Victor Sperandeo with T. Sullivan Brown (1991), John Wiley & Sons, Pgs. 30:31.

Clarence W. Barron. http://en.wikipedia.org/wiki/Clarence_W._Barron.

"Investment Management and Financial Innovations." Volume 3, Issue 3 (2006), Thompson ONE.

"The High Volume Return Premium." Simon Gervais, Ron Kaniel, and Dan Mingelgrin. The Rodney L. White Center for Financial Research.

"Volume, Variance, and the Combined Signal Approach to Technical Analysis." Camillo Lento, *Journal of Money, Investment and Banking*, EuroJournals Publishing, Inc., 2009.

"Relationship Between Trading Volume and Security Prices and Returns." Walter Sun, *Journal of Money, Investment and Banking*, Issue 7, 2009.

"Introduction to the Wyckoff Method of Stock Market Analysis."

"Frozen in Analysis Paralysis? Use Volume to Break Through the Ice." Todd Krueger.

"Identifying Trends with Volume Analysis." Stephen J. Klinger, CMT, *Stocks & Commodities*, V. 15:12, Pgs. 556–560.

"V" Is for Volume." David Penn (2005), *Working Money—Views from the Field*.

"Volume Spread Analysis." Karthik Marar.

"Wyckoff Laws and Tests." Henry (Hank) Pruden, Ph. D. and Benard Belletante.

"Is the Price-Volume Relationship Symmetric in the Futures Markets?." Imad Moosa and Marta Korczak (1999), *Journal of Financial Studies*, Vol. 7, No. 1.

"Testing for Temporal Asymmetry in the Price-Volume Relationship." Imad A. Moosa, Param Silvapulle, and Mervyn Silvapulle (2003), Blackwell Publishing Ltd and the Board of Trustees of the Bulletin of Economic Research 2003, Blackwell Publishing, Pgs. 373:374, 385.

"Is the Price-Volume Relation Asymmetric? Cross-Sectional Evidence from an Emerging Stock Market." Imad A. Moosa and Sulaiman Al-Abdul Jader (2006), *Investment Management and Financial Innovations*, Volume 3, Issue 3.

"Asymmetry in the price-volume relation: evidence based on individual company stocks traded in an emerging stock market." Khalid Al-Saad and Imad A. Moosa (2008), Applied Financial Economics Letters, Taylor & Francis, Pgs. 151–155.

"Trading Volume: Definitions, Data Analysis, and Implications of Portfolio Theory." Andrew W. Lo and Jiang Wang (2000), Nber Working Paper Series, Pgs. 1–3, 9:11, 35.

"Strategic Insider Trading with Imperfect Information: A Trading Volume Analysis." Andrea Marcello Buffa (2004), *Rivista Di Politica Economica*.

"A Bivariate Garch Approach to the Futures Volume-Volatility Issue." Marilyn K. Wiley and Robert T. Daigler (1999), Pgs. 1:4.

"Modeling Asymmetry in the Price-Volume Relation: Evidence from Nine Stock Markets." Talla M. Al-Deehani (2007), *Investment Management and Financial Innovations*, Volume 4, Issue 4.

"Volume and Price Formation in an Asset Trading Model with Asymmetric Information." Antonio E. Bernardo and Kenneth L. Judd (1996), Pgs. 1, 5–7, 22–24.

"A Model of Price, Volume, and Sequential Information." Gaiyan Zhang, Pgs. 2–5, 16.

"The Price Volume Relationship in the Sale and Purchase Market for Dry Bulk Vessels." Amir Alizadeh and Nikos Nomikos, Pgs. 1–6.

"The Empirical Relationship Between Trading Volume, Returns and Volatility." Timothy J. Brailsford (1994), Research Paper 94-01, Pgs. 2–5, 7:8, 10:12, 28.

"Trading Volume and Stock Returns: Evidence from Pakistan's Stock Market." Safi Ullah Khan and Faisal Rizwan (2008), *International Review of Business Research Papers*, Vol. 4, No. 2.

"Equity Trading in the 21st Century." James J. Angel, Lawrence E. Harris, and Chester S. Spatt (2010).

"Brokers Face Fines Over Role in 'Flash Crash'." *The Financial Times* (2010).

"Gene Noser's 5 Suggestions on How to Regain Our Market Back from the Robots." Tyler Durden (2010).

"The Matrix, But with Money: The World of High-Speed Trading." Jon Stokes (2009), *Ars Technica*.

"Regulators and Others Question the Need to Trade at Hyper-Fast Speeds." John D'antona Jr. and Peter Chapman (2010). http://www.tradersmagazine.com/issues/23_313/so-not-fast-106207-1.html?zkPrintable=true.

"Exclusive: SEC probing "spikey" U.S. quote traffic in markets." Jonathan Spicer and Rachelle Younglai (2010). http://www.reuters.com/assets/print?aid=USTRE68D4LX20100914.

"SEC Questions Trading Crusade as Market Makers Disappear." Nina Mehta (2010), www.bloomberg.com.

"Joint CFTC-SEC Advisory Committee on Emerging Regulatory Issues." Managed Funds Association (2010).

"FINRA Amended Trade Reporting Rules Effective August 3, 2009." Bracewell & Biuliani.

"Open Trade Cloud: Regulating the Next Generation of the National Market System." Carlos Mauricio S. Mirandola (2010).

"Consolidated Tape Association." http://en.wikipedia.org/wiki/Consolidated_Tape_Association.

"Consolidated Tape Association." 2007 FINRA/NASDAQ Trade Reporting Facility Exchange Operation Frequently Asked Questions. http://en.academic.ru/dic.nsf/enwiki/6906259.

"Why Do Numbers for Volume of Stock Traded Per Day Differ?." Episode 56, Andrew Horowitz (2010). http://winninginvestor.quickanddirtytips.com/.

"Have Human Traders Become an Endangered Species?." Pascal Willain, *Stocks & Commodities*, V. 26:12, Pgs. 58–61, Working Money, The Trading Ecosystem, Technical Analysis, Inc.

"Trading in Fragmented Markets: A Different Kind of Ballgame." Murat Atamer (2009), *A Guide to Global Liquidity: Asian Markets*.

"Floor Brokerages Remake Themselves: Downstairs Upstairs at the NYSE." Nina Mehta (2008). http://www.tradersmagazine.com/issues/20_285/101842-1.html?zkprintable=true.

"The Consolidated Tape: Yes Dark Pool Trades Are in There." 2009. http://blogs.wsj.com.

"Back to the Future: Lessons from the Forgotten 'Flash Crash' of 1962." Jason Zweig (2010). http://online.wsj.com/article/SB10001424052748703957604575272791511469272.html.

"Take Heed the Lessons from the 1962 Flash Crash." Ian Domowitz (2010). http://www.advancedtrading.com/showArticle.jhtml?articleID=225700888.

Bollinger on Bollinger Bands. John Bollinger (2002), McGraw-Hill, Pgs. 146–155.

Trading Chaos: Applying Expert Techniques to Maximize Your Profits. Bill Williams, Ph.D. (1995), John Wiley & Sons, Inc., Pgs. 20:60.

Value in Time. Pascal Willain (2008), John Wiley & Sons, Inc., Pgs. 11–13, 18:19, 27, 33, 40:41, 43, 47, 59, 61–67, 69:70, 81, 102, 105, 107, 113, 189.

Trading Without Fear. Richard W. Arms, Jr. (1996), John Wiley & Sons, Inc., Pgs. 15, 19, 35–55, 90-101.

"Charting the Stock Market: The Wyckoff Method." Edited by Jack K. Hutson (1986, 1987, 1990, 1991, 1998, 2000, 2009), Pgs. 3–51, 117–190.

Technical Analysis Explained: 3rd Edition. Martin J. Pring (1991, 1988, 1985), McGraw-Hill, Pgs. 31–105, 186:187, 271–313.

Technical Analysis. Charles D. Kirkpatrick II, CMT and Julie R. Dahlquist, Ph.D. (2007), Pearson Education, Inc., Pgs. 3–10, 30, 73–82, 125–152, 301–339, 411–430.

Technical Analysis of Stock Trends: Sixth Edition. Robert D. Edwards and John Magee (1992), New York Institute of Finance, Pgs. 3–7, 58–330.

Technical Analysis of the Futures Markets: A Comprehensive Guide to Trading Methods and Applications. John J. Murphy (1986), New York Institute of Finance, Pgs. 1–7, 24–33, 41–43, 55–68, 103–116, 136–155, 176–206.

"Bi Signal Indicator." Joseph Barics, *Stocks & Commodities*, V. 7:10, Pgs. 375–377.

"Money Flow Index." Money Flow Index.

"OEX and the Thrust Oscillator." Stuart Meibuhr, *Stocks & Commodities*, V. 11:3, Pgs. 127–132.

"Point Volume: A New Indicator." Richard W. Arms, Jr. (1984), *MTA Journal*, Pgs. 57–63.

"Tracking the 'Quality' of Investments with the Most Actives Money Flow." Bruce McCurtain (1984), *MTA Journal*, Pgs. 17–19.

"Financial Volume Index." Patrick Cifaldi, *Stocks & Commodities*, V. 7:8, Pgs. 246–248.

"A Survey of Volume Indicators." John Bollinger, CFA, CMT (2002), *IFTA Journal*, Pgs. 4–8.

"Arms Index (TRIN)." Thompson ONE.

"The Short-Term Trading Index: Have You Got It Figured Right?." John R. McGinley, Jr., Pgs. 7–10:15–16.

"The Speculator: An Investing Tool You Can Do Without." Victor Niederhoffer and Laurel Kenner, Thompson ONE.

"The Short-Term Trading (ARMS) Index Revisited." John R. McGinley, Jr., Pgs. 65–68.

"Market Breadth: A Directory of Internal Indicators." Investopedia.

"Q&A: Paul Desmond of Lowry's Reports." Barry Ritholtz, Thompson ONE.

"Lowry Without Tears." Stan Lipstadt, Pgs. 51–56.

"Planes, Trains & Automobiles: A Study of Different Market Internals That Can Be Used to Evaluate the Markets Momentum & How They Can Be Combined to Gauge the Markets Strength." 2009, Pgs. 1–14.

"Identifying Bear Market Bottoms and New Bull Markets." Paul F. Desmond (2002), *Journal of Technical Analysis*, Pgs. 38–42.

"Identifying Bear Market Bottoms and New Bull Markets." Paul F. Desmond (2002), Lowry's Reports Inc., Pgs. 1–19.

"Using Market Breadth in Trading Systems." Lawrence Chan (2007). www.futuresmag.com.

"Breadth of the Market Trends." Harold M. Gartley, Pgs. 67–74.

"Understanding Oscillators and Other Indicators: Used in *The McClellan Market Report*." Tom McClellan and Sherman McClellan (1995).

"Using the McClellan Oscillator for Bond Market Timing." Bob Kargenian (1991), *MTA Journal*, Pgs. 36–39.

"McClellan Summation Index." Thompson ONE.

"2004 MTA Lifetime Achievement Award Sherman and Marian McClellan: Technical Analysis in Los Angeles In the 1960s and 1970s." McClellan Financial Publications, Inc. (2004).

"The Well Traveled Road and the Not So Well Known Travels of the Negative and Positive Volume Indicators." George A Schade, Jr., CMT (2005), GASchadeArticle/August 2005.

"The Evolution of a Breadth Indicator or Teaching an Old Dog New Tricks." John Carder (1985), *MTA Journal*, Pgs. 35–39.

"Fundamental and Technical Analysis: Substitutes or Compliments?." Jenni L. Bettman, Stephen J. Sault, and Emma L. Welch, School of Finance and Applied Statistics, College of Business and Economics, Australian National University, Canberra, ACT, 0200 Australia.

"Volume Variations." Barbara Star, Ph.D., *Stocks & Commodities*, V. 11:5, Pgs. 215–219.

"Technical Analysis of Volume." Howard K. Waxenberg, *Stocks & Commodities*, V. 4:2, Pgs. 65–68.

"Volume and Forex, Together: Pump Up the Volume." Todd Krueger, *Stocks & Commodities*, V. 27:8, Pgs. 32–35.

"On a New Academic Paradigm: Henry Pruden of Golden Gate University." Thom Hartle, *Stocks & Commodities*, V. 16:9, Pgs. 434–442.

"The Holy Grail of Trading Is Within Us: Chuck Dukas of TRENDadvisor.com." Jayanthi Gopalakrishnan, *Stocks & Commodities*, V. 24:6, Pgs. 62–66.

"The Importance of Pattern Recognition: Henry "Hank" Pruden: What the Future Holds." Jayanthi Gopalakrishnan, *Stocks & Commodities*, V. 25:9, Pgs. 60–66.

"The Charts Know It All: Chart Patterns, Trading and Dan Zanger." Matt Blackman, *Stocks & Commodities*, V. 21:8, Pgs. 78–85.

"Working Money: He Knows Investors' Business, Daily William J. O'Neil." David Penn, *Stocks & Commodities*, V. 19:10, Pgs. 83–89.

"Steve Shobin of Merrill Lynch." Thom Hartle, *Stocks & Commodities*, V. 9:9, Pgs. 354–360.

"The Technical Song of Bernadette Murphy." Thom Hartle, *Stocks & Commodities*, V. 10:5, Pgs. 195–200.

"Real Life: Shearson's Jeffrey Weiss." Thom Hartle, *Stocks & Commodities*, V. 10:5, Pgs. 370–375.

"First Citizen of Technical Analysis: Arthur Merrill." Thom Hartle, *Stocks & Commodities*, V. 10:10, Pgs. 407–413.

"On the Bull Market of the Century: Louise Yamada." Thom Hartle, *Stocks & Commodities*, V. 16:8, Pgs. 387–393.

"The Ticker Tape: Yesterday, Today, and Tomorrow." Sam H. Hale, CMT (1995), *MTA Journal*.

"Steven C. Leuthold: Fundamentally Technical." Thom Hartle, *Stocks & Commodities*, V. 11:3, Pgs. 112–117.

"John Bollinger of Bollinger Capital Management." Thom Hartle, *Stocks & Commodities*, V. 11:7, Pgs. 277–284.

"A Buy Signal Isn't Just a Buy Signal, Contextual Trader Larry Williams." Thom Hartle, *Stocks & Commodities*, V. 15:7, Pgs. 318–322.

"Saving Money to Make Money: Measuring Risk." Lee Leibfarth, *Stocks & Commodities*, V. 24:11, Pgs. 20–26.

"Trading and Control: Walter Bressert." Thom Hartle, *Stocks & Commodities*, V. 16:3, Pgs. 145–151.

"Direction, Discipline, Risk and Leverage: Managing Money & Risk: Robert Deel." Jayanthi Gopalakrishnan, *Stocks & Commodities*, V. 21:10, Pgs. 82–89.

"On the Opening Bell: David Vomund of AIQ." John Sweeney, *Stocks & Commodities*, V. 17:10, Pgs. 449–457.

"Persistence of Money Flow (Daily Only)." AIQ TradingExpert Pro Reference Manual.

"Trading Strategies." 2010, *AAII Journal*, Pgs. 8–11.

"Market Fuel and Technical Analysis." D. Earl Essig, *Stocks & Commodities*, V. 9:12, Pgs. 488–491.

"Change Coming." Thompson ONE.

"Dynamic Visualization of Microarray Time Series." Bruce Peterson (2005), TeraStat/Peterson.

"Out of the Blocks." Doug Sandler, CFA (2006), Chief Equity Strategist.

"Missing the Ten Best." Paul J. Gire, CFP.

"Technical Analysis: Piecing the Puzzle Together." Buff Dormeier, CMT (2005), Fort Wayne Business Journal.

"A Six-Part Study Guide to Market Profile." Chicago Board of Trade.

"Enhancing On-Balance and Negative Volume." Phillip C. Holt, *Stocks & Commodities*, V. 14:6, Pgs. 265–269.

"Taking Stock of a Scary Market Signal." Michael Kahn (2010). Barrons.com.

"Focus on True Supply and Demand... And Better Your Odds for Low-Risk Entries." Sam Seiden (2005), *Stocks, Futures and Options Magazine*.

"Visualize Price Movement." Francois Bertrand, *Stocks & Commodities*, V. 23:6.

"The Better Volume Indicator... My Secret to Analyzing Volume." 2009. www.Emini-Watch.com.

"Stock Trading Using Wyckoff's 5 Step Method."

"Different Types of Volume." Mike Estrey, Thompson ONE (2007).

"Trading Volume Spread Analysis." Lamont Adair (2009).

"A Primer on Volume Spread Analysis." Todd Krueger.

"A Study in Volume and Price Alerts." David Bryan (1996), *MTA Journal*, Pgs. 57–60.

"Understanding Stock Volume." Christina Pomoni (2010), Thompson ONE.

"Volume Analysis: Part 1." John C. Lawlor, *Stocks & Commodities*, V. 6:1, Pgs. 37–39.

"Websites for Traders." David Penn, *Stocks & Commodities*, V. 22:6, Pgs. 86–88.

"Technical Analysis: Key Papers."

"Trading Stock Index Futures?: ETF Volume Can Be More Accurate." Todd Krueger, *The Official Advocate for Personal Investing*, Pgs. 29–32.

"Price/Volume Divergence." Henry O. Pruden, Ph.D. (1983), *MTA Journal*, Pgs. 35–44.

"Market Profile Basics." Forex & Stock Trading Library.

"Stock Chart Volume: How Traders Use Volume on a Stock Chart." http://www.swing-trade-stocks.com/stock-chart-volume.html.

"Volume in the Stock Index Futures Market—Part One." http://traderfeed.blogspot.com/2008/04/volume-in-stock-index-futures-market.html.

"Find Non-Displayed Liquidity on NASDAQ." NASDAQOMAXtrader.com.

"Dark Pools of Liquidity." Keith Caplan, Robert P. Cohen, Jimmie Lenz, and Christopher Pullano. Price Waterhouse Coopers.

"SEC Issues Proposals to Shed Greater Light on Dark Pools." Thompson ONE.

"Strengthening the Regulation of Dark Pools." Thompson ONE.

"Exposing the Identity of Dark Pools in Real Time Could Hurt Institutional Traders." Ivy Schmerken, Thompson ONE.

"Rappin' It Up with Dark Pools of Liquidity." David Silverman. www.sfomag.com.

"The HFT Interviews: Walter Hendriks, ABR Financial." www.highfrequencytradingreview.com.

"Ending the ban against locked markets could benefit our national market system." Manoj Narang. www.imagazine.com.

"The HFT Interviews: Sal Arnuk, Themis Trading." www.highfrequencytradingreview.com.

"Q&A." Don Bright, *Stocks & Commodities*, V. 26:10, Pg. 51.

"Don't Be Afraid of the Dark Pools." Alexandra Zendrian. Forbes.com.

"The HFT Interviews: Peter Green, The Kyte Group." www.highfrequencytradingreview.com.

"A Defense of High Frequency Trading by NYSE Euronext." Stacy-Marie Ishmael. www.ft.com/alphaville.

"The HFT Interviews: Ari Burstein, Investment Company Institute." www.highfrequencytradingreview.com.

"Stock Traders Find Speed Pays, in Milliseconds." Charles Duhigg. www.nytimes.com.

"The HFT Interviews: Manoj Narang, Tradeworx." www.highfrequencytradingreview.com.

"The Trading Ecosystem: Have human traders become an endangered species?." Pascal Willain, *Stocks & Commodities*, V. 26:12.

"SEC Proposes Regulation of Dark Pools." Morrison–Foerster (2009).

"Dark Pools and Algorithmic Trading." George Sofianos, *Algorithms in Action*.

"Fast, Loose, and Out of Control: Trading billions of shares in the blink of an eye has made stock martes more responsive—and volatile—than ever." Matthew Philips (2010).

"Tradeworx, Inc. Public Commentary on SEC Market Structure Concept Release." Manoj Narang (2010), TradeWorx.

"The Heretics of Finance: Conversations with Leading Practitioners." Andrew W. Lo.

"Buff Up Your Moving Averages." Buff Dormeier, CMT, *Stocks & Commodities*, V. 19:2, Pgs. 48–56.

"Bollinger on Volume Indicators." David Penn, *Stocks & Commodities*, V. 19:14, Pgs. 128–129.

"Putting the VPCI to the Test." 2005. www.activetradermag.com.

"A Survey of Volume Indicators." John Bollinger, CFA, CMT (2002), *IFTA Journal*.

"Market trends in composite averages: Wyckoff method of trading stocks: Part 3." Jack K. Hutson, *Stocks & Commodities*, V. 4:3, Pgs. 105–108.

"Market Strategy: The Wyckoff Method of Trading: Part 15." Jack K. Hutson, *Stocks & Commodities*, V. 5:11, Pgs. 364–368.

"Wyckoff Tests: Nine Classic Tests for Accumulation; Nine New Tests for Re-Accumulation." Henry (Hank) Pruden, Ph. D. (2001), *MTA Journal*.

"Anatomy of a Trading Range." Jim Forte (1994), *MTA Journal*.

"Life Cycle Model of Crowd Behavior." Henry O. Pruden, Ph.D. (2003), *Journal of Technical Analysis*.

"Editor's Commentary 'Behavioral Finance': What Is It?." Henry O. Pruden, Ph.D. (1995), *MTA Journal*.

"The Cup-With-Handle Pattern." Gregory Kuhn, *Stocks & Commodities*, V. 13:3, Pgs. 107–111.

"Identifying the Cup (With or Without the Handle)." Giorgos Siligardos, Ph.D., *Stocks & Commodities*, V. 24:2, Pgs. 36–42.

"Identifying Trends with the K st Indicator." Martin J. Pring, *Stocks & Commodities*, V. 10:10, Pgs. 420–424.

"Broad Bottom Configurations and Their Applications to Investment Strategy." William S. Doane.

"Weinstein's Theory of Relativity." Larry Swing, *Stocks & Commodities*, V. 27:2, Pgs. 46–47.

"Wyckoff Method of Trading Stocks: Part 8, Trendlines: Refinements in Charting." Jack K. Hutson, *Stocks & Commodities*, V. 4:9, Pgs. 340–342.

"Probabilities, Not Certainties: Martin Pring and the Relevance of Price Trends." J. Gopalakrishnan and B.R. Faber, *Stocks & Commodities*, V. 27:10, Pgs. 50–56.

"Is It Possible to Time Swings and Trends?: Timing the Move." *Stocks & Commodities*, V. 19:8, Pgs. 70–72, 78–79.

"Determining Capital Amounts for Trading." Ajay Jani, *Stocks & Commodities*, V. 12:4, Pgs. 165–170.

"Are You Piloting Your Trading with Safety?." Ana Maria Wilson, *Stocks & Commodities*, V. 7:10, Pgs. 355–356.

"The Holy Grail of Trading is Within Us All: Van K. Tharp, Ph.D." Thom Hartle, *Stocks & Commodities*, V. 17:4, Pgs. 186–192.

"Trader's Progress: Better Trading with Risk Control." Daryl Guppy, *Stocks & Commodities*, V. 20:9, Pgs. 22–29.

"Trading Is a Business: Four Decades with Joe Ross." Thom Hartle, *Stocks & Commodities*, V. 13, Pgs. 530–537.

"The 10 Pillars of Trading." Sam Baum, *Stocks & Commodities*, V. 26:10, Pgs. 96–98.

"Mathematics of Gambling." Edward O. Thorp (1981), *Gambling Times*.

"Trading Educator's Corner." John Bollinger. www.esignallearning.com/education/marketmaster/jbollinger/default.aspx.

"The Pring Money Flow Indicator." Martin Pring, *Stocks & Commodities*, V. 15:5, Pgs. 243–245.

"Wyckoff in Action." David H. Weis, *Stocks & Commodities*, V. 4:4, Pgs. 136–138.

"John Bollinger and Group Analysis." Thom Hartle, *Stocks & Commodities*, V. 15:4, Pgs. 170–178.

"5 Simple Questions to Know Before Investing." 1986, *MTA Journal*.

"Putting It All Together." Henry O. (Hank) Purden, Ph.D., *MTA Journal*.

"Time and Indicator Design." Gilbert Raff, *Stocks & Commodities*, V. 11:2, Pgs. 92–97.

"A 'Scenario Planning' Approach to Optimal Money Management." Ralph Vince (1993), *MTA Journal*.

"Getting to Know Technicals." Darrell Jobman (2006). www.sfomag.com/ Trading_Stocks_News-Getting_to_Know_Technicals-par911.aspx.

"'Why' Doesn't Matter to the Technical Trader." Michael Covel (2007). www. sfomag.com.

"What is Risk?." Gary Anderson, *Stocks & Commodities*, V. 16:4, Pgs. 183–188.

"The Wyckoff Method: Trading and Investing in Stocks." Jack K. Hutson, *Stocks & Commodities*, V. 4:1, Pgs. 14–17.

"Why Does Technical Analysis Work? Looking for Entry/Exit Points? It's All in the Charts." Kira McCaffrey Brecht (2003). www.sfomag.com.

"Read This to Avoid Unpleasant Surprises: Retail Trading Myths." Don Bright, *Stocks & Commodities*, V. 19:4, Pgs. 64–66.

"Introducing the Volume Price Confirmation Indicator (VPCI): Price & Volume Reconciled." Buff Dormeier, CMT, *Journal of Technical Analysis*.

"The Tragic Neglect of the Old Masters." James Alphier, *Stocks & Commodities*, V. 6:10, Pgs. 395–396.

"Price Activity Charts: An Innovative, Profit-Generating Way to... Visualize Price Movement." Francois Bertrand, *Stocks & Commodities*, V. 23:6, Pgs. 46–50.

"Trading a Stock Using Technical Analysis." Thom Hartle, *Stocks & Commodities*, V. 12:7, Pgs. 306–309.

"Designing a Money Management Strategy." Ray Overholser, O.D., *Stocks & Commodities*, V. 18:5, Pgs. 38–46.

"Maximizing Profits with Stop Orders: The Wyckoff Method of Trading Stocks: Part 11." Jack K. Hutson, *Stocks & Commodities*, V. 5:6, Pgs. 192–194.

"The Basics of Managing Money." Robert P. Rotella, *Stocks & Commodities*, V. 10:6, Pgs. 261–264.

"Detecting New Trends Early." David R. Steckler, *Stocks & Commodities*, V. 17:11, Pgs. 494–498.

"Visualizing Stock Behavior Patterns: Discerning Portfolio Patterns Using Data Animation." Bruce Peterson, Ph.D., *Stocks & Commodities*, V. 27:2, Pgs. 48–51.

"The Universal Applicability of Technical Analysis." Robert R. Prechter, Jr., CMT (1994), *MTA Journal*.

"The Dow Theory: William Peter Hamilton's Track Record Reconsidered." Stephen J. Brown, William N. Goetzmann, and Alok Kumar (1998).

"Volume Speaks Volumes." Dennis Peterson (2001). www.premium.working-money.com/wm.display.asp?art=184.

"Why Technical Analysis Matters." Michael Kahn, *AAII Journal*.

"Perspectives on Technical Analysis." Jasmina Hasanhodzic (2009), *Market Technician*.

"A Theoretical Foundation for Technical Analysis." Gunduz Caginalp, Ph.D. and Donald Balenovich, Ph.D. (2003), *Journal of Technical Analysis*.

"Trading the Indicators: Be Your Own Analyst: Understanding Volume." Kira McCaffrey Brecht (2005). www.sfomag.com.

"Fundamentally Speaking, Again." Phillip Gotthelf (2004). www.sfomag.com.

"Book Review." David Nassar (2004). www.sfomag.com/Trading_Stocks_News-Book_Review-php76.aspx.

"Quantitative Technical Analysis in Tactical Asset Allocation Models." Campbell A. R. Gorrie and George S. Lucas (1989), *MTA Journal*.

"Quantitative Strategy: Does Technical Analysis Work?." Credit Suisse Equity Research (2002).

"Fundamental Analysis vs. Technical Analysis." Dr. Jerry Blythe.

Technical Analysis Explained. Martin J. Pring (1980), McGraw-Hill Book Co.

"The Stock and the Company." Ralph J. Acampora.

"Ben Graham on the Efficient Market Theory and the Manic Depressive Market." 2010. www.topgunfp.com.

"Master the Markets: Taking a Professional Approach to Trading & Investing by Using Volume Spread Analysis." 1993, TradeGuider Systems, Pgs. 12–98.

"The Importance of Self-Analysis." Vak K. Tharp, Ph.D. (1989), *MTA Journal*.

"The Quantification Predicament." Timothy W. Hayes, CMT (1996), *MTA Journal*.

"Guidelines for Risk Management." George R. Arrington, *Stocks & Commodities*, V. 11:2, Pgs. 89–91.

"On System Development: Part 1." Mark Vakkur, M.D., *Stocks & Commodities*, V. 16:6, Pgs. 277–284.

"Measuring Risk." Lee Leibfarth, *Stocks & Commodities*, V. 24:11, Pgs. 20–26.

"Developing a Trading System." Curtis Arnold, *Stocks & Commodities*, V. 11:8, Pgs. 333–337.

"The Trading Plan." Cory Mitchell, *Stocks & Commodities*, V. 27:3, Pgs. 44–49.

"Successfully Evaluating the Offensive and Defensive of Stocks, Groups and Sectors." Gary Anderson.

"Risk Management, Position, Sizing and Probability." Brian Auit, *Stocks & Commodities*, V. 27:9, Pgs. 38–44.

"Measuring Trend Values." P.N. Haurlan, Trade Levels, Inc.

"Samurai Trader!: Homage to Homma." John Needham (2008). www.financialsense. com/asia/danielcode/2008/0120.html.

"Homma Munehisa." en.wikipedia.org/wiki/Homma_Munehisa.

"Arms on Arms." Thom Hartle, *Stocks & Commodities*, V. 9:7, Pgs. 293–297.

"OVR—A New Indicator." Fred Purifoy, *Stocks & Commodities*, V. 6:4, Pgs. 142–144.

"Demand Oscillator Momentum." Thomas Aspray, *Stocks & Commodities*, V. 7:9, Pgs. 282–285.

"Money Flow Analysis." Steven B. Goldstein and Michael N. Kahn, *Stocks & Commodities*, V. 6:2, Pgs. 79–81.

"A Price and Volume Based System." Alex Saitta, *Stocks & Commodities*, V. 14:3, Pgs. 103–105.

"Right on Target." Richard W. Arms, Jr., *Stocks & Commodities*, V. 8:9, Pgs. 345–347.

"Increasing OBV Reliability with Stock Index Futures." Gerald Appel, *Stocks & Commodities*, V. 8:1, Pgs. 40–43.

"Ratio Accumulators." William Mason, *Stocks & Commodities*, V. 7:9, Pgs. 278–281.

"WRB Analysis—Understanding the price action prior to the appearance of trade signals." www.thestrategylab.com/WRBAnalysis.htm.

"VSA5 Professional: Volume Spread Analysis." *Stocks & Commodities*, V. 17:13, Pgs. 637–639.

"Volume Spread Analysis (Part 1): A New Way to Look at Markets." Larry Swing. www.mrswing.com/artman/publish/printer_4212.shtml.

"Candlestick Charting Explained." Candlestickshop.com. www.daytradingcoach.com/daytrading-candlestick-course.htm.

"Normalized Volume." Dr. Shumiloff (2008). codebase.mq14.com/3571.

"Investor/RT Tour—Volume Breakdown." www.linnsoft.com/tour/techind/vb.htm.

"Normalized Volume Oscillator." Dr. Shumiloff. codebase.mq14.com/3747.

"Trade Guide." Jayanthi Gopalakrishnan, *Stocks & Commodities*, V. 24:11, Pgs. 52–54.

"Money Flow Indicator." *Stocks & Commodities*, V. 11:2, Pgs. 61–69.

"Volume-Weighted Average Price." George Reyna, *Stocks & Commodities*, V. 19:5, Pgs. 48–56.

"Market Trend and MIDAS." Andrew Coles and David Hawkins, *Stocks & Commodities*, V. 27:7, Pgs. 32–37.

"Applying MIDAS to Daily and Weekly Charts." Andrew Coles and David Hawkins, *Stocks & Commodities*, V. 27:8, Pgs. 54–61.

"The MIDAS Touch." Andrew Coles, Ph.D., *Stocks & Commodities*, V. 26:9, Pgs. 24–33.

"MIDAS—Technical Analysis Method." technical-analysis-addins.com/def-MIDAS.php.

"Technical Analysis: Institutional Trading and Money Flows: The Lessons of Stock Week." Laszio Birinyi, Jr. and Susan L. Field (1987), *MTA Journal*.

"Intraday Swings with Wave Charts: The Wyckoff Method of Trading Stocks: Part 12." Jack K. Hutson, *Stocks & Commodities*, V. 5:7, Pgs. 236–238.

"Q & A." Don Bright, *Stocks & Commodities*, V. 22:10, Pg. 47.

"Volume-Weighted Average Price." Mark Whistler. www.fxstreet.com.

"Q & A." Don Bright, *Stocks & Commodities*, V. 22:8, Pg. 86.

"Tick Volume—Technical Analysis Indicator." www.mysmp.com/technical-analysis/tick-volume.html.

"The MIDAS Touch: Part 1." Andrew Coles, Ph.D., *Stocks & Commodities*, V. 26:9, Pgs. 24–33.

"Cycle Analysis and Intraday Trading." John F. Ehlers, *Stocks & Commodities*, V. 11:2, Pgs. 84–88.

"MIDAS and Intraday Charts." Andrew Coles and David Hawkins, *Stocks & Commodities*, V. 27:9, Pgs. 14–20.

"Volume-Weighted Average Price." Michael Tanksley, Ph.D., *Stocks & Commodities*, V. 18:12, Pgs. 32–39.

"Volume and Volatility." Bishop Brock, *Intraday Volume Analysis*.

"How to Reduce the Risk of Executing VWAP Orders? New Approach to Modeling Intraday Volume." Jedrzej Bialkowski, Serge Darolles, and Gaelle Le Fol (2006).

"Trading with Equivolume." Dick Arms, realmoney.com.

"The Market Facilitation Index Update: 1/89 to 3/90." Charles F. Wright, *Stocks & Commodities*, V. 8:11, Pgs. 413–416.

"New Dimensions in Market Charts." Salvatore J. Chiappone, DDS, *Stocks & Commodities*, V. 15:12, Pgs. 572–577.

"Market Facilitation Index." Charles F. Wright, *Stocks & Commodities*, V. 7:10, Pgs. 365–368.

"The Market Facilitation Index." Gary Hoover, *Stocks & Commodities*, V. 12:6, Pgs. 253–254.

"The Market Facilitation Index." Thom Hartle, *Stocks & Commodities*, V. 14:8, Pgs. 348–352.

"The Critical Head & Shoulders Test." Matt Blackman, *Stocks & Commodities*, V. 21:13, Pgs. 41–44.

"Detecting Breakouts." Markos Katsanos, *Stocks & Commodities*, V. 21:4, Pgs. 26–38.

"Spike Up the Volume." Giorgos Siligardos, Ph.D., *Stocks & Commodities*, V. 23:6, Pgs. 30–37.

"A Tale of Two Indicators." Andrew Tomlinson, *Stocks & Commodities*, V. 22:10, Pgs. 22–27.

"The Overlooked But Profitable Volume." Cory Mitchell, *Stocks & Commodities*, V. 26:6, Pgs. 26–30.

"Did decimalization hurt institutional investor?." Sugato Chakravarty, Venkatesh Panchapagesan, and Robert Wood, *Journal of Financial Markets*.

"Why Has Trading Volume Increased." Tarun Chordia, Richard Roll, and Avanidhar Subrahmanyam (2008).

"Accumulation Distribution Indicator." www.1st-futures-broker.com/accumulation_distribution.htm.

"Technical Analysis from A to Z." Steven B. Achelis. www.equis.com/free/taaz/williamsaccumdistr.html.

"On-Balance Volume." en.wikipedia.org/wiki/On-balance_volume.

"Price and Volume Trend." en.wikipedia.org/wiki/Price_and_Volume_Trend.

"Accumulation/Distribution Index." en.wikipedia.org/wiki/Accumulation/distribution_index.

"John Bollinger on Consolidations." Currency Trader Staff (2005), *Currency Trader*.

"Using Volume Indicators to Improve Trading." Dave Goodboy, TradingMarkets.com.

"Volume Indicators." John Bollinger, CFA, CMT (2000).

"Interpretation of Technical Indicators." Robert Deel.

"Unlocking Volume Analysis." Todd Krueger (2009). www.YTEmagazine.com.

"Chaikin Money Flow (CMF)—ChartSchool—StockCharts.com." www.stockcharts.com.

"Twiggs Money Flow." www.incrediblecharts.com/indicators/twiggs_money-flow.php.

"Technical Analysis of Stocks & Commodities." *The Traders' Magazine*.

"Positive Volume Index." Dennis Peterson, *Stocks & Commodities*, V. 21:4, Pgs. 63–65.

"All in One: Price, Volume and Open Interest." Larry Williams (2007). www.futuresmag.com.

"Using Money Flow to Stay with the Trend." Markos Katsanos, *Stocks & Commodities*, V. 22:6, Pgs. 40–51.

"Profitability of the On-Balance Volume Indicator." William Wai Him Tsang and Terence Tai Leung Chong, *Economics Bulletin*.

"What Does the Volume of a Stock Mean?." www.isfaq.com/business/31081.html.

"Volume Zone Oscillator (VZO)." Waleed Aly Khalil. www.ifta.org.

"Of All the On-Balance Volume Indicators, Which Is the Best? Using Oscillators with On-Balance Volume." Carl F. Ehrlch, *Stocks & Commodities*, V. 18:9, Pgs. 22–29.

"The Force Index." John A Sarkett. www.option-wizard.com/features/force.shtml.

"Market Monograph: Technical Analysis & Stock Market Commentary." Fred Goodman. www.marketmonograph.caom/a/goodman/keyIndicators/pvCharting.asp.

"Volume Basics." Martin J. Pring, *Stocks & Commodities*, V. 18:7, Pgs. 36–41.

"The Use of Volume as an Early Warning Signal." Richard C. Orr, Ph.D.

"Volume Averaging." MarketVolume.com.

"Volume Oscillator." MarketVolume.com.

"Ease of Movement." www.investopedia.com/terms/e/easofmovement.asp.

"Arms Ease of Movement: Volume-Weighted MovAvg Difference." www.neuroshell.com.

"Ease of Movement." www.paritech.com.au/education/technical/indicators/strength. ease.asp.

"Force Index." en.wikipedia.org/wiki/Force_Index.

"Force Index Feature." option-wizard.com/features/force.shtml.

"Money Flow Analysis." MarketVolume.com.

"William's Accumulation/Distribution (A/D)—Forex Technical Indicator." www.forexrealm.com.

"Discovering the Force Index—Part 1: Introduction." Jason Van Bergen. www.investopedia.com/articles/trading/03-031203.asp.

"Ease of Movement." www.primeequant.com/help/node18.html.

"Do You Need Volume to Move Stocks Higher?." Michael Carr, *Stocks & Commodities*, V. 27:12, Pg. 8.

"Volume Flow Indicator Performance." Markos Katsanos, *Stocks & Commodities*, V. 22:7, Pgs. 50–60.

"William's Accumulation—Distribution." www.fxwords.com/w/williams-accumulation-distribution.html.

"Most of What You Need to Know About Technical Analysis." Matt Blackman, *Stocks & Commodities*, V. 21:5, Pgs. 44–49.

"A Tool Everyone Knows But Few Recognize: The Overlooked But Profitable Volume." Cory Mitchell, *Stocks & Commodities*, V. 26:6, Pgs. 26–30.

"Triangles." David Vomund, *Stocks & Commodities*, V. 16:7, Pgs. 352–355.

"Into the Money Flow: Sorting Out the Volume Indicators." S. Yamanaka, *Stocks & Commodities*, V. 24:13, Pgs. 62–66, 92.

"The Volume Indicators." Bruce R. Faber, *Stocks & Commodities*, V. 14:5, Pgs. 204–206.

"Volume-Weighted Relative Strength Index." Russell R. Minor, CMT (1997), *MTA Journal*.

"Arms Equivolume Charting System." Dr. James S. Gould, *Stocks & Commodities*, V. 7:12, Pgs. 442–444.

"What Volume Is It?." Richard W. Arms, Jr., *Stocks & Commodities*, V. 7:12, Pgs. 456–457.

"Intraday Intensity Index." www.investopedia.com/terms/i/intradayintensityindex. asp.

"Worden Discussion Forums: Basic Info on BOP, TSV and MoneyStream." www.forums.worden.com/default.aspx?g=posts&t=7365.

"Cumulative Volume: Intraday Intensity." Dennis Peterson. technical.traders.com/tradersonline/display.asp?art=521.

"The Klinger Volume Oscillator (KVO): A Theoretical Model." Stephen J. Klinger, CMT (1995), *MTA Journal.*

"Volume-Weighted RSI: Money Flow." Gene Quong and Avrum Soudack, *Stocks & Commodities*, V. 7:3, Pgs. 76–77.

"Money Flow." en.wikipedia.org/wiki/Money_flow.

"Speeding Up the Oscillator." Grady Garrett, *Stocks & Commodities*, V. 7:6, Pgs. 177–179.

"Investor/RT Tour—Money Flow Index." www.linnsoft.com/tour/techind/mfi.htm.

"Technical Analysis, Studies, Indicators: Money Flow Index (MFI)." www.marketvolume.com/technicalanalysis/mfi.asp.

"Money Flow Index (MFI)." www.smallstocks.com.au/technical-analysis/money-flow-index-mfi/.

"Money Flow Index (MFI)." www.stockcharts.com.

INDEX

W–Z

FINANCIAL TIMES

In an increasingly competitive world, it is quality
of thinking that gives an edge—an idea that opens new
doors, a technique that solves a problem, or an insight
that simply helps make sense of it all.

We work with leading authors in the various arenas
of business and finance to bring cutting-edge thinking
and best-learning practices to a global market.

It is our goal to create world-class print publications
and electronic products that give readers
knowledge and understanding that can then be
applied, whether studying or at work.

To find out more about our business
products, you can visit us at www.ftpress.com.